795

D1134768

DATE DUE		
DEC 9 '76	AUG 2 7 1986	
JAN 24 '77	JUL 0 2 1995	
APR 21 '77		
MAY 3 '77		
MAY 27 '77		
DEC 2 6 1978		
MAY 2 0 1980		
MAR 1 0 1981		
JUN 1 8 1981		
APR 2 4 1984		

Richmond Public Library
Richmond, California

WATCH OUT FOR GEORGE WALLACE

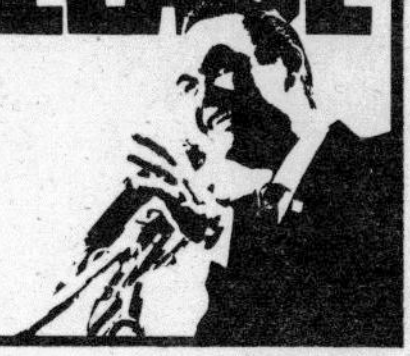

B
Wallace, G. C.
c.1

WATCH OUT FOR GEORGE WALLACE

By
Wayne Greenhaw

PRENTICE-HALL, INC.
Englewood Cliffs
New Jersey

Watch Out for George Wallace, by Wayne Greenhaw
Copyright © 1976 by Wayne Greenhaw

All rights reserved. No part of this book may be
reproduced in any form or by any means, except
for the inclusion of brief quotations in a review,
without permission in writing from the publisher.

Printed in the United States of America

Prentice-Hall International, Inc., London
Prentice-Hall of Australia, Pty. Ltd., Sydney
Prentice-Hall of Canada, Ltd., Toronto
Prentice-Hall of India Private Ltd., New Delhi
Prentice-Hall of Japan, Inc., Tokyo

10 9 8 7 6 5 4 3 2 1

Library of Congress Cataloging in Publication Data

Greenhaw, Wayne.
    Watch out for George Wallace.

    Bibliography: p.
    1. Wallace, George Corley, 1919–   I. Title.
F330.W3G73   976.1′06′0924 [B]   75-40153
ISBN 0-13-945790-9

In
Memory of
My Father
Harold Reed Greenhaw

ACKNOWLEDGMENTS

Thanks are in order to so many people that I could not begin to name them all. I appreciate the generosity of the hundreds who gave of their time to talk about the man and his politics. Without their help this book could not have been written.

First, I would like to thank Dorothy deSantillana, who first encouraged me to write a book about Wallace, and who saw the germ of worthiness in the subject. Most of my colleagues at the Alabama *Journal* lent supporting advice, especially when the project was in its final phase. The able secretarial and research assistance of Pauline S. Jackson and Marci Levin was valued. Without the treasured aid of my agent, Al Zuckerman, the project would never have gotten off the ground in the beginning. And throughout the struggle my most cherished and helpful assistant was my wife, Sally.

PROLOGUE

I was fourteen years old when I met Circuit Judge George Corley Wallace in a small-town barbershop. At the time he was south Alabama campaign manager for former Governor James E. "Big Jim" Folsom, who was seeking a second term. My father, a traveling beauty- and barber-supply salesman, had always voted Republican in a country that adored Franklin Delano Roosevelt. But Daddy never minded telling anybody his political preference. That afternoon in the barbershop you would never have thought Daddy even knew how to spell Republican, much less vote it. It was hard to tell who talked more, but Wallace mostly talked about himself. He probably didn't say ten words about Jim Folsom. I do remember that he went on and on about how the people of Alabama were damned good and tired of the Yankees telling us what to do and when to do it. And I remember my father agreeing with every word.

After more than an hour in the shop, Daddy and I got back into his car, which always smelled of after-shave lotion and permanent-wave mixture. On our way toward the next town, Daddy said, "That man's not going to stop until he's governor of Alabama."

Almost two years later I met George Wallace for the second time. Again I was with my father, and we were in another barbershop in another small town in south Alabama. He was doing some business and taking me and my best friend to the Gulf Coast for a week in the sunshine. When Wallace came through the door, he bounced straight over to me, his arm outstretched, and he said, "How are you, Wayne? Who's your friend?" And again, he and my father spent time bantering about what was on their minds.

I liked George Wallace. If I could have voted, I would have voted for him. I knew no other adult who remembered my name after meeting me only one time and not seeing me for two years. He was an impressive man.

When he stood in front of my father he looked like an erect dwarf. My father was tall and heavyset. Wallace was a half foot shorter, his chin was thrust upward, his lips full but taut, and his hair slickly combed with a wave beginning at the top of his forehead and sweeping back.

Nearly ten years later, when I became a reporter for the Alabama *Journal* in Montgomery, I met Wallace the governor. He recalled the first two meetings and asked about my father, whom he called by name.

My first "big" story for the *Journal* was an exposé of a huge printing press some Wallace cronies had sold to the state for more than one hundred thousand dollars. The equipment had been bought more than a year before and it still sat unused in the basement of the State Highway Department.

During the following decade I covered the governor sporadically, watching him wheel and deal with the state legislature, experiencing his phenomenal success on the campaign trail, and studying his day-by-day maneuverings. He is a fascinating politician. It is extremely difficult to be an indifferent Wallace-watcher. He is an accomplished demagogue, but he is also amazing in his ability to feel out the fundamental issues of any given day. He is amazing in his ability to remember names and events. This talent, along with many others, has undoubtedly helped him become the most dangerous politician in America today.

In 1963, when he stood on the steps of the Alabama capitol and promised the people of his state segregation forever, he became a symbol of opposition. Today he is the rebel *with* a cause. Twelve years ago he could be sloughed aside as the cocky hero of a handful of racists. Since that time his power base has grown; he has moderated his stance, and he has become the idol of vast numbers of people who think "the system" is working against them.

Regardless of his talent, the question remains: Would he make a good president? I will answer that question in this book. I will show what makes George Wallace run. He has been called the Sammy Glick of American politics. And he has been labeled the dark side of the country's political life. He is a determined man who is convinced that if he does not become president he will influence drastic changes in the system. He has looked death in the face twice and he is still alive. He believes that God saved him for a purpose.

Wayne Greenhaw
Montgomery, Alabama

PLAYING POLITICS

THE TIME WAS SPRING 1963, and George Corley Wallace was the superman of the segregationist set. After he shouted "Segregation now! Segregation tomorrow! Segregation forever!" he became known throughout the world as the champion of the white supremacists. Media representatives from as far away as New Delhi and Tokyo paraded into Montgomery, the capital of Alabama, to see the number-one subject of interest: the governor.

As the temperature and the racial tension in the South grew hotter, Wallace made himself the enlightened leader of The Cause. He began waving the stars and bars of the Confederacy with more zeal than ever before, and he screamed louder than any other politician south of the Mason-Dixon Line.

Because of his far-right stance on the race issue and because he had suddenly become a national figure, he was invited to appear on *Meet the Press*, his first nationally televised interview program.

Excited to the point of being little-boylike, he telephoned his good friend and confidant, Grover Cleveland Hall, Jr., editor of the Montgomery *Advertiser*. He told Hall about the invitation and hurriedly added, "You've got to go with me. I'll need your help up there."

Hall quipped, "I've never known you to need anybody's help."

"I'll need yours," Wallace assured Hall seriously.

Hall agreed to accompany Wallace, and two days later they

flew toward Washington, D. C., in the governor's new Lockheed Lodestar. As quickly as they were airborne Wallace began nervously to point out features of the plane. "Look here, Grover, it's even got a built-in coffeepot. You want a cup?"

With his characteristic dry wit, Hall asked if the plane had a bar.

Wallace only stared at him and then let the words pass. Hall was aware that Wallace had quit drinking whiskey several years before and had promised the voters of Alabama he wouldn't serve alcoholic beverages in the governor's mansion —a promise he intended to keep.

Halfway to the capital, Wallace began to squirm in his seat. The governor's nervousness was nothing unusual. He hated to even sit at a desk very long. He liked to be up and moving about. And he despised flying. It was merely a convenience, he told friends.

After a few minutes of shifting his shoulders, twisting in his seat, he finally leaned forward and said, "I've got to have a foreign policy."

Grover Hall looked at the governor incredulously.

"Those boys are going to question me about my beliefs tomorrow. They're going to want to know about what I think about things in this nation. And they're going to want to know about my foreign policy. If I'm going to run for the presidency next year I've got to have a foreign policy."

Hall, decked out in his customary tailored suit with a rose in his lapel, crossed his legs, saying nothing. He oftentimes appeared bemused at his friend's political naiveté as well as his political brilliance.

Wallace went on about what he assumed the media reporters would ask. His speech did not dwindle until the plane landed.

All the way to their hotel Wallace talked about and verbally worried about what he would answer when asked about a foreign policy.

The next morning a knock interrupted Hall's sleep at an early hour. Wallace entered, his teeth gripping a cigar, and he paced the floor, saying over and over that he had to have "a foreign policy to tell 'em about."

Finally Hall told him not to worry. On the way to the studio Hall ripped a news column from the *Wall Street Journal*. "That's a perfect foreign policy," Hall assured Wallace, who began immediately to read the type. He read the story a half dozen times. Before going on the air, he stuffed it into his shirt pocket.

After the show Wallace strutted into the lobby, where his friend was waiting. He lighted another cigar. He wadded the clipping and threw it into a waste can. "I don't need a foreign policy. All they wanted to know about was niggers, and I'm the expert," he announced proudly.

Racism was the easy way to power for George Wallace. After he became governor of Alabama he made himself virtual dictator of the state. During the thirty-year span of his political career, he has been hellbent on a course that would eventually lead him to the White House.

Since 1963, when he took office as governor, he has run the state continuously with the exception of thirty-five months when his wife's lieutenant governor succeeded her after she died in office. It was no secret that she had been a stand-in for her husband. Counting her term, Wallace had been elected governor four times by the mid-1970s. Even counting only the three terms that he won under his own name, he has broken all Alabama records.

There was not one board or commission in the state that he did not control in 1975. There were only a handful of

3

appointments out of the more than five thousand appointed jobs in the state that he had not made personally. Such absolute control had previously never been possible when governors were not allowed to succeed themselves. Powerful board positions had been staggered over a six-year period, with terms ending every two years. In that way, a new governor would have at least one appointment, and perhaps two, but he could not control the board because at least one appointment would not serve until the next governor's term. During Wallace's back-to-back administrations, 1970–74 and 1974–78, every board membership would come open for reappointment. By the end of 1975 there were only a few positions that had not been appointed by him.

When the state senate defeated his succession bill in the last year of his first term, Wallace put the evil eye on those who voted against him. He exercised his power with supreme vindictiveness. Among those who had fought him, the ones who ran for reelection were defeated, several didn't run, and one committed suicide. The next legislature, which was thoroughly Wallace-dominated, passed a succession bill into law early in the session.

"He has always played the game ruthlessly. He has played it without regard to principle or philosophy. He's a racist, that's the one thing you know about him; but after that he might be liberal one day and conservative the next, according to the shifting tides of public opinion. George Wallace has no political principles. He has no political philosophy. He believes in helping George Wallace. Every move that he makes is motivated with self-interest in mind. Of that you can be sure," a former Wallace associate summed up the politician.

George Wallace came of age in a time that was riddled with complex political issues. When he was a boy he listened to the radio in Clio, Alabama, and he heard the many tales of the greatest southern politician of them all—Huey Pierce Long.

As he grew older Wallace studied the unique politics of that powerful figure, Huey Long, who spoke for a region of destitute people living from hand to mouth in the Great Depression. Wallace placed Long next to his other heroes: Andrew Jackson, John C. Calhoun, William Lowndes Yancy, and Robert E. Lee. A student of the Civil War, Wallace believed deeply that the South has never been brought out of the time of Reconstruction. The South was never given back all of its rights, which were lost when it rebelled, he was taught. He holds to the theory that Huey Long was on the way to becoming the spokesman that the South needed, but that Long never accomplished that task. Perhaps he is correct. Long served only one term as governor of Louisiana and was assassinated before his first term in the U. S. Senate expired.

Wallace has bragged that his own populism is much like that of Long. They were both rip-roaring dyed-in-the-wool southerners. Both exuded the cocky façade of fast-talking demagoguery. Like Long, Wallace built his own image. He was the maker of himself. Neither were plastic-style twentieth-century politicians molded of soft putty by an advertising company. Neither Wallace nor Long needed the public-relations men who seemed to walk side by side with other modern politicians. Both Wallace and Long had strong personalities. They were one-man shows. Their entire political operations revolved around them. Each was the center of his own spotlight.

George Wallace was born and raised in a small rural town in south Alabama. His father owned several small farms nearby. The family was never destitute, but Wallace looks back on the time of his growing up as though he, his mother, his father, two brothers and sister were always on the edge of starvation. In reality, the Wallaces were far from the wealthiest people in Barbour County, but they were not dirt poor. Huey Long also had a way of low-rating his own childhood environment in Winn Parish in north Louisiana. Both men were from the farmlands, however, and both could talk the language of the country people. From these people came the original nucleus of their votes. Huey Long would stand in front of these folks and brag about being born and raised in a log cabin. George Wallace has long wished that he could make the same claim.

Both George Wallace and Huey Long loved power. Both knew the importance and necessity of a power base, especially when they planned to use it as a pad from which to launch a national campaign for the presidency. Like Wallace, Long could not succeed himself as governor. In 1932, while still serving as governor, the Kingfish ran for the U. S. Senate and was elected. He also didn't wish to give up his home power. He chose Oscar K. Allen, one of his floor leaders from the state senate, to run for governor. Long campaigned for Allen, who won; it was no secret that he was a stand-in for Long. Wallace used a different tactic when his first term as governor was running out, but he, too, found a way to stay in power. He attempted to pass a bill through the legislature to amend the Alabama Constitution and allow succession in office. After the state senate stood against him, he ran his wife, Lurleen, who was obviously his stand-in. Like Long, Wallace did not let the traditional political system stand in the way of his power seeking.

Both men recognized issues and knew how to deal with them, whether complex or simple. Clifford J. Durr, who became a Federal Communications Commissioner during the New Deal and who retired near Montgomery at his old home place until his death in the summer of 1975, once witnessed Huey Long deliver a rabble-rousing speech evoking all sorts of evil images to a Democratic caucus in a smoke-filled room in Washington. That afternoon Durr's brother-in-law, then U. S. Senator Hugo Black, had a complex piece of legislation that

6

would regulate big business. "Who are your main supporters?" asked Durr. Without hesitation, Black said his support came from the senator from Louisiana, Huey Long. Durr was amazed. "Why, I saw him operate this morning. The man's a raving maniac," Durr said. "Wait and see," Black said. Several hours later Durr was present when Huey Long dissected the legislation with splendid accolades on the senate floor. "He displayed a marvelous legal mind, probing directly to the heart of the matter, and his speech was clear and illustrative. It almost reminded you of some of Churchill's orations," said Durr.

Wallace was himself a rabble-rouser to the first degree. His talks have brought out the hate for Negroes, distaste for changes in social conditions, and distrust in federal courts. He also has the ability to simplify the complex in near-poetic terms. During the regular legislative session of 1975 he was having a fight with the Alabama Education Association, which had bowed its back against his appropriation schedule. Wallace asked the lawmakers to take $48 million from the special education trust fund, which held a surplus of about $150 million. When he asked, the AEA screamed and placed its own budget in the legislature. It became obvious that the teachers' group had more votes committed to it than Wallace had in his back pocket. The governor went on state-wide television. He explained what was happening. Three fruit jars sat on his desk. Two were almost empty. These represented the State Department of Mental Health and the State Highway Department. The third was running over with nickels. Of course, it represented the education trust fund. He took a few nickels from the jar that was running over and put them into each of the other two, demonstrating that the trust fund could afford to take care of highways and the mentally ill. The next day mail poured into the capitol asking legislators to reconsider their stand for the AEA. The people were behind Wallace. He had made his point—beautifully and simply and powerfully.

Both Wallace and Long knew how to wield their power in useful as well as vengeful ways. After Wallace's three-jar speech, some of the legislators still bucked the governor's plan. Wallace called the rebellious lawmakers into his office. "If we don't get this money for our highway system," he warned, "your counties are not only not going to get road money, the bulldozers will start tearing up the blacktop." One legislator commented several days later that a constituent had telephoned him and said, "They've got the tractors next to the road." The harried politician told the man not to worry, he'd vote for Wallace's program, which passed shortly thereafter.

In the same vein, Huey Long maneuvered his power not only for votes, roads, bridges, and the like, but also for more mundane matters. To Huey Long, the Louisiana State University football team was no laughing matter. Once when an opening game was not sold out because the Ringling Brothers and Barnum and Bailey Circus was scheduled for Baton Rouge on the same night, Governor Long called circus owner John Ringling North. After Long explained the problem, North haughtily took the stand that the circus never rescheduled its shows once a contract had been signed. Long asked North if he was familiar with Louisiana's dip law. As he interpreted the law, Long said, animals crossing the state line would have to be dipped, then placed in quarantine for three weeks. "Did you ever dip a tiger?" Long asked. "Or how about an elephant?" North immediately agreed to reschedule the circus for New Orleans on the night in question.

Both Long and Wallace believed deeply that they were agents of the people. Long once remarked, "A perfect democracy can come close to looking like a dictatorship, a democracy in which the people are so satisfied they have no complaint." At another time, he said, "A man is not a dictator when he is given a commission from the people and carries it

8

out. I believe in democracy, and the people of Louisiana ain't never going to have anything but a democracy. You know and I know that if people want to throw me out they're going to do it. They like what I'm giving them and what they're getting." As soon as Wallace took a grasp on the power of the governor's office, he willed "the people put me here to represent them, and that's what I'm doing." When he entered three presidential primaries in 1964, he said, "The people of Alabama sent me up here to tell y'all about what's happening to us." When he attempted to pass the succession bill in his first term, he explained, "All I want is a vote of the people. If they want me, they'll pass the amendment. If they don't, they'll throw me out." After the bill lost in the senate and he decided to run his wife, he declared, "It's time for the people to show those mealy-mouthed politicians a thing or two. If the people want George Wallace, they'll vote for his wife."

Both Long and Wallace were demagogues. Wallace would fit into the category of the mass leader, a term presented by Eric Hoffer in his book, *The True Believer*. Huey Long's magnificent biographer, T. Harry Williams, suggested that Long was in this classification, too. Both became Hoffer's mass leader, who "articulates and justifies the resentment dammed up in the souls of the frustrated. He kindles the vision of a breathtaking future," and he moves to "harness man's hungers and fears to weld a following and make it zealous unto death in the service of a holy cause." The mass leader, according to Hoffer, has certain qualities: audacity; iron will; faith in himself and his cause and his destiny; a recognition that the innermost craving of a following is for "communion" or a sense of collectivity; unbounded brazenness, which enables the leader to disregard consistency; and a capacity for hatred, without which he could be deflected from his goals. However, according to Harry Williams, Long's capacity for hate had its definite limits. He wrote,

> *Many people, especially his enemies, think that he was
> filled with hatred, that he was vindictive, spiteful. He
> hated many things that conservatives stood for and he did
> hate some men. But he hardly ever acted out of hatred.
> He could seem vindictive, he could seem beside himself
> with rage, he could seem to destroy an enemy in
> passion—but in every case he was actually calculating,
> cool, and detached, and always his motives were political
> rather than personal. If he eliminated a man, it was only
> because that man stood in the way of one of his objectives
> or had become unnecessary to his plans. "I don't know of
> a single case where Huey took after an individual or kept
> after him just for the sake of harming him," said one
> intimate. "The minute a man ceased to be a threat, Huey
> lost interest in him."*

The same could be said of Wallace. When he went out of his
way to defeat the senators who had stood up against him and
his succession plans, he wanted them out of his way during the
upcoming legislature. A state politician close to Wallace said,
"He forgives very easily. When a man runs against Wallace, all
he has to do is call up after he's been defeated and
congratulate Wallace. The governor loves it and will take the
man under his wing. It's incredible."

Their most glaring difference, primarily, was that of basic
goals. Huey Long worked diligently to develop a program
which he called Share Our Wealth, to enhance the future for
the poor people of the land. He wanted to help the whites and
the blacks of the United States. Guard against wealth, take
money from the rich, divide prosperity, and make sure all had
enough to eat; Long pronounced, "Every man is a king!" On
the other hand, George Wallace's bright future for his average
citizen (he never speaks directly to the poor, because that
might mean black in the political-code-word system) was that
suburban home, two cars in the driveway, a clean school for

the children, and not one black in the neighborhood other than those who are bused in to clean, wash, and cook.

Both Long and Wallace lost their first bids for the governorships of their states, but they reacted very differently. Long based his campaign on the fight which he had been waging as a Louisiana Public Service commissioner against the power and evils of Standard Oil. The next time Long ran he went after the same enemy with even more gusto. In Wallace's first campaign for governor he was branded the more moderate of the two candidates in the runoff, and the Ku Klux Klan support went to his opponent. In a private party after losing, Wallace declared, "I'll never be out-niggered again." And in his next race Wallace ran on a pledge to "stand in the schoolhouse door" to keep them from being integrated.

Huey Long admitted openly that he was a segregationist, but he wanted all people to be lifted out of poverty. When he advocated Negro Share Our Wealth Clubs in Louisiana and across the nation, he was denounced for his "un-American attitude." The chief Kluxer, Dr. Hiram W. Evans, announced he was going to Louisiana to campaign against Huey. When asked by reporters what he would do about Evans's invasion, Long said, "Quote me as saying that that imperial bastard will never set foot in Louisiana, and that when I call him a son of a bitch I am not using profanity but am referring to the circumstances of his birth." If Evans came into the state, he said, he would leave with "his toes turned up." Evans never got to the Pelican State.

After his first years of power Wallace, however, never admitted being a segregationist, much less a racist. He said that when he stood in the schoolhouse door he was standing up for a principle: The federal government didn't have the right to invade a state. He said he believed in the state law at that time, which was segregation. Ten years later he said he believed in the state law at that time, which was public desegregation. But he continued to speak out against forced busing, federal court decisions, and rule by bureaucracy. He never came forward with a substantial positive program to help the financially distressed.

Again, each ran his campaigns differently. Long never thought race or religion were political issues. When he was asked once to compare himself to Hitler, Long roared, "Don't liken me to that son of a bitch. Anybody that lets his public policies be mixed up with religious prejudice is a plain goddamned fool." The only issue that he thrust to the forefront of his campaigns was economics: Standard Oil was stealing the people's money, he said; people needed to Share Our Wealth; poor people were starving to death and needed a chicken in the pot. He always offered positive programs. But with Wallace race was always on the periphery if not the dead center of his issues. His were negative campaigns, anti-integration, anti-busing, anti-courts, anti-politics. He never offered positive solutions. He offered himself in his state-wide races. If the people voted for him, "you will give me a mandate, and I will go out and tell America about you and your problems," and the crowds went wild with enthusiasm.

Huey Long enjoyed himself. He not only liked a cocktail or two, he appreciated an occasional woman in his suite at the Roosevelt Hotel in New Orleans or Heidelberg Hotel in Baton Rouge. He admitted once to his wife, Rose, "I can't live a normal family life." He also enjoyed playing the clown. A relatively handsome man with a jowly face and a bulbous nose, he stood five feet eleven inches tall, and often received journalists in bed wearing silk pajamas. Wallace enjoyed an occasional drink when he was a young man, but discovered he couldn't handle whiskey. He gave it up when he discovered it was a good campaign issue in 1962 to announce he would not serve alcoholic beverages in the governor's mansion. Before an assassin rendered him paralyzed below the waist, Wallace, too, enjoyed occasional affairs with women at a friend's apartment in a downtown Montgomery complex. Wallace would never poke fun at himself in public. Self-conscious about his size, he stood on a four-inch elevated platform during his inauguration in 1971 because his new bride, Cornelia, was taller.

Both men made themselves great politicians. Through sheer personal magnetism, intelligence, fortitude, and hard work, they placed themselves higher on the political ladder than any other southern leaders. Their names will be remembered among the greatest and most unusual politicians in the history of the United States. They were very different, yet very alike. They were the South's answer to Machiavelli's *The Prince*; they sought to gain power and worked to keep it.

When he was a boy Wallace listened to the men who hung out around the barbershop and hardware store. The major subject of conversation was politics. As he grew older he watched, listened, and talked nothing but that subject which was dearest to his heart. During these years, the late twenties and middle thirties, the dominant figure in Alabama politics was Bibb Graves.

Graves won his first governorship in 1926 with the support of the revitalized Ku Klux Klan. Wallace was seven years old that year and listened to all the talk that was generated by this vital personality. When the KKK turned to racist violence in 1928 and 1929, Graves turned against the group. He tried but failed to pass an antimask law through the legislature. Before his term was finished he was backing the New Deal. He followed the leadership of FDR into the thirties. Walking at his side were Hugo Black, Lister Hill, John Sparkman, and other progressive Alabamians.

"He was a gentleman," said former U. S. Congressman Carl

Elliott of Bibb Graves. "He was a cultured, well-bred person, and married his first cousin Dixie Bibb who was as lovely as he was handsome," said Elliott.

The tall, stern-faced, dark-eyed, and thin-lipped Graves, descendent of Alabama's first governor, William Wyatt Bibb, was a graduate of Yale Law School, a veteran of World War I, and later capitalized on his war record for American Legion votes.

In his first term he was one of the most active and powerful governors the state had ever produced. A record was set with a $25 million highway program and a two-cent gasoline tax. With an iron hand, he pushed a $600,000 education program through the legislature.

When George Wallace was sixteen years old, Bibb Graves was elected to his second administration. By this time the young Wallace had been actively interested in politics for more than three years. He was very aware of Graves-style politics.

When Graves's Tunstall Revenue Bill hit the floor of the legislature, newspaper reporters wrote about the governor putting a tax of fifteen percent on cigars, cigarettes, and tobacco. People from every hamlet within miles of Montgomery poured into the capital. Letters of criticism were mailed in by the hundreds. But Graves pulled a slick trick. He formed a committee that would later be called "Graves's Steamroller" in the state senate. The bill was rewritten in committee. The tax burden was switched from the people to utilities: railroads, telegraph and telephone companies, and the coal and iron industries. The "Steamroller" pushed the bill through.

Wallace was a student in the University of Alabama when Roosevelt appointed Hugo Black to the Supreme Court. Graves named his wife Dixie to fill Black's unexpired term in the U. S. Senate. The student politician listened while people criticized Bibb Graves for putting his wife in the high position, and he was also aware when that talk died and others spoke of reelecting Graves to a third term.

Graves had already announced his candidacy for a third term—and most felt no one could have defeated him—when a recurring kidney infection flared up. He was recuperating in Florida when he died March 14, 1942.

During that spring of 1942 George Wallace was courting pretty Lurleen Burns after he finished law school. He also worked in the campaign of his fellow Barbour Countian Chauncey Sparks. Wallace had a job driving a truck that summer, but in the evenings Lurleen would walk with him through residential areas where he'd knock on doors and ask people to vote for Sparks, whom he knew as a circuit judge in Eufaula. Of course he always introduced himself when he walked from door to door.

Sparks was a pleasant, soft-spoken bachelor who had been a lawyer and legislator as well as a judge in Eufaula. He was far from the dynamic politician young Wallace later became. It was certain that Wallace did not take speaking style or campaigning mannerisms from Sparks. "Governor Sparks had great integrity, and I always hoped that I would have half as much," Wallace was once quoted. Sparks ran for governor at the insistence of his old friend W. W. "Billy" Watson, a frontier character who sold everything from shoes to Bull-of-the-Woods chewing tobacco. Throughout the years Wallace would seek advice from Watson and would seek the support of Sparks.

When Wallace ran for his first term in the Alabama House of Representatives, James Elisha "Big Jim" Folsom was running for the governor's chair. Four years earlier Folsom had run second to Sparks. But in 1947, "the little man's big friend," a six foot eight inch, overgrown country boy with wide brown eyes and massive jawbones and a shock of dark brown hair falling over his broad forehead, was headed for Montgomery with a suds bucket in his hand. He campaigned from courthouse to courthouse telling people it was time to "scrub out that capitol building."

Wallace was a serious young man who made no moves that were not calculated to further his career. He pushed through a bill which to this day carries his name. At that time it was considered daringly progressive, even liberal. The Wallace Act, frowned upon by big business in the state, was an invitation to out-of-state industry to relocate in Alabama. It offered a Cinderella gift of municipal bonds to finance housing for the industry, plus absolutely no property tax for at least forty years. The bill passed with Folsom's blessing.

While Wallace was building a name for himself by working diligently and doing his homework and making few enemies, "Big Jim" was having fun in the governor's mansion. He was always on the go. He went to a dinner in his honor in Washington with President Harry Truman, Senator Lister Hill, and Justice Black. The two Alabamians escorted the governor on to New York where forty young models greeted him. He kissed each one, after which the national press always referred to him as "Kissin' Jim." He bought a fleet of planes, one of which flew almost constantly back and forth between Alabama and California, where he dated Virginia Warren, daughter of then-Governor Earl Warren. When that courtship waned, he eloped with a young secretary who worked for the state, Jamelle Moore. Following their honeymoon he purchased a ninety-five-foot yacht for $140,000 in state funds and named it *Jamelle*. The same yacht was sold by Wallace when he became governor; he said Alabama's governor didn't need a yacht on which to entertain.

One of Folsom's favorite late afternoon pastimes was to pull off his huge shoes, lean back in the rocking chair on the veranda of the mansion, drink bourbon from an iced-tea glass, and wave at the rush-hour traffic on South Perry Street. But

Folsom was not all buffoonery. He took after the "Big Mules" with gusto. He passed prolabor legislation. He pushed for Negro suffrage, attempted over and over again to repeal the poll tax, and hammered home the "one man, one vote" theory. He raised old-age pensions. He boosted a state sales tax and a graduated income tax to provide a farm-to-market road system. He had promised blacktopped roads from the farms to the county seats, and he delivered. Before he went into office there was less than one mile of paved road in Jackson County in the northeast corner of the state, and when he left there were more than a hundred miles paved.

In his Christmas message of 1949 Folsom pleaded for equal justice for black people. "As long as the Negroes are held down by deprivation and lack of opportunity, all other people will be held down alongside them. Let's start talking fellowship and brotherly love and doing unto others," he said.

George Wallace perhaps did not listen to every word Folsom uttered, but the older politician influenced the legislator in 1948 to the point that Wallace, a delegate to the National Democratic Convention, did not join the Dixiecrats who walked out and formed their own party. Wallace stayed behind with the Loyalists.

When Wallace went to the governor the second time for help in passing a bill, Folsom made him promise he would do anything he asked. Folsom put his weight behind a bill creating five trade schools in the state, and placed one in Wallace's U. S. Congressional District at Napier Field near Dothan. At Wallace's request Folsom named it after the legislator's father, George Wallace. At the time Wallace was thinking that he might run for Congress in the future.

About four years later Folsom decided he would seek a second term. He called Wallace.

"You remember what you promised," Folsom said.

"Yes, I said I would give you my support," Wallace said.

"No, you said you would do anything I asked, and I am asking you to be my south Alabama manager," Folsom said.

Wallace, who later said he did not want to get involved with Folsom, went to Chauncey Sparks and asked him what to do. "Did you promise?" Sparks asked.

"Yes, I guess I did," Wallace said.

"Well, you'd better go ahead and do it then, because you can't break your word in politics," the elder politician advised.

Wallace said that he told himself, "Well, maybe I can have a good effect on Jim's administration," adding that that was how "I salved my conscience." The campaigning for Folsom had not hurt Wallace. At that time Folsom was the most popular name in the state, beating eight opponents without a runoff.

After Folsom went back into office in 1955, Wallace, who was then a circuit judge for Barbour and Bullock counties, asked to be appointed to the board of trustees of all-black Tuskegee Institute. Still watching out for his own future, he told a Folsom aide, "You've got to have the Negro vote from now on if you expect to run for anything, and I'm going to lay my groundwork right now."

He said he did not stay with the Folsom camp because "I saw that those around him were drinking and stealing, and I got out because I figured they would all wind up in the penitentiary."

Wallace ran for governor in 1958 and was defeated by John Patterson, the son of the Attorney General-elect Albert Patterson who had been assassinated four years earlier when he swore to clean up Phenix City. Patterson had served his father's term as attorney general and had received the Ku Klux Klan support in the runoff, after which Wallace told friends, "I'll never be out-niggered again."

Jim Folsom made one last serious try for the governorship in 1962. He campaigned vigorously. He would have gotten into a runoff with Wallace had he not appeared intoxicated on state-wide television the night before the primary. He burped, chirped, and hooted like an owl. He could not remember the names of his own children. He called Wallace and company the me-too candidates, then refrained, "Me too! Me too! Me too!" in a singsong voice. Later he complained that he had not been drunk but drugged by an aide before the show. His lieutenants accompanying him on the campaign trail had videotapes that could have been substituted for the live telecast at the last minute. But he had insisted on appearing live. The next day the votes were cast and he missed the runoff by about two thousand.

Since then Folsom has run in every race for governor. He has polled as many as twenty-five thousand and less than ten thousand. The old die-hards have fallen by the wayside. In the summer of 1975, when his former protégé, George Wallace, was gearing up to run for the presidency a year later, Folsom was presented with a lifetime membership award by the Alabama Civil Liberties Union. Charles Morgan, Jr., an Alabamian who was director of the national office of ACLU, said of Folsom, "The things we believe, he believed before us. The things we say, he said before us. The things we fight for, he fought for before us."

While most politicians of his time and his state have faded into the background, George Wallace has persevered. He has brought briar-patch politics out of the backwoods and thrust it upon the national scene. He has learned from those who went before him. He has always been aware of his position, and that awareness has vaulted him into the political limelight—his chosen place to exist and prevail.

THE NATIONAL CAMPAIGNS

IF THERE HAD BEEN a clown prince in the presidential campaigns from 1964 through 1972, it was certainly George Wallace. He was the bantam rooster of the bunch, a proud, cocky, irascible little southerner who dared anything that stepped into his path. His was a one-man show in '64, '68, and '72, but he swore and be-damned if he would play such a circus act in 1976. He was serious about the Democratic nomination, he declared. And his campaign workers, most of whom had been with him through the disastrous day when he was shot in the stomach in the spring of 1972, were as positive as he.

Previously the candidate from Alabama had operated in a vacuum, fighting against the marathon rat race of politicking with lame stabs at federal bureaucracy, the Supreme Court, and the guidelines and rulings put forth by each. He was the bizarre fashion in the midst of a wild crew of politicians. Suddenly he was bound and determined to turn respectable—if that was the only way he could have the nomination.

Back in 1964, when the bantam from Barbour County decided to "take the Alabama story to the people of the nation," his outfit consisted of a handful of country boys and a half dozen tough-looking state troopers. His first outing was a whirlwind tour of Ivy League campuses beginning at Harvard, where the majority of students hissed his outline of the South's role in the Civil War. From the rostrum of Sanders Auditorium he told the students that they didn't know what a "full-blooded African Negro" looked like. "When we speak of the Negro in the South, the image in our minds is that great residue of easy-going, basically happy, unambitious African, who constitutes forty percent of our population, and who the white man of the South, in addition to educating his own children, has attempted to educate, to furnish public health services and civil protection," he told his audience, which had stopped its hissing to listen to his words. "Let me pass now to the cold, stark, realistic, political reason why the racial issue has been so violently precipitated on the American scene at this time, after a hundred years of slowly working out its own solution in an evolutionary way, the only satisfactory way, and historically the only permanent and just way," he said, rising occasionally on his heels, rocking forward, always pointing his forefinger toward the roof. The same speech was used again at Dartmouth, the Universities of New Hampshire, Maine, and Pennsylvania, as well as Yale, Brown, and Princeton. At each the groups came to hiss. They stayed to listen with unbelieving ears to his patronizing revelations. "Let us look at the 1954 school case, Brown versus Topeka, the lawyers call it. It did not, I assure you, as some seem to think, spring instantly into existence full-grown and ready for action equipped with injunctive process, preferred appeal, set bayonets and all its accouterments like Botticelli would have us believe Venus came to the shores of Greece full-grown and full-blown on the breath of Boreas," he continued. He outlined the history of the decision, including attorney Thurgood Marshall stating, "We've got to get by those boys down there," speaking of the southern whites. He said "the big kill," when the U. S. Constitution was "wantonly destroyed," happened on May 17,

1954. Speaking loudly, clearly, and quickly, Wallace stated, "From the heart, the people of the United States do not hate the Negro. The people of the South do not hate the Negro. They have carried him on their shoulders and have endowed him with every blessing of civilization that he has been able to assimilate. They want him to rise just as high as his capacities and his industry will carry him, and the higher he rises, the lighter will be their load and the happier their hearts. . . ." He was singing, but the students were staring open-mouthed as they listened to his words. "To ask us to equate our children, classroom for classroom, with a race that is two years behind at the sixth grade and three years behind at the twelfth grade is to ask us to deprive our children of the education to which they are entitled, and, in the effort to give this, we strain our resources to the utmost. It is our problem, not yours. Your problem here is yours, not ours. We ask you to believe that we are civilized, humane, and considerate of human rights. We give you the credit for being and we ask you to extend us the same consideration," he finished, and a polite applause followed. After a short question-and-answer period, Wallace prepared to leave. But the crowd outside had apparently felt the hostility of his words more than those who had remained inside. Someone cut the tires of Massachusetts Governor Endicott Peabody's limousine, put at Wallace's disposal while he was in the state. Pickets had surrounded the auditorium. Wallace was scurried away by local police through an underground tunnel.

After he attempted to explain his own not-so-unique brand of racism to New England, he carried it west through New Mexico, Arizona, and into California. Ostensibly he was in California and later the Northwest to persuade businesses to relocate in Alabama. He talked about his home state, but most of the talk was centered on George Wallace: what he had done for Alabama and what he planned to do for the country.

22

During a press conference at the Conrad Hilton Hotel in Chicago, a Negro minister who called himself Prophet William A. Lewis stepped to Wallace's side and announced, "You are definitely right, Governor Wallace, integration is contrary to God's law. You are the only white man in America I believe in."

Time after time the small entourage ran into rowdy pickets, whom Wallace called "dirty, filthy beatniks." Once a group outside an auditorium where he had spoken carried a coffin on their shoulders. A banner down the side of the coffin read: Mister Segregation.

That spring he entered three northern primaries: Wisconsin, Indiana, and Maryland. He made basically the same speech he had given on campuses, but dropped the stress on history. Although Wallace Press Secretary Bill Jones later said the campaign group found "these Wisconsin people are more die-hard segregationists than Alabamians," the candidate had several confrontations with religious groups because of the race issue. The Protestant Oshkosh Ministerial Association protested his candidacy. The president of that group, Reverend Jack LaMar, pastor of the Bethany United Church of Christ, asked, "Would you object, Governor Wallace, to your daughter marrying a Negro?" Wallace answered, "I most certainly would. I am against that." LaMar pushed, "Why would you object to such a marriage?" Wallace repeated his answer, and LaMar charged, "I think you are evading the issue." Wallace snapped back, "I'm not evading the issue at all. I don't think interracial marriages are good for either race and I am against it. That's not evading the question." During a Milwaukee speech in which Wallace said there was more racial peace in the South than in most northern cities, Reverend Earling Robe of St. John's Lutheran Church stood up and charged, "The trouble in the South has caused all the trouble in the big cities. We didn't have any difficulty in

Chicago until you had all that trouble in Arkansas, Alabama, and Mississippi." Wallace calmly pointed out that the 1943 riot in Detroit killed thirty-four persons. When the votes were tabulated in Wisconsin, the favorite son, Governor John Reynolds, a Lyndon Johnson stand-in, received nearly twice as many as Wallace, who got about one hundred thousand. Running third was Congressman John Byrnes with some sixty-six thousand votes. An on-the-spot analysis by Reynolds estimated that few Republicans crossed over and voted in the Democratic primary. "I would interpret the [Wallace] vote as a prejudicial vote. The people who vote for Governor Wallace will basically be voting for him because he is for segregation."

Wallace's makeshift advance team in Indiana was two Ku Klux Klansmen. Asa Carter, who led his own Klan group in Birmingham during the fifties, and Robert S. Shelton, Jr., leader of the largest KKK organization in the United States and a fellow Alabamian, traveled in search of friendly segregationists. "We went to every little town in southern Indiana and that led us to some of the suburban areas. What we found was a lot of very dissatisfied people. They were ready to take up arms. They wanted something to be done in a hurry. They were ready for George Wallace," Shelton remembered.

In Terre Haute Wallace told a reporter, "I am not the racist many people have been led by the left-wing, liberal press to believe. We in Alabama, along with ever-growing and imposing groups of other Americans, have made it known that we are concerned over the continuing trend toward autocratic government—that we will not willingly relinquish the basic tenets of our system. We ask no more or no less than that you attempt to understand that our actions are based on a premise of acting lawfully under the Constitution of the United States. My campaign is based on an attack on the fact that the federal government in Washington is reaching into every facet of society and encroaching on the rightful powers of the state. Through the so-called Civil Rights Bill, Washington is planning an additional invasion of the lawful prerogatives of the state. It is reaching into homes, schools, businesses, farms, and labor." The reporter asked, "What about all the federal aid Alabama receives?" And Wallace answered, "No one turns down federal aid if it is good, but actually we don't get any federal aid, because there is no such thing. It is taxpayers' aid, because it is your money and my money, and they just return a small portion to us after throwing most of it down a rat hole somewhere."

U. S. Senator Birch Bayh sent letters throughout Indiana urging Democrats to vote for Governor Matthew Welsh, the stand-in candidate for President Johnson.

When Wallace spoke in South Bend, more than five thousand attended and another five hundred circled outside with pickets. The governor had a field day. Shouting louder than the demonstrators could sing "We Shall Overcome," he said, "Northern hypocrisy is a problem that must be contended with. What is termed a race riot in the South is called civil disobedience in New York or Chicago. Take, for example, integration in Washington, D. C., which is supposed to be the personification of what is good. In Alabama we don't take what Washington does as divine—when Washington schools integrated the proportion of white in the schools was high. Now the proportion of Negroes there is high and all the whites are taking children to Virginia and Maryland. In fact, I flew over Washington last week and saw they are building a new bridge over the Potomac—for all the white liberals fleeing to Virginia."

The final results were almost a carbon copy of Wisconsin. Welsh polled 368,401, Wallace drew 170,146.

The campaigning was the same in Maryland. A tired Wallace trudged across the state. He spoke his same brand of demagoguery. Like the other states, there was a stand-in candidate opposing him, this time U. S. Senator Daniel Brewster, who took a positive stance on the Civil Rights Act. Wallace lost Baltimore and Montgomery County, near Washington, D. C., by about two to one. But he won about forty-three percent of the vote. Brewster received 267,106 to Wallace's 214,849. While the state was relatively the same as the previous two, it pointed out something far more real to the Wallace advisers: He had a strong chance of winning Maryland in the future.

Wallace swept through the South, speaking at every crossroads that would have him. He tried to woo other southern leaders, but his candidacy was dead. On Sunday, July 19, he made his withdrawal statement on national television's *Face the Nation*. According to at least one account, a millionaire textile baron, Roger Milliken from South Carolina, a Goldwater backer with high stakes in the game, bought off Wallace and promised to help in future campaigns. But his name does not appear on lists of large contributors in the 1968 and 1972 campaigns. One of Wallace's closest friends said the real reason he did not continue his fight was because "he couldn't get a single important southern politician to support him."

Johnson won by a landslide, after which Wallace said of Goldwater, "He's a good man, but a poor candidate. He didn't have the massive support that we have among the working people."

In 1964 he was the oddest bird on the political trail. Journalists wrote about him, described his antics, were fascinated with his racism, and were certain that he was only the passing fancy of a few far-rightists.

By 1968 his strength had grown not only in the South but throughout the country. He had appeared politically damaged when his own legislature would not allow him to succeed himself, but he ran his wife for governor and she won handily.

At the end of the '64 campaign Wallace had met right-wing columnist John Synon, and he could not forget Synon's Virginia Plan. It continued to echo in his mind. If he could throw the election into the House of Representatives, he could make some changes and the people would know it. His position would be strengthened considerably.

Synon had outlined his plan, based on the 1960 election. Kennedy had received 303 electoral votes. He needed only 269 to be elected. Fourteen Democratic electors would not vote for Kennedy. One elector refused to vote for Nixon. This gave Senator Harry Byrd 15 electoral votes. If the 43 Democrats from Mississippi, Alabama, South Carolina, Louisiana, Arkansas, and Georgia had been free not to vote for Kennedy, then the election would have been decided by the House. Wallace dreamed of the time when the Democrats and the Republicans would arrive at his doorstep to beg for his support.

He called together the best political minds in the state. He outlined his idea. He would bypass the Democratic party and would run on the American Independent party ticket. This group of maverick ragtag politicians, mostly from the Alabama legislature, were quickly organized into a campaign effort.

It was not difficult to persuade former Georgia Governor Marvin Griffin to act as temporary vice-president while the Alabamians worked to get their man's name on the ballots. Griffin was a believer in the Wallace brand of politics.

The politicos ran into good times and bad times in the foreign states. In California, state senators Pierre Pelham and Alton Turner took turns wooing the third-party people, and they found Wallace friends abundant in Orange County. Former legislator and cabinet member Bob Kendall did not find the going so easy in Ohio, where he visited the secretary of state, a staunch Democrat. Asked how the Wallace people could get on the ballot, the secretary replied, "There's no way." Asked again for the rules, the secretary said, "You don't understand, Mr. Kendall, it's impossible for your man to be on the ballot in Ohio." It took a court order, but the deed was accomplished.

In early March, in Nebraska, Wallace set a record for qualifying for ballot position. After landing at the Omaha airport to a welcoming party of about 1,500, including a brass band, Wallace arrived at the convention in the city's Civic Auditorium, which was overflowing. He needed 750 signatures to qualify. All had to be under one roof. Seven and one-half minutes after he arrived he had 802 signatures. Before he left that night he had 2,207 signatures.

Among those who campaigned with him was Texan Chill Wills, the whiskey-gravel voice of Francis the Talking Mule in the fifties and a character actor in movies and on television in the sixties and seventies. "I like George Wallace because he's more human than most of these politicians you see running around screaming about poor people not getting enough welfare," Wills said between campaign tours. "George Wallace has appeal with these poor people the others are screaming about. They know ol' George'll take care of 'em. You see 'em looking at him. They've got love in their eyes. They know that he cares about them, and they care about him. It's a real love affair between a lot of people and one man."

On the southern tour and the western tour, Wills whooped up the crowds and called for Wallace with a lump in his throat the size of a baseball while "The Battle Hymn of the Republic" played in the background.

As soon as Wallace got to the rostrum, hands outstretched, smiling, nodding, feeling the glory of thousands of shouts and screams and hand-claps, he said, "I bring you greetings from my wife, the governor of Alabama, who, as you know, has been under the weather in recent weeks. But she has given me a job to do—appointed me head of the highway beautification program. And you have no idea how boring it can be to go planting magnolia trees up and down the road."

The laughter filled the rooms. Wherever he happened to be, they knew him; they knew her; they caught the obvious punch lines of his down-to-earth humor.

If a heckler attempted to harass him, he'd come back with a remark. "Hey, fella, you got a boll weevil in your beard?" The Confederate flags would wave in a fury. "That's right, George. You tell 'em, George," they'd shout.

He had most of them in the palm of his hand. It was a time of war in Vietnam. People were more prosperous than they had ever been. The working man was paying more taxes, but he was reaping the benefits of fat paychecks. He had time to think about the problems that existed out there on the street and three thousand miles away in Southeast Asia. He did not like the government taking big chunks of money out of his check and giving it to poor blacks in the ghettos. Hell, they'd only squander it on a color television and two-year-old Cadillacs. His people were the low-class whites, the lower-, middle-, and upper-middle-class whites called "the backlash vote" by the press.

"Now, what are the real issues that exist today in these United States?" Wallace asked them. "It is the trend of the pseudo-intellectual government, where a select, elite group have written guidelines in bureaus and court decisions, have spoken from some pulpits, some college campuses, some newspaper offices, looking down their noses at the average man on the street, the glassworker, the steelworker, the auto worker, and the textile worker, the farmer, the policeman, the beautician and the barber, and the little businessman, saying to him that you do not know how to get up in the morning, or go to bed at night, unless we write you a guideline. . . ."

His code words were more sophisticated than they had been

in 1964. He had a wide variety by now. There was no doubt about what he meant when he said "pseudo-intellectual" or when he spoke of the "bearded professor who thinks he knows how to settle the Vietnam War when he hasn't got sense enough to park a bicycle straight." He pinpointed them. He had them dead to rights. There were thousands of pseudo-intellectuals that minute writing guidelines in Washington which the federal judges would use to change local institutions.

"When I get to be President," he told them, "I'm gonna call in a bunch of bureaucrats and take away their briefcases and throw them in the Potomac River." And they loved it. Take the briefcases! Throw them! That was what the country needed, his followers agreed.

"You've got five hundred and thirty-five big-talking members of Congress, and only six of them have got their children in the public schools in Washington. And yet they tell us how to run our schools." Again, they loved it. They clapped and whistled.

In Pittsburgh he told them, "I don't care what you people up here decide to do with your children. You can put your little children on a bus every morning and send them all the way across the state, if that's what you want to do. But when is it that the people of Pittsburgh don't know what they want to do without some pseudo-intellectual bureaucrat—usually with a beard—to write them a guideline?"

He said there was "not a dime's worth of difference" between the Democrats and the Republicans. Both parties supported the "so-called open-occupancy bill that would put you in jail without a trial by jury if you don't lease or sell your property to who they say."

When he became President in 1969, he said, there would be some changes made. "We're going to put through a legislative act that will do away with that court decision that says a Communist can work in a defense plant without a security clearance." And the people brought the roof down with applause.

In his view the top issues of the election were the war and the breakdown of law and order, which he said "are coupled. Those people who advocate a breakdown of law and order eventually wind up in Havana and Hanoi and Moscow."

In his administration, he said, policemen would not be "second-class citizens." He hit the law-and-order issue hard, telling, "If we were President today, you wouldn't get stabbed or raped in the shadow of the White House, even if we had to call out thirty thousand troops and equip them with two-foot-long bayonets and station them every few feet apart. If you walk out of this hotel tonight and someone knocks you on the head, he'll be out of jail before you're out of the hospital, and on Monday morning, they'll try the policeman instead of the criminal."

A master of sarcastic mockery, Wallace put the hook into the mouth and twisted it. "But some psychologist says, 'Well, he's not to blame—society's to blame. His father didn't take him to see the Pittsburgh Pirates when he was a little boy.' Well, I was raised in a house that didn't even have an indoor toilet. My mama couldn't even buy me a dollar-and-fifteen-cent cowboy suit that I saw in the Sears, Roebuck window. But I didn't go and bust the window out to get it."

He had been talking about professors for years. In his 1968 speeches he always used them as targets. "There's a professor out in California," he said, "that advocated revolution. Said, 'We ought to burn the town down.' Well, I can tell you this, if any professor in Alabama advocates burning the town down, my little wife's gonna see to it that he's a fired professor," he sneered in his dramatic manner.

Softening his voice, becoming personally sincere, he leaned forward. "I know there's good people here tonight who sincerely believe we should not be involved in Vietnam. I

31

respect their opinion. I believe in the right of dissent. But when somebody advocates a Communist victory, he's advocating the killing of American boys, and that's treason. He ought to be drug before a grand jury and put *under* a federal jail."

George Wallace was feeling his oats on every stage. He was like a vaudeville entertainer. He kept the same act from town to town. He changed it in subtle ways, cutting out words and phrases which did not get foot-stomping response, adding new lines now and then, forever perfecting the rhythm and timing. He would say anything or do anything that would make the people respond to him.

After one speech in Bloomington, Indiana, he turned to a *New York Times* newsman who had been traveling with the group in the DC-6. "All of these people love me," he told the reporter. "They don't act like that with Hubert Humphrey. You've seen him. They don't jump up and down and scream and shout. They wouldn't fight anybody over him. But look at them. They'd fight you over me. They love me."

That's what he'd been searching for in every face in the crowd—love. They didn't just walk into a voting booth and pull the lever for a political ideology. That was pure nonsense, and he knew it. They got in their cars, traveled miles, stood in line in the rain, and voted for George Wallace because they loved him. Why else?

He bullheadedly fought the newspapers of the nation the way he had battled them back home in Alabama. He talked about The *New York Times*, The *Washington Post*, The *Time*, and The *Newsweek*. "*The New York Times* calls me a racist. Well, it's a sad come-off when you can't favor law and order without somebody asking if you're a racist. Anyway, who writes their editorials? It's just one man, and his opinion is no better than mine—not as good, in fact. Why, they even said Mao Tse-tung was a good man, and they called Castro the

Robin Hood of the Caribbean," he said in more than one speech.

If the newsmen questioned him about his Ku Klux Klan support, he said that "the *Communist Daily Worker* supported President Johnson, but that doesn't make the President a Communist." And if he was asked about the John Birch Society supporting his bid for the presidency, he responded that "the Birch society is anti-Communist, and I have no objection to anyone who is anti-Communist."

While he flew from town to town, about one dozen young people followed in vans. While one pair arrived two days before his speech in Milwaukee, another pair would leave Des Moines and head for Wichita. Recruited from posters in the Montgomery YMCAs, they were having fun, working inside politics, and making a little summer money. They carried flat straw hats with WALLACE written in red, white, and blue around the sides. Thousands of bumper stickers were packed into the vans. Big boxes contained "Wallace for President" buttons. Smaller boxes were crammed with George and Lurleen Wallace commemoration coins.

Two brothers crisscrossed from West Palm Beach to Tampa to New Orleans to Houston, back to Montgomery, then up through the Midwest. One eighteen years old and the other twenty-one, they had the time of their lives. In Louisiana they swapped Wallace coins for gasoline fill-ups. In Florida they bribed a Miami policeman who had stopped them for exceeding the speed limit with a half dozen stickers. They had fun with the Wallace Girls, pretty leggy teen-agers dressed in miniskirts and go-go boots, who passed the money buckets at the rallies. When they arrived at the site of a speech the boys set up booths, did chores, and sold the Wallace memorabilia to the eager audiences. The profits went into the campaign chest. They were part of the down-home fever, the electric atmosphere Wallace generated.

In May, after Governor Lurleen Wallace died at the mansion in Montgomery, the campaigning was halted for a month.

However, during that time the local politicians still worked at getting Wallace's name on all the ballots. After the campaign was reopened, the Alabama legislators continued their work in the field. By the first of July names were on all ballots but a handful. In the middle of July the petitions for the last state, Oregon, were signed and delivered.

On the Wednesday night before the Fourth of July, the fanfare build-up was in process in Minneapolis when a large group of young people entered the auditorium. Wallace was warned that this might be a rough crowd. He shrugged it off as he always did. As soon as "The Battle Hymn of the Republic" started its stirring sound, he stepped forward to the rostrum.

Smiling, raising his arms, he was met with more boos than cheers. He began speaking, but the hecklers continued with their loud shouting. "Y'all lose your manners somewhere?" he asked. They didn't hear him. His smile faded as the group stood and began chanting, "Down with Wallace! Down with Wallace!"

Several of his most ardent admirers in the crowd attempted to push the demonstrators aside, but were met with stronger shoves and were seated again quickly.

Wallace's bodyguards had moved to surround him as soon as the people stood and began marching in a circle in front of the rostrum.

The city police providing security called other help. By the time the other policemen arrived, the place was in shambles. The people who had come to see and hear Wallace had moved out of trouble's range. Wallace was ushered out the back door of the auditorium.

On the morning of the Fourth, President Johnson issued a statement from the LBJ Ranch near San Antonio. He told his country, "Americans of every viewpoint must be deeply concerned over the intolerance which prevented presidential candidate George Wallace from speaking in Minneapolis last night. Freedom to speak, freedom to listen, and the full and open right to communicate and reason together are essential to our system of government and our fulfillment as individuals. However ardently we may disagree with what a man says, we must stand with Voltaire in our defense of his right to say what he will.

"It is from our diversity, our tolerance of diversity, our reasoning together from the main differences of opinion we hold that the chief strength of our people derives. The conduct of a handful who interfere with the rights of others to speak is the antithesis of what we began one hundred and ninety-two years ago today. Every American should again resolve on this fourth day of July, 1968, that he will again hear every point of view, that he will test all against his experience and his reason, that he will afford everyone—and see that others do—the right to express their point of view, and that he will lend all his energies to decide for himself what is best for his country. Having done these things, we must within the framework of order under law and by the ballot through which American citizens direct their destiny, with tolerance and understanding, gently and humanely, but clearly and firmly steer the nation on that course which will fulfill that promise while truth is free for all to see we never fear any ideology or candidacy."

With the demonstration stopping him from speaking and the President's message hitting the headlines both in newspapers and magazines, on television and radio throughout the country, Wallace's candidacy was boosted even stronger. He began privately to sound as though he might have a chance of winning. Peering out the four-engine plane's window he was heard to murmur, "Just think! Someday I'll be President of all that!"

According to his own propaganda, Wallace could conceivably have won with as little as twenty-five percent of the vote. A "position paper" drawn up by his press people stated, "With three candidates in the race, Wallace would need only thirty-four percent of the vote if the other two candidates split the remaining sixty-six percent. With four candidates running, Wallace could conceivably win with only twenty-six percent of the vote. It is even possible for a candidate to win by carrying twelve of the larger states with only twenty-five percent of the vote."

The paper cited two similar incidents from the past which would point up its conclusions. For instance, in 1824 Andrew Jackson led John Quincy Adams in electoral votes, but neither had a majority and the House of Representatives voted and elected Adams. Again, in 1876 Rutherford B. Hayes trailed Samuel J. Tilden by some 250,000 popular votes, but Hayes won the presidency by one electoral vote.

If he could have kept the candidates from gaining a clear majority of electoral votes, the candidates from the two major parties would come to him. At that time, he planned to release his electoral votes to the candidate who would make "a solemn covenant with the American people [to form] a kind of coalition government like they have in some other countries."

The candidate who sought his votes would have to promise publicly that the federal government would abandon open-housing proposals, control of schools would return to the states, as would apportionment of state legislatures, and foreign aid to Communist countries such as Yugoslavia would be terminated.

Behind-the-scenes dealing was not counted out if the election had been thrown into the House of Representatives.

Much speculation was made concerning the election. Editorial writers worked overtime attempting to discover how many votes Wallace would get, from which party he would draw his support, and how he would do if he came up with a formidable running mate.

It was also speculated that if everything went wrong, this might be termed a "warm-up race." This came from some of the Alabama viewers who were accustomed to politicians running in a gubernatorial race and losing before actually winning the number-one spot.

Wallace envisioned himself as a prime influence in the realignment of liberals and conservatives. He felt that his strength in 1968 would bring both parties back toward the middle of the road rather than being too leftist.

After the American Independent party convention in Dallas, where everything went according to the Wallace-written script, the money started rolling in. The workers, who had been flying tourist and staying in roadside inns rather than downtown hotels, suddenly found that they had first-class privileges. "Put on a good show for everybody," they were told. And they did.

Arriving in Montgomery after the Dallas convention, the bosses of that campaign—Seymore Trammell, the finance director in Wallace's first administration; Gerald Wallace, the governor's younger brother; and others—carried four traveling trunks filled with cash to the downtown headquarters in the renovated Veterans Administration building in the warehouse district. The trunks were placed inside an office cubicle, where they remained for three days.

Money was pouring in. Sizable contributions were made by conservative-oriented millionaires, including H. L. Hunt. On one occasion Trammell was sent to Hunt's home in suburban Dallas to pick up a check which he later said totaled $500,000.

In October in Pittsburgh, after Seymore Trammell made several quick trips to the West Coast, a press conference was called to name Wallace's running mate, retired Strategic Air Command boss General Curtis E. LeMay. "Everything was downhill from that point on," commented Alton Turner, one of three Wallace aides who accompanied LeMay around the country during the final nineteen days of the campaign.

In Boston, where Irish Catholic voters dominate the electorate, LeMay came out in favor of abortions. "He could have easily sidestepped the issue," explained Turner. "It wasn't what you'd call a hard question. The reporter just asked him what he thought about abortions. The general could have said simply that he didn't have an opinion or that it wasn't an issue in the race. But no, he had an opinion on everything. He started talking about how in certain cases abortion was the right thing. He might have been correct ideally, but you don't say it in Boston.

"In Miami, where some of our southern leaders were meeting, LeMay bragged to them about how he integrated the Air Force just as easy as one, two, three. That didn't turn those folks on, I'll tell you that," Turner continued.

By the time the election came, the Lewis Harris poll indicated Wallace had peaked about six weeks earlier when he had nearly twenty percent of the nation's votes behind him. When the votes were counted Wallace had about thirteen million or ten percent. Richard Nixon was the winner.

The January 1972 busing decision by U. S. District Judge Robert R. Merhige, Jr., in Richmond, Virginia, boosted Wallace's candidacy that year. Since Richmond's student population was seventy percent black and thirty percent white in 1972, with most of the parents of white children sending their youngsters to private schools, it was mathematically impossible to distribute the children in such a way that some schools would not remain with a majority of black children. In answer to this problem Judge Merhige combined two adjacent counties, Henrico and Chesterfield, and ruled that the three systems must combine efforts. The suburbs must bus their white children into the central city and the city must bus its black children to the suburbs, thereby providing a correct ratio under the law.

Although this decision was to be reversed in June of 1972, its immediate ramifications dealt frightening blows to the minds of Florida voters who were listening to a large field of candidates in its primary. Wallace, who had a brilliant slogan, "Send Them a Message," had a firm grip on the busing issue. There was no doubt in anybody's mind where he stood.

Early in March, while he was campaigning in Florida, he analyzed his own campaign on the Op-Ed page of *The New York Times*: "The American people are fed up with the interference of government. They want to be left alone. Once the Democratic party reflected true expressions of the rank-and-file citizens. They were its heart, the bulk of its strength and vitality. Long ago it became the party of the so-called intelligentsia. Where it once was the party of the people, along the way it lost contact with the workingman and the businessman."

Appearing before record-breaking crowds not only in the Florida panhandle, which has been called an extension of Alabama, but also in the metropolitan areas of Miami, Tampa, and Jacksonville, he tore into busing with his old vitality. He termed Nixon a "double-dealer, a two-timer, and a man who tells folks one thing and does another." He put the busing decision on Nixon's back. He said Nixon was only another part of the government in Washington which was run by "bureaucrats, hypocrites, and uninterested politicians," repeating his phrases from previous campaigns. "If you opened all their briefcases you'll find nothing in them but a peanut-butter sandwich," he said. Of his opponents—Lindsay, McGovern, Muskie, and Humphrey—he said they were all "hypocrites

. . . They're like a bunch of cats on a hot tin roof. They're a-hemmin' and a-hawin' and they're about to break out in Saint Vitus' dance. . . ."

When he put his finger directly on *the* issue, he complained, "This senseless business of trifling with the health and safety of your child, regardless of his color, by busing him across state lines and city lines and into kingdom come, has got to go!" He said the entire business was "social scheming" imposed by "anthropologists, zoologists, and sociologists." With the applause breaking up his sentences, he became wound up. His delivery was fast, as powerful and enunciated as ever. He was sending them his message, saying that busing was "the most atrocious, callous, cruel, asinine thing you can do for little children," and that the national politicians were the "pluperfect hypocrites who live over in Maryland or Virginia, and they've got their children in a private school," and told those same politicians that "tomorrow the chickens are coming home to roost. They gonna be sorry they bused your little children and had something to do with it. So, my friends, you give 'em a good jolt tomorrow. You give 'em the Saint Vitus' dance."

And the next day the electorate did hand out a jolt. Wallace received forty-two percent of the vote, leading the ticket even in liberal Dade County, most of which is covered by Miami. In the primarily Jewish precincts of South Miami Beach he was running third after Humphrey and Henry Jackson.

According to Theodore H. White's *The Making of a President 1972*, "Wallace, it became obvious that night, was not just a southern phenomenon—he was much more than a state-wide Florida phenomenon. He was a national phenomenon."

He campaigned vigorously in Michigan, pounding on the busing issue with ever-growing strength, and finally in Maryland, where he had done well in the two previous attempts.

On a hot Monday afternoon, the day before the primaries, he had finished speaking to a crowd in a Laurel, Maryland, shopping center when an assassin's bullets ripped through his stomach. He was taken to Holy Cross Hospital in Silver Springs, where emergency surgery was performed.

The following day he won both Maryland and Michigan. He carried thirty-nine percent to Humphrey's twenty-seven and McGovern's twenty-two in Maryland. He had a clear majority with fifty-one percent in Michigan, where McGovern won twenty-seven and Humphrey sixteen percent. *Newsweek* stated that two factors caused his overwhelming Michigan victory: first, the antibusing sentiment in Detroit and suburban Pontiac; second, a crossover of 250,000 Republicans voting for Wallace, which accounted for one third of his total vote.

The twin victories placed Wallace first in the entire Democratic field. He had accumulated a popular vote of 3.3 million with 2.5 million for Humphrey and 2.1 million for McGovern. At this early date he had more than enough delegates to assure him an important voice at the convention in Miami. In some behind-the-scenes circles, including the Humphrey camp, the possibility of a Wallace vice-presidency was beginning to be discussed.

As quickly as he was shot, Wallace gained respectability. On the day of the shooting incident, Humphrey, Senator John Sparkman of Alabama, and Mrs. George McGovern visited the hospital and spoke with the governor's wife, Cornelia. The day following the primaries President Nixon and Mrs. Ethel Kennedy, the widow of Senator Robert F. Kennedy, telephoned Mrs. Wallace and wished the governor well. During the next two weeks, President Nixon and Vice-President Spiro Agnew visited Wallace; Democratic National Chairman Larry O'Brien visited and assured him that there would be a welcome mat at the national convention; Senators Muskie and Edward Kennedy dropped by to wish him a speedy recovery;

and U. S. Representative Shirley Chisholm, also a candidate for the nomination, visited. When McGovern arrived on June 10, he told the Alabamian he "wouldn't rule out" offering a cabinet post to Wallace if McGovern won the nomination and was elected president.

Every day after the shooting his professional crew issued statements. Wallace Press Secretary Billy Joe Camp told newsmen that the governor would continue his campaign from the bed. He would go to the convention "a strong, viable candidate," Camp reported. National Campaign Director Charles Snider said videotaped political advertisements would be sent to New Mexico, Oregon, and Rhode Island—the last states where Wallace's name was to appear on the ballot. Six supporters were designated to speak for Wallace in these states: former Governor John Patterson, who beat Wallace in the 1958 gubernatorial race; Senator Jim Allen, former lieutenant governor during Wallace's first administration; Representative Walter Flowers from Tuscaloosa; Representative Bill Nichols from Sylacauga; Dr. Max Rafferty, former right-wing superintendent of education in California before he moved to Alabama's Troy State University as dean of the School of Education; and Bill France, millionaire sports entrepreneur and longtime Wallace friend.

Despite his absence from the scene, Wallace ran second in Oregon. McGovern won with 505,350 votes to Wallace's 323,000. Humphrey had 294,350.

However, in Rhode Island Wallace placed fourth with only fifteen percent of the vote, while McGovern tallied forty-one percent, Muskie twenty-four, and Humphrey twenty.

Back in Alabama, Lieutenant Governor Jere Beasley, who had led a prayer vigil on the steps of the Capitol on the night Wallace was shot, became acting governor when Wallace was out of the state twenty consecutive days. He made several speeches for Wallace, but primarily attended to the business at hand. "I did only what he told me to do," Beasley commented.

But Wallace, who had been improving steadily although he had lost control of his bowels and kidneys with the shooting and had been paralyzed from the waist down by a bullet which lodged in his spinal column, needed the office of governor before he faced the Democratic national convention. An itinerary was set up whereby he would land in Montgomery, roll in his wheelchair onto Alabama soil, then fly away toward Miami, governor again.

At least three thousand persons crowded into a private section of Montgomery's Dannelly Field. More than one hundred reporters were on hand. The plane landed, a special door opened, and he descended slowly, propped up in the wheelchair, waving at the crowd. Very pale, skinny, one hand shaking and the other gripping the side of the chair, and perspiration pouring off his forehead, he said, "I'm going to insist that they adopt a platform that tells the average citizen we are responsive to his needs and conscious of his desires. The average citizen in this country agrees with my position on these issues. And my campaign should make it clear that the average citizens are now the kings and queens of American politics." After his twelve-minute speech the Troy State University band struck up the state song, and Wallace ascended via the elevator-type doorway, disappearing into the jetliner.

At the Miami International Airport he was greeted by U. S. Representative Wilbur Mills of Arkansas, who said later the governor looked very weak.

On his second evening in Miami, Wallace made his first public appearance before his delegation. He entertained at a cocktail party at his hotel. His speech, brief and subdued, again showed his weak condition. Although all three thousand delegates were invited, only about one thousand attended the festivities. The only governor to show up was John C. West of

South Carolina. The true hit of the evening was eleven-year-old Lee Wallace, who gave her own speech. Despite her father's "accident," she said, he could still be a good president "and do all the things other people can do."

At his first press conference three days later, Wallace declared, "The Democrats cannot win in November without the support of the people drawn to my candidacy." If the convention did not respond suitably to his perspectives and philosophy, he warned, "then there is always, of course, the possibility of a new party movement."

During the following two days both Wallace and his staffers dropped their stubborn hold to the fragile dream of his eventual nomination. Now they spoke optimistically of his role as a "man of influence" in the convention deliberations.

Wallace spent most of his time meeting with the four hundred-odd delegates pledged to him. He wanted them to vote correctly on the minority platform reports. "What is in the platform is a key item. I wouldn't want to support a candidate, for instance, running on a platform that doesn't repudiate busing or one that advocates the weakening of our national defense," he remarked.

An associate who had worked for him since the 1958 governor's race, Pierre Pelham of Mobile, was working constantly to obtain a speaking spot for Wallace. Before this no candidate had ever addressed the convention. Pelham, who had been president pro tem of the Alabama senate, put Wallace on the stage. "Even a few minutes before he was to talk, he turned to me and expressed doubt. 'What if the Democrats do choose McGovern? The people of Alabama won't like that. They won't be able to vote for him. What will they feel about me talking to this convention?'" Pelham remembered. "I told him, 'They'll be proud of you. An Alabamian will be the first candidate for the nomination to speak to a national convention. You will be speaking your piece. They can't be anything but proud of you.' And he went up there and outlined his program and was the real star of the convention," Pelham continued.

After his speech, in which he Sent Them a Message, Wallace could have forced a roll call. But at that time it would have only been a delaying tactic, and such a move would have been difficult to hide from the millions watching on television. But AFL-CIO consultant Robert J. Keefe later recalled that Wallace had a "desire for a harmonious convention. We had some discussions on the platform with several of the candidates. Clearly the governor wanted his message to be heard, but he didn't think there was a hope of carrying it, and to push it would only create greater confusion. The governor sincerely seemed to want to promote harmony within the party at that time." Another political professional, Max M. Kapelman, an adviser to Senator Humphrey and a New York attorney, remembered, "I, for one, was impressed with the activities of the Wallace representatives in the period from the California primary [where Wallace received only a handful of votes as a write-in choice] through the convention. I got the message that this force was looking ahead to working within the Democratic Party. I was impressed with the number of questions from Wallace people about the rules, as though to say, 'Hell, if these are going to be the rules, we're going to master them for the future and understand them and see what they can do to help our objectives in the future.' There were meetings that took place during the week prior to the convention dealing with the California credentials; and during the convention week, meetings took place with a view toward action at the convention, and for the future. I don't think a meeting took place at which Wallace's representatives were not present. I thought that the clear message of the no-roll-call vote on platform was that they didn't want to embarrass or hurt the Democratic Party by requiring people to stand up and be counted on issues that might hurt them in the general election or might hurt them somehow within the Democratic Party."

Also, unlike some other delegations, Wallace advised the Alabama delegation to vote in favor of Senator Thomas Eagleton as vice-presidential nominee. "The man who gets the nomination should have his choice of Vice-President," Wallace said plainly and simply.

That night Wallace developed a fever and other complications. A physician had to be discreetly called to his bedside in Miami. The doctor prescribed a pain-killing drug and massive doses of antibiotics to stop the infection from spreading.

Early the next morning, one week from the day he had arrived, Wallace was rushed to the University Hospital in Birmingham. "He came within an inch of dying," said Charles Snider. "He told me before we went to Miami, 'I'm going if it kills me,' and it almost did. He felt that he had to deliver his message in person. He didn't go down there to fool around. He went down to fight fair and that's what he did," Snider added.

Physicians drained an abscess, then operated through an old incision to correct tissues that had grown together wrongly. The doctors indicated that there would be much more work of this nature to mend his body.

After the operations he went into a deep depression. His campaign workers announced that he would not seek the presidency on the third-party ticket. Joe Azbell, his information specialist who remained with the organization, said, "We never planned to enter any kind of third-party movement. That was what had us stopped when the governor was shot. We couldn't go in the other direction then. He had ordered that we were bound for the Democratic nomination. There was no moving into second gear."

Azbell also said that after Eagleton was taken off the ticket because he had failed to tell McGovern about three previous bouts with mental illness, McGovern people came to Birmingham. "They talked to the governor about the possibilities of his being a running mate with McGovern. It was obvious that the governor was very ill. And Governor Wallace told them he didn't think such a ticket would be compatible," Azbell said.

Wallace never endorsed McGovern during the campaign that followed. Nixon won every state with the exception of Massachusetts and the District of Columbia.

Although Nixon did win overwhelmingly in 1972, the behind-the-scenes Republican workers were worried about the final outcome during the campaign. Jeb Stuart Magruder, deputy campaign director for the Committee for the Reelection of the President, commented that CREEP hoped Wallace would not go the third-party route because he would take more votes from Nixon than he would from McGovern. The former White House staffer, who was later to serve a prison sentence for his part in the Watergate scandal, said, "We felt that it would have been a mistake, from the standpoint of the electorate, to have a third-party candidate whose views were so closely associated with the views of the President in many domestic issues and foreign policy, too. I think if you go down the issue orientation of Governor Wallace, in most cases you'll find it very close to the President's. There was a lot of talk by the press at that time that Wallace supporters were really McGovern supporters. But the Wallace supporters turned out to be Nixon supporters by a huge majority, and I think we felt that from the beginning."

In a Kennedy Institute of Politics—Nieman Foundation for Journalism seminar held at Harvard University in January following the general election, the professionals talked about the phenomenon of the "Wallace vote." Ben J. Wattenberg, adviser to Senator Henry Jackson and coauthor of *The Real Majority*, stated, "The use of the phrase in the Democratic Party now somehow suggests that something called the Wallace vote is something very dirty and difficult and racist and a whole lot of other things. In point of fact, when you're talking about the Wallace vote, you're also talking about 'resurrecting the FDR coalition.' Every Democratic president in recent years—Roosevelt, Truman, Kennedy, and Johnson— won because they were able to attract the Wallace vote. That is a very cold facet of electoral politics in the United States."

Pollster Patrick H. Caddell said he had spent a great deal of time studying the Wallace vote, particularly in the South. "First of all, the Wallace vote is much more complex than is often thought. It's clear that the '68 Wallace voters and the '72 Wallace voters were really different blocs. The '72 bloc was much more expanded. There are two parts to the Wallace coalition, one of which is a very ideological, racial bloc. But by '72, most Wallace voters were people who tended to be a great deal less ideological and extremely alienated from the political process. They were people who were very strong in favor of things like expanded health care and a number of social-welfare programs. The Wallace vote in '68 in the industrial cities of Ohio, for instance, broke heavily for Jack Gilligan in his Senate race against William Saxbe—in very large numbers. Gilligan tended to outrun Humphrey in most precincts in Cleveland, Youngstown, Toledo, and those areas. In '70 the Wallace vote in the South overwhelmingly went, on almost every occasion, into either more moderate or more populist Democrats like Dale Bumpers, Reuben Askew, Lawton Chiles, and Jimmy Carter, while throwing out establishment conservatives.

"Taking that nonideological Wallace vote, as distinguished from the racial vote, was a very key part of what we were trying to do from late '71 on. Those people had those strong indications of alienation. The decision [for McGovern] to go to Ohio when he was running with only half the vote that Humphrey had was premised on the fact that most Wallace voters were in the undecided column and weren't sure where

48

they were going. And certainly in Kenosha and Milwaukee it was a tremendous battle, especially among young blue-collar workers, between Wallace and McGovern. I think you have to look at the Wallace vote on a very broad spectrum. The CBS survey on election day, with a massive eighteen thousand interviews, showed that the southern Wallace voter went very heavily for Nixon but that in the North it was much closer," Caddell said.

At another point in the discussion Allen L. Otten, Washington bureau chief of the *Wall Street Journal*, directed his inquiry again to Caddell. "During the early primaries some people started developing the theory that the Wallace vote and the McGovern vote were part of one big 'alienation' pot. It seemed to me at the time that it was a rather questionable theory. What really gave the McGovern people the idea that the Wallace vote was potentially theirs?"

Caddell, one of the most brilliant young poll-surveyors in the United States, said, "I think you have to go back to distinguishing which voters you're talking about. In surveys we began very early [for McGovern], we didn't look for the people who said they were voting for George Wallace; you never get an approximation of his votes that way because of what we call the 'closet Wallace vote'—people who won't say, but who are going to vote for him. But if you start picking out certain criteria, you can identify them pretty well. The Wallace vote in '72 was different from '68, but it was still partly a racial vote or ideological vote. Then you've got a lot of blue-collar workers, particularly young blue-collar workers, who are extremely alienated voters but who never voted for Wallace before.

"When we went into Wisconsin and looked at it, it was clear that Wallace was starting off at about eight percent but really had potential up to thirty. And so we made a concerted effort at that vote, on issues of tax reform and whether

49

anybody cares about the voter. In a state like Massachusetts our prospect was won pretty handily. Wallace was showing at six percent in surveys, but there was a potential Wallace vote of eighteen percent. Our whole campaign was devoted, in the blue-collar areas in the cities, to chipping away at that vote. People who were undecided going into most of the primaries were people who were very highly favorable to Wallace and most likely to vote for him. Three weeks before the Ohio primary, with Wallace not in the race, Humphrey was running at about thirty-five; Muskie was running at about twenty-two; McGovern was running at about fifteen. But because of the undecideds and their attitudes about the other candidates, it was very clear that McGovern could pick up most of those votes, and that's exactly what he did—particularly blue-collar workers under the age of forty."

According to Charles Guggenheim, media adviser to McGovern and a documentary film maker from Washington, "We were very encouraged that the Wallace vote could be had until the perception of McGovern changed. What the Wallace voters began to understand later about McGovern, they disliked more than the things they liked about him. I think that the turn began just after Ohio and Nebraska. McGovern felt that Jackson really started that trend—I don't know if that's fair. But we felt a start of that trend, and then Humphrey picked it up in California and put it to bed."

Dick Stewart, who had been press secretary to Muskie and was once Washington correspondent for the Boston *Globe*, recalled seeing an early poll relating to Florida. "I was fascinated by it because it showed that the second choice among Wallace voters was John Lindsay," Stewart said. "As it was explained to me by people who are supposed to know something about these things, the reason Wallace voters had Lindsay as their second choice was that their only perception of him at that point was gleaned from *The Tonight Show* with

Johnny Carson. They saw this tall, handsome mayor of New York, who looked good on the Johnny Carson show and said glib and funny things. But they also perceived him as a maverick of sorts outside the party structure, and the guy who liked Wallace was not part of the establishment."

What happened to Wallace in the 1972 primaries?

In the ten states where he was on the ballot in the primaries, he counted 3.4 million votes but racked up only 376 delegates.

On the other hand, McGovern was entered in fourteen primary states and received 3.8 million votes. But he got 660 delegates.

For instance, Wallace came in second in Wisconsin although he had no organization there and made only a few speeches. He polled 250,000 votes for twenty-two percent. He failed to get one single delegate. Humphrey, who placed third, counted thirteen delegates.

Wallace went into Pennsylvania only once. He finished second with 287,998 votes, falling behind Humphrey. But Wallace only got two delegates. These individuals had filed as Wallace delegates with the proper authorities, but without assistance from the Wallace organization. McGovern came in third and got fifty-six delegates. Muskie was fourth and got thirty-nine.

Looking back in retrospect, Wallace Press Secretary Billy Joe Camp analyzed the situation, "The initial decision was to go to Florida. We had to win there. But assuming that we would, on to Wisconsin, Indiana, West Virginia, North Carolina, Michigan, Maryland, and Tennessee, of course. We later dropped West Virginia. We entered the state, but we did not campaign there. We just simply found the support for Senator Humphrey too great to go in; we did not have the time or the money to get in and fight that support.

"I would say the biggest mistake of the Wallace campaign

was the delay in getting into Wisconsin after the Florida primary. We spent ten days to two weeks in Montgomery—I don't know what we were doing—when we should have been in Wisconsin. We did not have a single staff person in Wisconsin. When we went there eight or more days before the election, we realized almost immediately that the polls showing Governor Wallace running fifth were simply not true. Senator McGovern had been on the air, and he had a good organization—a well-oiled machine, you might say; his support was tremendous. But I think all of us realized from the beginning that if Governor Wallace worked hard and campaigned extensively, he could possibly move up to three and have an outside chance of beating Senator Humphrey for second place—which he did. We were a little surprised. It was our biggest mistake—not getting into Wisconsin immediately following the Florida primary, or, for that matter, having some staff people there before the end of the Florida primary."

Wallace came in second behind Humphrey in the Indiana primary. With a more effective machine, Wallace might have won. Although he lost to Humphrey by only forty thousand votes out of more than seven hundred thousand cast, Humphrey got fifty-five delegates to Wallace's twenty-one.

Weaknesses in the Wallace organization showed up again and again. In North Carolina, Tennessee, and Maryland, the three primaries he won, his people failed to file complete delegate slates. And in many cases the delegates he did win were actually McGovern supporters. In Tennessee, for example, only one of the forty-nine delegates he won was a true Wallace supporter.

Camp said that the idea of going directly to Wisconsin after Florida never entered the organization's collective mind in the planning stages. "I can just say that we erred—we erred grossly," he admitted. "The other states that we made a mistake on were Ohio, Illinois, and Pennsylvania. Although we made the decision to go into Pennsylvania, we did not have the knowledge of the rules and reforms of the party that we needed. We didn't have a slate of delegates. It would have been a simple process, in the two or three days that we had after we decided to enter, to get an uncommitted slate of delegates that we could have later promoted in our advertisements as a Wallace slate. I think we would have come out of Pennsylvania with a good number of delegates. But we didn't do that, and we realized soon that it was a mistake—certainly after we got some twenty percent of the vote without more than two speeches there by the governor. These were staff mistakes."

Camp said he believed the reason Wallace did not go more heavily into nonprimary states was "because of a lack of knowledge about the reform rules of the party on the part of people directing the campaign [Snider]. There was a general feeling that if we got good votes out of the primaries, some of the nonprimary states would fall in line. Maybe in the past they have, but it's just not going to happen with the new rules. Obviously we realized that this was incorrect thinking later on, and we did get into Texas and we were going into some other states. At the time that the governor was shot [May 13], we felt reasonably sure that we would win Michigan and win big, and we thought we had a good chance of winning in Maryland. From there we were going to move into some nonprimary states. I still think the pressure would have been enough for him to move into New Mexico and wage a campaign there, and probably into California for a few days for a write-in vote. All of this is projection, of course."

One of the problems with the Wallace campaign from the very beginning was the lack of money. Camp explained, "First of all, we had no money to begin with in Florida. So we went to people who had contributed to Governor Wallace before, by direct mail and other means, and asked them for assistance.

Of course, having been involved in 1968, we did have a pretty good mailing list compiled by primary time. I can say our percentage figure would be eighty percent or better of small donations. That gave us the money for Florida. From that point on, it was a matter of what you do in this primary determining how much money you have in the next primary, or at least the ease or the difficulty of getting it. We did have a serious financial problem at times—actually throughout—it just fluctuated as to degree. It's very expensive when you're campaigning in about five states at the same time and trying to fly staff people back and forth to all of them; and obviously the candidate cannot spend a lot of time in each place, so you feel you've got to be on television two or three times a week or more with a good substantive political program."

However, the Wallace group paid little or no attention to the nonprimary caucus states—even four southern states he had carried in the 1968 presidential campaign. In Louisiana he gathered only three delegates in the caucus process. He did not collect a single caucus delegate from Arkansas, Georgia, Kentucky, Mississippi, Oklahoma, South Carolina, or Virginia.

In the southern primary states he captured eighty-four percent of the delegates. If his people had worked the same magic in the caucus states, he would have gone to the convention with about two hundred and fifty more southern delegates. If he had been able to put together delegate strength with his vote-getting strength in the northern primary states, he would have had at least six hundred more delegates at convention time.

"We never thought he could win the nomination in 1972," said Charles Snider afterward. "We thought we might come close. We thought we might influence the platform. We honestly and truly wanted to get the Democratic Party back into a middle-of-the-road position which would appeal to the masses."

Camp reiterated, "The governor has always viewed himself as a man who, regardless of whether he attains the presidency or not, could go down in history as having had a tremendous influence on the direction of this country in his lifetime. By getting out in the primaries as a Democrat and putting forth his position on the issues, he felt that he could send a message to the party and to the voters throughout the nation, regardless of their party affiliations, for that matter, that would be helpful to the country."

If his people had paid attention to the rules, learned the caucus system, and had had the money with which to operate effectively, he could possibly have gone to the convention with more than twelve hundred delegates pledged to him. Many of these would have been subtracted from the McGovern total. He could have forced a lengthy convention, keeping McGovern from a win on the first ballot and allowing time for negotiations in the smoke-filled back rooms. If his power had been this visible, he would have doubtless had even more influence on the party and its direction.

THE PRIMARY SCENE

THE WALLACE PEOPLE WERE paying attention to the rules of the Democratic party by 1976. The campaign machinery in the downtown Montgomery offices in the Executive Building had been cranking away at breakneck speed for at least two years. The offices had spread over two floors. Multimillion-dollar computers were running around the clock to provide instantaneous communications between the headquarters and the Richard A. Viguerie Company in Falls Church, Virginia, the center of the direct-mail operations.

Walking from the elevator, the headquarters looked like the offices of an efficiently run construction company. Charles Snider, a native Montgomerian who has been interested in politics most of his life, had a background in engineering and construction. An amiable graduate of nearby Auburn University, Snider spent five years honing his political workshop to the fine edge he was seeking. "I don't want this place run like most campaigns. I remember being in the George McGovern office in Washington in 1972 and it was a madhouse. Gary Hart was running from office to office. Frank Mankiewicz was shouting at somebody. Underlings were hopping from desk to desk. Nobody appeared to have any direction whatsoever. It was just wild. I mean, it wasn't hard to see why they lost the general election. There was no organization at all."

56

Snider looked like a youthful version of General Dwight David Eisenhower as he sat behind the wide desk, his arms winged outward and crooked at the elbows.

On the wall behind Snider were a half dozen photos, drawings, and paintings of George Wallace. STAND UP FOR AMERICA, an old poster from the 1968 campaign blared. SEND THEM A MESSAGE, stated another from 1972. And the most prominent was GET IT ALL TOGETHER for 1976. Outside the window a revolving sign announced to the Montgomery public that it was ninety-five degrees at 2:56 this August Friday afternoon. Inside the room the temperature was a comfortable seventy-two. In fact, everybody on the seventh and eighth floors of the Executive Building looked cool and comfortable.

Snider had everything planned.

Leaning back in a chair in front of Snider's desk was the tall, blond, ruggedly handsome young man who was attempting to keep everything running smoothly between the Wallace organization and the National Democratic Party. Mickey Griffin, a twenty-seven-year-old member of the executive committee of the Democratic National Committee, crossed his legs and looked vaguely interested.

"We're working like hell everywhere in the country," said Snider, his prominent chin thrust forward as he leaned into his elbows.

Snider said the Wallace professionals were uniting. More than one hundred and fifty paid workers went out into the field as early as winter 1974, laying the groundwork for the campaign, which would commence more than a year later.

"We picked people from precinct chairmen to Ph.D.'s in political science. We taught them in seminars and told them everything they should know about the Wallace candidacy at that time. Since then they have been working constantly toward one purpose: Nominate George Wallace on the

Democratic ticket," said Joe Azbell, media director for the national campaign.

"This is a more sophisticated outfit than we've ever had in the past," bragged Azbell, who fidgeted with a ballpoint since giving up four packs of Kools a day. A longtime Wallace worker, Azbell began putting out *The Wallace Stand* for the 1968 campaign on a part-time basis. Once city editor of the Montgomery *Advertiser* and Alabama *Journal*, he was from the old school of small-town journalism. A pleasant fellow with a slight lisp, Azbell prided himself on the content and layout of his political propaganda. "We're not trying to do things differently, it's just coming out that way because we're better prepared. We're not going into this campaign blind like the last three times. This time we're prepared for anything."

The first controversy to arise from the Wallace machine in 1975 concerned money. Looking into the records of the Government Accounting Office, reporter Christopher Lydon of *The New York Times* discovered that sixty-five cents of every dollar that was sent to the Wallace campaign headquarters was being spent with the Richard A. Viguerie Company for direct-mail work. Lydon wrote his article detailing how the Wallace people were not collecting the kind of money they had been bragging about because the greatest majority was going back to Viguerie. He also outlined the everyday working men and women who were sending their hard-earned dollars to Wallace, and the money was being eaten up by a huckster outfit. The entire operation sounded like a massive flimflam scheme.

Charles Snider screamed. George Wallace reacted by calling a press conference and attempting to explain the process. But nothing was made clear in the wake of publication of the article.

Later Snider took the mechanics of the direct-mail function apart detail by detail. First he said he had been sending sixty-five cents from every dollar contribution to Viguerie for prospecting purposes during 1974. "If I could have given him eighty-five cents out of every dollar, I would have," Snider maintained. "I wanted every dime that didn't have to go into the operation of this office to go for prospecting before 1975," he said.

Prospecting is the process of sending out, say, one million direct-mail advertisements and getting back fifty thousand with checks inside. The office then knows that the fifty thousand are solid contributors. These names go into the Wallace computer bank.

"I wanted all the names we could get before the campaign spending limits went into effect," Snider said. "None of that exploration work we did in 1974 counted against us. As a result we gathered more than ten times the solid contributors that any other proposed candidate had at that time. If they prospect for names now [1975–76], which is what Jackson and Carter are doing, all the money they spend counts against their limit," he added.

Each candidate was limited to two million dollars for fund-raising purposes from January 1, 1975, through the national convention in 1976. With this two million dollars, another ten million could be raised and spent on politicking. However, during the summer of 1975, these figures were raised by fourteen percent to account for inflation, which boosted all costs. Thus the politicking figure rose to $11.4 million; half of this figure could be matching funds provided through the federal campaign-funding law.

Snider was counting on the Wallace campaign paying its own way without matching funds from the government. "But if we're a million dollars short of the limit, and it might mean that much spent between getting and not getting the nomination, we will accept the matching funds. The governor believes it would be in the best interest of the people to go ahead and take it rather than turn it down and lose the nomination," Snider continued.

"But wouldn't that be something?" Snider said enthusiastically. "If we could run the campaign without taking federal matching funds, we would be another jump ahead of the field."

Richard A. Viguerie, a slight man with thinning hair and a quiet, thoughtful manner, was relatively unknown in political circles when he became the Wallace fund-raiser. But he was well known as a direct-mail expert. His efforts had been the mainstay behind the massive fund-raising of the National Rifle Association.

After dropping out of law school the Houston, Texas, native was introduced to the direct-mail approach to fund-raising when he became executive secretary of the Young Americans for Freedom. He went into business for himself in 1965 after working strenuously in the Goldwater for President movement.

He was the personification of the young conservative Republican. Then thirty-one years old, Viguerie signed up a number of clients akin to his political philosophical beliefs: the Anti-Communist Book Club, the Reverend Billy James Hargis's Christian Crusade, and the Legal Foundation of the National Rifle Association. He represented such right-wing Republicans as Strom Thurmond of South Carolina, Representative Philip Crane of Illinois, and Dr. Max Rafferty, who had been superintendent of schools in California and who ran for the U. S. Senate there in 1966.

Through the early years of hard work and vast knowledge of conservatives, Viguerie compiled the largest list of conservative donors within one computer, totaling more than 1.5 million names.

During the early months of 1972 Viguerie was wheeling and

dealing with the White House staff over a contract to raise money for the campaign to reelect President Nixon. When it came down to the wire, he said, he backed off. "I rejected the job on principle," he said proudly. He inspected such unconservative moves as the Nixon administration's wage-and-price-control policy and, mainly, the detente with China and the Soviet Union. "I could not in good conscience take such a contract," he said.

"But as my wife said at the time, 'When the good Lord closes a door, he opens a window.' It took me a few months to see what that window was, then it became perfectly clear that the Wallace people needed my help," he said.

Viguerie saw his participation as not only the direct-mail expert to bring in cash, but as a go-between for Governor Wallace and former Republican Governor Ronald Reagan of California. When he spoke of the political marriage of the two men, he talked with quiet passion. "If the two could combine forces, such a development would bring about the strongest conservative third-party movement we have ever seen in this country," Viguerie maintained. "It's my fervent hope that George Wallace and Ronald Reagan will team up as the ticket of a new party. I don't know who should run for what. That's up to them," he added.

But Wallace was making no sound about such a ticket. He met with Reagan once in the spring of 1975 in Cullman, Alabama, for a dinner speech. He declared afterward that they had "made no arrangements" concerning a political merger. "I am a Democrat," Wallace stated flatly.

Under the new rules, no more than one thousand dollars may be obtained in contributions from any one contributing source. And like any good direct-mail person, these rules delighted Richard Viguerie. In a forest of computers he was like an artist in the Louvre.

When Viguerie took control of the Wallace account in

August 1973, the campaign was almost two hundred thousand dollars in debt. Viguerie proposed to advance the campaign all the fund-raising materials it needed, and defer debt for these materials to a point in the future. In return, Viguerie would own the list of new contributors which he would develop. He could use the names for another conservative cause after he completed the Wallace fund-raising.

For a full year, until August of 1974, the average contribution from new Wallace contributors was $9.70, but the process of finding the new contributor cost $11.40. As both Viguerie and Snider pointed out, the money brought into the campaign was not the most important item at that time. The important and valuable asset was the new name, someone who would more than likely contribute again when asked.

For instance, during 1974 one mailing of 6.4 million letters were mailed at a cost of $1.12 million. It raised only $934,000. But 96,000 new contributors were found through the process, which cost the campaign $186,000. "The next time we ask these people for contributions we'll get an eighty-five to ninety percent response," Snider pointed out. "That will cost less and bring in more money. If we needed $500,000 by next month we could get it quickly with one mail-out," he added.

By the beginning of 1975, when the new rules went into effect, Viguerie said the Wallace campaign had paid off "straight down the line. He paid us off the top of what we got in every mailing. As the money came in, he would pay our bills. That's standard operating procedure for us."

Earlier the loan-collect method used in the Wallace-Viguerie arrangement was questioned by other Democratic candidates who were not pulling in money as rapidly as Wallace.

Although a deficit had grown in the Wallace account through 1974, Viguerie explained that it was his company's fault for not billing until late. "We are not worried about raising money legitimately for George Wallace—not now or later," he stated.

But everything was not running so smoothly. The Wallace forces had been to the Democratic miniconvention in Kansas City in 1974 and had experienced a thorough whipping at the hands of Party Chairman Robert Strauss. A rule that Wallace opposed was passed by Strauss's quick gavel. In essence, the rule kept the same old political power structure intact. It stated that each candidate had to show where his organization used affirmative action to have blacks, women, young people, etc., on his slate of delegates in each state. If the preconvention credentials committee determined that the candidate's organization did not show affirmative action in its choice of delegates, that delegation could be replaced by another. But the miniconvention failed to hand down guidelines as to exactly what constituted affirmative action. "What it gets right down to is there's still going to be politics in politics. It'll be the same old folks doing the same old things," commented Pierre Pelham. "They [the Wallace workers] are going to have to watch every step they make or the credentials committee will kick their delegates out just as fast as they kicked Mayor [Richard] Daley's Chicago delegation out in 1972 and replaced it with Jesse Jackson's people. Hell, it's the same old ball game with the same old players."

Snider said that his people were traveling down the political highways carefully. "We're bending over backward to stay within the rules of the Democratic party," he added.

Snider had his organizational chart filled out as early as January of 1975. By midspring he had the United States divided into twelve regions. He had a professional working directly under him taking care of each region. "Each of these regions has been covered with a fine-toothed comb," Snider said. "Our men are full-time, paid professionals with the decision-making powers. The people working under them in the regions don't come to me, they go to the regional man. I don't see them or hear from them.

"This is the only campaign with such an organizational setup. People come in here from out of town, journalists and other political people, and they say the first thing that impresses them is the fact that we have one boss, me, and they know exactly who to go to." Snider was obviously proud of his organizational abilities.

The next thing he did was work out how much money had to be spent where. "If you analyze how much money is allotted for campaign purposes under the new rules and divide it equally among the primary states, you come out spending very little in some key areas. But on the other hand, if you start spending, say, what we will spend in Florida in Massachusetts, Maryland, Illinois, Indiana, Wisconsin, etc., you come out way over the top figure you are allowed to spend. So we had to take a close look at all the primaries.

"I sat down with the governor after I had gone over the proposed campaigns, and we decided first of all to go heavy in Florida. As I told you, we believe that's a significant area. Of course, we want to win big in Florida.

"Then we will spread our money out more or less evenly between Wisconsin, Illinois, Indiana, Maryland, Michigan, and Massachusetts. If we can, say, come in second in Massachusetts, that will be a big incentive for the Wallace voters of Ohio, New York, and California to turn out at the polls and vote for their man. We will be saving up our strength for New York and California. If we can get a substantial percentage of the vote in those two states, it's altogether possible that we will go to the convention with enough votes for a first-ballot nomination." When he said those words, "first-ballot nomination," Snider's face lit up like a homemade Christmas tree.

"You look at the statistics on paper, it's there. Every vote is right there." He stared at the computer printout.

Asked if there had not been other elections that figured beautifully on paper but never at the polls, he quickly replied, "Sure, sure, but we're trying to be as scientific as possible. The Wallace campaigns have never really been scientific in the past. People have sort of felt their way along in the darkness, so to speak. The leaders, people like myself, like Joe and Mickey, we haven't really known exactly what was going on. All the shots were called by the governor. He knew by instinct what to say, what to do, where to go. But he didn't know by instinct in 1972 to go into Wisconsin because the Wallace vote was big up there at that time. He didn't know by instinct what the Democratic party rules were. This year we believe we will be prepared for anything. We're hoping for the very best, but we're prepared for anything."

Governor Wallace said he knows "there are Wallace voters everywhere. When we say Wallace Country, we don't mean just Alabama. Wallace Country is a state of mind. It's all over this country where people are dissatisfied with the way things are going and they want a change. They know George Wallace stands for the principle of efficiency and honesty in government. They know that George Wallace won't put up with any foolishness from a bunch of namby-pamby bureaucrats and federal judges."

But aren't computers and long-range strategy going against the grain of Wallace's appeal to the masses? Isn't his instinctive approach to politics what made him the unusual figure that he has become today? "Sure, it is his instincts, and we sure aren't going to take that away," answered Snider with his best public-relations approach. "We are just putting his instincts into the computer, feeding them in and seeing what we come out with. It's the mass production of genius, if you will." Again he smiled hugely. "We know the major programs of George Wallace. We know his ideas. We know what he plans to say where."

What if the audience demanded to hear something else? "He has always been flexible, and he will remain flexible. But if you look at all of his speeches in 1968 or all of his speeches in 1972, they were all very much alike. He changed small things here and there, but that's the great thing about Wallace. He knows how he feels about an issue and he's not going to change just because he's in Boston, Massachusetts, or Los Angeles, California, like some of the other politicians who try to give the people exactly what they want. If George Wallace came out with great liberal statements nobody would believe him. He's not a liberal. He's a conservative. He speaks with a conservative tongue. He has and he will," Snider contended.

Like a medieval knight dressed in double-knit armor doing bid for his master, Snider was leading his forces toward the great army that awaited him. He was insistent on the fact that the Wallace voter would at last vote for the candidate for whom he had been named. "You see, this organizational chart starts up here with me, but of course the governor is over me, up here, but it goes all the way down to the everyday voter. He's the man on the bottom, down here somewhere. In between is this series of command. And it works, it works well. Down at the county level, say in Okaloosa County, Florida, in the early spring we had a lot of people wanting to work on the Wallace campaign down there. There's this one person who hasn't had a great deal of experience with running a campaign, but she's been a Wallace supporter for years and she's a nice person and she's very enthusiastic and willing to give her time and energy to the campaign. Well, we named her coordinator, and she's got all these other workers under her. Now, between that time and the primary, along comes a very popular mayor or county commissioner or somebody like that, somebody who can get you votes and you know it, and they're interested in the campaign and they want to help Wallace because helping him will mean helping himself, or whatever; then you call in your coordinator and introduce her to Mayor so-and-so and tell her that you want her to be the first to know that Mayor so-and-so will be named chairman of the county campaign. Well, she's coordinator and she's happy with that, and you are letting her in on the decision-making process and it builds up her pride, you're keeping her informed. That's just plain good politics, but it's something not too many of the presidential candidates ever think of. Most of them believe that if they take care of the major issues, those little things will tend to themselves. George McGovern was a brilliant example. People all the way down to the bottom of his organization were biting backs, fussing, arguing over the most mundane little things. Nobody was kept informed, and everybody wanted to be the big dog. It made them look silly in the general election. On the other hand, Richard Nixon's people did just the opposite. He had too many chiefs, and that might have been one reason for Watergate; it grew directly out of the campaign. With us, I keep Governor Wallace informed about everything I do. I know that he's the number-one man. And these people who work for the campaign understand where I am on the chart."

Before he came up with his beloved organization, the people working directly under Snider came to him about every menial decision. "They even came and asked me what band or music group to hire for a rally. Jesus, that's ridiculous! I don't care about that kind of thing. Now they know how much they can spend. They know every detail of the budget. If their job calls for them to hire Minnie Pearl for Jacksonville, Florida, they go about doing that job without running to me every five minutes. If something comes up big and they can't handle it, however, I want them to come and ask," he continued.

Snider depended on Michael G. Griffin to keep the communications open between the national campaign headquarters and National Chairman Bob Strauss. That was the specific reason Mickey Griffin was Wallace's choice to sit on the twenty-five-member executive committee of the party.

Griffin, the Robert Redford of the Wallace camp, has a one-track political mind with his favorite subject: George Wallace. He was given a job: Get Wallace on the inside track with Bob Strauss. Apparently he pulled off the coup with flying colors. He has been the receiver of the blunt end of Strauss's personal jokes on numerous occasions, and only the insiders become the receivers of such.

Strauss, a gambling man, took Griffin with him to Keeneland track in Kentucky. He gave the youth some inside hints on how to bet the ponies. "Nothing but a few pointers, you know. We don't want you hillbillies to come up here and win all the loot they put out for us high rollers," Strauss joked. And Griffin took it like a grateful young man seeking advice from the experienced pro, and Strauss loved it.

On their way to Frankfort for a luncheon with top Kentucky Democrats, Strauss told Griffin, "Remember to keep your shoes on and your mouth shut and maybe these folks won't discover you're a redneck." Griffin beamed.

Afterward, clapping Griffin on the back, Strauss said, "He's a boy after my own heart. He eats turnip greens with a spoon." Griffin grimaced slightly, but with a smile.

On another occasion Strauss introduced Griffin's pretty little wife, Colley, to other members of the executive committee. "Now this is really the one Governor Wallace sent to the committee. That old country boy is just her husband." They both loved it.

Griffin worked long and hard for his place on the organizational chart. As a twenty-year-old student at the University of Alabama, he volunteered to work on the campaign trail during the 1968 election. He became one of those low-paid youths who followed the trail in vans, peddling Wallace buttons and Wallace Country ties into the middle of the night. In 1970, still a student on campus, where anti-Vietnam War demonstrations were the order of the day, he made a valiant effort to drum up support for his man. And when Wallace was booed off the stage of Foster Auditorium, the same building he had stood before in 1963 to keep two black students from entering, Griffin felt that he had not done his job. But Wallace turned the booing into votes. Afterward, when he campaigned in rural sections of the state, he talked about those radicals at the college "saying bad things about your sons who are dying in Saigon." The people applauded as loudly as ever before.

In 1971 Griffin was put on the regular payroll. He was sent off to the hinterlands to organize Wallace supporters just in case the boss wanted to take another swing at the third-party route. When Wallace decided to travel the primary highway, Griffin switched to that effort.

The opinions within the Wallace camp varied about Griffin. Snider complimented him for his previous, present, and future work. "He's one of the most competent young men we've ever had the good fortune to have work for us," he said. However, a former Wallace-backed legislator said, "He's a kid. He plays kids' games. At the convention in 1972, when he was supposed to be running the show, there he was out on the floor with some kind of damn walkie-talkie. That was the status symbol down there. If you had a walkie-talkie, you were in. Here's Mickey Griffin with one over in this corner. And there's John DeCarlo with one over in that corner. One of 'em says, 'Bella Abzug's making a statement to CBS.' The other says, 'Shirley MacLaine's got on a see-through blouse.' It was ridiculous."

Ridiculous or not, Griffin made his way to the executive committee. He cracked the door to the inside workings of the Democratic party. But what did it look like from the inside?

"We've accomplished a lot by just getting in," said Griffin. He had tried to talk to Larry O'Brien, the former chairman of the party, but O'Brien lent only a deaf ear. When he approached Strauss he found a more friendly person. "I think Bob Strauss really sees the usefulness of George Wallace within the Democratic party. He knows that the party has to swing back toward the right. He recognizes the fact that it went too left in 1972, and that's the reason it was whipped so badly. He may not be for George Wallace that much, but I don't think he'll be working that much against George Wallace. At least not like some of the others have done in the past," Griffin added.

When asked about Griffin, Strauss was all compliments. "He's quick, he's alert, and he is one of the fastest learners I've ever seen. You have to be all those things in this business to survive, and Mickey Griffin is surviving pretty well," Strauss said.

But Strauss has grown accustomed to handing out compliments as well as friendly verbal jabs. He has gambled his own political future on the Democratic party the same way he placed hundreds of dollars on the nose of a horse in the fifth. By mid-1975 he was working overtime to keep everybody within the party happy. He knew he couldn't keep them all satisfied, but he was trying. A native of Lockhart, Texas, who grew up in the only Jewish family in the tiny west Texas town of Stamford, he has become a master at the glad hand. A graduate of the University of Texas Law School in 1941, just two years before Wallace graduated from Alabama, Strauss did brief duty with the Federal Bureau of Investigation before entering into law practice. He got rich wheeling and dealing across the flat and treeless central Texas plains. He was made a partner in a Dallas law firm, chairman of the Valley View Bank, bought pieces of radio stations here and there, and was made a member of the board of directors of Columbia Pictures. Throughout it all he played the game of politics. He rubbed shoulders with Sam Rayburn, whom he considered the best political maneuverer to ever place a bare toe on sandy Texas soil. He was a friend of Lyndon Johnson and John Connelly, both of whom received his money-raising support on various occasions. He became treasurer of the national party, and pulled the party down from $9.5 million in debt to $2.5 million indebtedness. He wheeled and dealed just as he had done in Texas. And on several occasions he tiptoed down that narrow line between legality and illegality. He once collected a total of fifty thousand dollars from an official of Ashland Oil in Louisville as a party contribution. The sum was revealed when Ashland appeared in federal court to plead guilty to making a corporate contribution to the DNC. It was against the law for corporations to contribute to campaigns, but Strauss maintained that he thought the money was a personal contribution from the head of the company. He had listed it simply as a miscellaneous contribution. Under the Federal Corrupt Practices Act he was required to list the specific amounts and names of donors of all gifts amounting to more than one hundred dollars. When Strauss was told the contribution was illegal, he refused to give it back. Instead he appointed a committee to study the matter. In the meantime the Democratic-controlled Congress in 1974 reduced the statute of limitations for campaign violations from five to three years. In a letter from the special prosecutor's office, which had investigated him, Strauss was informed that the case was being closed since the statute of limitations had run out.

When Strauss spotted the vulnerability of Chairman Jean Westwood, who had single-mindedly supported George McGovern in 1972, he put on the move that vaulted him into the chairmanship. Since then he has continued to wheel and deal with a Texas Jewish gambler's calculated recklessness.

That was the kind of politicking that young Mickey Griffin was exposed to at the tender age of twenty-five. And when he stated emphatically, "I think Governor Wallace will win the nomination in 1976 or he will come so close that he will scare the britches off some very important people," some people listened to what he said.

THE DEMOCRATIC CONVENTION

DESPITE WHAT APPEARED TO BE near-impenetrable odds, Wallace and his company of professionals believed they could arrive at the 1976 Democratic National Convention in New York with the nomination in their back pocket. Shy of the nomination, they were sure the Wallace forces would be able to call the shots on major planks in the platform and could certainly hand the nomination to some other candidate of their choice.

With such a heavy load to tote, the Wallace people never hesitated in their strutting. They took their cues from their man. When Wallace strutted, they strutted. And he was strutting beautifully as he headed toward the primaries.

Wallace had been to many conventions. He went to his first back in 1948. That was when he put in his first two cents' worth for his segregation-forever philosophy and his antifederal-power beliefs. His people today look back on that convention and attempt to hoodwink liberals into believing that Wallace was progressive back in those days. He was no more progressive than Senator Strom Thurmond of South Carolina, who led the walkout of the Dixiecrats and later became the States Rights party's candidate for president. Wallace chose to fight from within the party. He was less than thirty years old. He saw a long career ahead of him. His congressman was George Andrews, who even then was no spring chicken, and Wallace had his eye on Congress. He knew the only way to be elected representative from his district was as a Democrat. But he also knew he had to be a right-wing Democrat to get anywhere near first base. He also knew that when he decided to run for a higher office (he was state representative), he would have to take the same stance. When the Dixiecrats walked, he remained. When the platform was read, the delegate from Alabama bounced to his feet. In that down-home south Alabama drawl which later became famous, he challenged every word in every paragraph of the civil-rights plank. When it came time to nominate, Wallace would not yield Alabama to any other state. He stood in the spotlight and made a rousing speech for Senator Richard Russell of Georgia. After that choice was defeated, Wallace came to his feet again to nominate Russell for Vice-President. His thrusting of the southerner to the front of the convention, swelling his pride, was later recalled when during the Maryland primary of 1964 Russell spoke in favor of Wallace on the floor of the Senate. Stating that he did not believe the Wallace victory in Maryland would defeat the Civil Rights Bill in the upper chambers, he added that when the people of the country "understand the impact the so-called Civil Rights Bill would have not only on their social order, but on their property rights and their right of association, there will be a nationwide political revolution. Either the law will be repealed or the pressure groups that are so powerful today and exercise such great influence in the Congress will finally drive us to a system of laws entirely, and become a government that will be directed by a man on a horse," thereby adding fuel to Wallace's flame.

At any rate, Wallace feathered his own nest. He certainly proved himself no loyalist simply by staying behind when the others walked out. When they walked out, they left him a forum on which to state his segregationist's creed. He was recognized by Mississippi Governor J. P. Coleman, among others, to be the up-and-coming spokesman for southern racism. Eight years later Coleman named Wallace chairman of the Dixie delegation on the platform committee, and Wallace became the chief gunner of the squad that shot holes in that year's civil-rights plank of the Democratic platform. After the Wallace wrecking crew was finished, an NAACP leader complained, "The civil-rights plank is as weak as a wet splinter." And Wallace received glowing support from southern leaders such as Leander Perez, Coleman, and others.

In 1964 he would have had a handful of delegates from the South ready to vote for him, but he stepped aside early. And in 1968, with another handful, he decided to go all the way with the third-party move. That year he attended the national convention of the American Independent party in Dallas. It was an open-and-shut case for Wallace. He was the man of the conservative hour. He was nominated unanimously.

In 1972 he came back to the Democrats. He attended the convention to "send them a message," delivering his speech to the delegates from a wheelchair. He had gone into that convention, after being shot in mid-May, with approximately thirty-five percent of the popular vote cast during the pre-California primaries.

"There was no way we could have gotten the nomination in 1972," recalled Charles Snider. "Even if the governor had not been shot, we would have had an uphill battle all the way. It would have been virtually impossible. We didn't know the rules the way the McGovern people did. But as I've said before, we know the rules this time—and we're going to pick up some votes on the way to New York."

With the convention being held in Madison Square Garden in 1976, the Wallace-ites planned to invade the Big Apple with a very large sack filled with delegates. But when they arrive on

New York's West Side the Wallace people expect trouble. They know they aren't headed for a picnic, but most of them believe it will be just like throwing Br'er Rabbit into the briar patch. "Wallace has been there before. He doesn't mind being there again with all the marbles in his pockets this time," explained Azbell.

However, the main problem facing the Wallace people (and they recognized the problem) was the fact that Wallace cannot fight every battle. If he could fight off the challenges personally, his people wouldn't worry. But he has to depend on others, just as he had to depend on them in the 1972 primaries when they let him down. The kingpin of the Wallace followers, Snider, reiterated that he was aware of the political problems and that efforts were being made to find top-notch lawyers to stave off any frontal attacks. "When we go before the credentials committee, we know it's going to be rough," Snider said. He thought every Wallace delegation would be challenged before the committee. If the challenges were valid, the delegation would be replaced by one more suitable to the committee. "No candidate would be able to withstand much of that," Snider said.

"That's only one way they could try to keep the nomination out of our reach," he said. With the affirmative-action rule in effect, there remained a distinct possibility that more than one Wallace delegation would be struck down by the committee for lack of such action. "It's the same old political game that has always been played," said Snider.

But there was another possibility in 1976 and not before. The Wallace people had moved and apparently the DNC agreed to have all open meetings shown over national television. "If the Wallace delegations are thrown out for no apparent reason, even after we prove in each case that we have fulfilled the requirements for affirmative action, such action will be detrimental to the Democratic party. In fact, such a show would effectively kill the Democratic party.

"Of course if the twenty-five member committee decides, no matter what the results might be, to throw us out, we have no recourse to their decision. But we will scream if they carry out their threat: 'I don't care if you show up with two thousand delegates, you aren't getting the nomination.' We will scream so loud that people will hear us in every corner of this country. They will have seen it on television. They will have read about it in their newspapers. They will know by then that the Democratic party has left them standing out in the cold.

"We hope that such a scene will not happen. We are working within the Democratic party. The governor is a Democrat. He has proven that before. He will prove it again. He has said over and over that he's a Jeffersonian Democrat in the populist tradition. That is what he is. But if the Democrats wish to shove him out the back door, then he will do what he can to destroy them.

"But Wallace is not going to the convention to disrupt it. He didn't do that in 1972. He won't do it in 1976. But he said in 1972, 'I'm going down there if it kills me. I want to explain the basic principles of my platform to the millions of people who support me.' And it damn near killed him, but he went and he delivered his message.

"At that convention we fought fairly. We bent over backward. We were not there to destroy the Democratic party. We were there to help it, to attempt to get it back into the mainstream of life in America. The party had strayed too far out in left field. We were there in an attempt to get it back in the middle of the road.

"More than any other time in our history, the average voter in the United States will be watching the conduct of the politicians at the conventions. If they try to pull something behind the backs of the people, the voters will react. People have seen too many shenanigans in the Watergate hearings to turn their backs on the politicians when they try to pull more stunts. The people trust George Wallace and Wallace trusts the people.

"Our ace in the hole at the convention will be our prior record. The professionals who will be running things will know they cannot run roughshod over George Wallace like they have done in the past. He is now a respectable candidate. He will demand their respect, and I believe he will get their respect. I think there is enough sanity in the party to recognize the cold, hard fact that we will not be pushed around. It's as simple as that," Snider concluded.

If anybody could doubt Charles Snider, they had only to listen to his boss. Heading down the final stretch toward the primaries, Wallace was full of himself. He was absolutely dead sure that he had a cinch on the nomination.

"I have no doubt that they will roll out the red carpet for me and my people when we go to the convention," the governor predicted. Using that cocky twist of his head to emphasize his words, he warned, "If they don't, there will be trouble across the country for the Democrats.

"Sure, I've been feeling my oats as a candidate. I expect to feel them more by the summer of 1976. And by the fall of 1976 I expect to be leading the Democratic banner across the country. All the people who have been working for the Democrats who are running just to be running against me will see their little kingdoms fall in domino fashion when we come out of the starting gate. There's a great number of people in the country who know I'm the only person running who can save America for them."

Never once letting his confidence falter, Wallace talked

constantly about winning—why he would win and what he would do if he won. "One of the reasons [I want to be President] is I've become involved over the years and have a certain constituency in the country who do feel that I represent their viewpoints better than any other contemporary man in government. I really believe that one of the great issues of the day, social and economic, is whether or not the middle class in this country is going to survive," he touched on the main theme of his 1976 campaign.

To the National Lieutenant Governors' Convention he stated, "There is a festering sore of discontent in this country that could lead to a revolt of the middle class, whose survival in 1976 and from hence on is the great economic issue facing the country."

Sitting high above the more than one thousand persons gathered for the political dinner in Gulf Shores, Alabama, Wallace said, "Under this serious tax burden and inflation which now plagues them, they have lost much hope—although they're the kind of people whose resilience is pretty tough and that can be rekindled because it's there—and they are frustrated. I think that in order to help them survive, in order that the institutions of this country survive as we've known them, I think we're going to have to have somebody as president that they don't think is a tool of anything big, whether it's big government, or big anything else."

He continued, "When the middle-class revolt comes it will be at the ballot box. Big government is an enemy of the people, and the people want to be left alone. Look at the income tax. Nothing is more unfair to the great bulk of our population than the income tax. Those on the bottom are looked after, and those super-rich on the top get by for nothing. I do believe the middle class will survive, because they're survivors. They survived the Great Depression, they survived World War II, and they will survive other catastrophes in the future. They will survive this mess we are in today."

Asked later what he would do, given the opportunity, to change the existing economic trend, Wallace answered in his usual vague style. "I would do what I could to change the situation," he said. "A vote for me from the people who care, that great middle class, would see that changes took place over the long haul. It would show the politicians of this country that they are sick and tired and fed up to here with the way things have been going in this country. I believe there are more than fifty percent of the people in this country who are tired of the mess we're in. I really do believe they are.

"I don't believe a person could make any radical changes in a short period of time in view of the fact that the problems we now face came on us after a period of many years of overspending, of extravagance in government, of a gradual takeover by the nonproducers of the country, like the intelligentsia and the bureaucracy in government. They're the ones that have been parasitic, living off the people, taking away their life's blood," he said.

This line of talk was nothing new for Wallace. He had been expressing anti-intellectual sentiments since his first major political speeches during the Democratic National Convention of 1948. He had always been after the federal bureaucracy since those days.

"The first thing I would do [if elected President] is establish the fact that big government has at least been defeated in the sense that the expression has been made at the polls by the people that they want government trimmed down and some government taken out of their lives," he told an interviewer. "We recognize we can't take *all* government out of our lives because there are matters we have accepted that are for governmental regulation. But I think the first hundred days [of his administration] would be more of a rekindling of hope in the breast of middle-class America, letting them know they are going to be the kings and queens of this country; they ought to be, because they are the producers, they are the ones who've made it go, they've paid the taxes."

Reiterating the same theme, Wallace wrote in the June 1975 issue of "The Wallace Stand" that our government is supposed to provide life, liberty, and the pursuit of happiness. But he stated that during these times "these things are being taken from average citizens more and more each day until there is only left an insecure, constant government interference, and a blurring of the true meaning of freedom. For years, we have seen this constant erosion of the rights of average citizens. The situation has now reached a crisis. Our people cry out for an end to what is happening to them. They want a new day and a new attitude in our government so that they can get back into control of their lives."

He had already started playing the tune which the country would be destined to hear over and over again during 1976. He would continue to play it until everybody knew the words before he even opened his mouth.

"One of the main reasons I want to be President is because as it stands now I'm one of the few who has a constituency that does not contain many members of the hierarchy of the Democratic party, many members of Congress, many of the party leaders, many of the intelligentsia, many of the bureaucracy, many of the nonproducers. And those are the people that the great mass of people today resent, and are blaming for their ills and the troubles that they now face.

"I feel that were I a successful candidate, the people would feel that they had someone who related to them. Frankly, I believe it would help the country in the sense that this mass of people who support me would feel there was some hope for the future—my future, their future, the country's future," he said.

In outlining his beliefs, Wallace met the issue of civil rights head-on. "People know that I'm for civil rights," he said, as though he had never made a racist speech in his life. "That's nothing new," he added. "Everybody's for civil rights, and we here in the South have accepted a policy of nondiscrimination," he continued. But he did not add the list of fights, led primarily by Wallace himself, that blacks had to face before being allowed basic rights such as voting, using public facilities, or going to school with whites.

"Every citizen is entitled to his civil rights under the Constitution, regardless of who the citizen happens to be," he said. Again he failed to add his own prejudices of 1963, when, if he had made such a statement, he would have been the most progressive governor in the South. He failed to state that he screamed, "Segregation forever!" and became the most belligerent fighter of civil rights.

Then Wallace hit upon the major object of his scorn. "This asinine matter of busing is opposed by people of all races—all except a few exotic noisemakers, whereas the average man who works each day for a living and pays the taxes and holds the country together—he's ignored. And it's just this kind of thing that has made the American people feel their government is remote from them. As a personal matter, I'm strictly opposed generally speaking to the matter of busing to acquire racial balance. And I believe that the people ought to eventually have this matter rectified in the courts and in the law," he said.

Most recently, he stated, he believed the schoolchildren should be able to attend the school of their choice. Wallace fought freedom of choice back in the early sixties. But he maintained that he had not changed during the years. "The law changed. I didn't change. It was the law in Alabama in 1962 that people of different races be segregated. I became governor and I swore to uphold the law," he said. According to Wallace, the Brown vs. Topeka Board of Education decision by the U. S. Supreme Court in 1954, which stated emphatically that so-called separate-but-equal school systems were illegal, was not in effect in Alabama in 1962. "We were still fighting that decision in the courts. When the decision was later upheld, our laws were changed. Since then we've been living by the ruling," he said.

However, he has forgotten now that he fought the freedom-of-choice method. "I would suggest to the federal courts," he said, "I would suggest to the federal Congress that freedom of choice as adopted in the southern states back in the early sixties allowed people to go to the school of their choice regardless of their color. You could go across town or stay in your neighborhood. If you went across town to a school of your choice you'd be afforded transportation. And under that system the city of Boston or the city of Birmingham could let anybody go to any school in any section of town they wanted to go to, but you didn't force anybody to go from that section to any section if they didn't want to go.

"Now that is certainly democratic, but it didn't suit the theoreticians and the judges and the intelligentsia who thought that they knew what was best because they felt that we should have a quota and a percentage, which I thought was ludicrous and asinine. That's one of the things people object to: that *we* think our child should go to this school but the *theoretician* in Washington thinks he ought to go to this school. But the child belongs to us and we're the ones concerned with his welfare each and every day. And they also note through intuition and through factual reading that some of the ones who drew these guidelines don't send their children to schools that they don't want them sent to and they are sort of fed up with all this hypocrisy."

Wallace also had his words opposing gun control. "I wish that you could take every handgun in the nation and do away with it, if that were possible, but it isn't. I'd like to take all the guns out of the hands of everybody. I'd be for that. But a man who will shoot you and rob you would also violate the gun-control law. As for sporting guns and rifles, I think people shouldn't be restricted on them. If we had started a long time ago, like they did in England, that would be one thing. We wouldn't have had such a proliferation of them. I worry about gun control in the sense that you're going to wind up taking guns from good people and all the thugs will still have them. And I don't want that to happen. The false liberalism that has brought on legislation for gun controls is the same liberalism that has brought us heroin addiction in the streets, disaffected youth, crime and violence, an ever-bottomless pit of taxation against the middle-class citizen, the use of four-letter words, which is now commonplace in most college publications in the guise of academic freedom and expression of free speech."

Wallace could see the light at the end of the tunnel. Every time he faced a new election it was like this. Something happened inside him. He was all words. He was as quick with a speech as Hubert "The Happy Warrior" Humphrey. And like Humphrey, he believed what he said.

If you wanted to hear about pornography, he'd talk about pornography. "It's everywhere, and people are getting tired of it. The courts say they can't tell what's indecent—what's indecent to one is not indecent to another. But any average man walking down the street knows what pornography is, knows what indecency is, knows what is obscene. And any court ought to know this too. And the average man feels the old moral values have broken down under this permissiveness

—the kind that allows you to take your clothes off in public but you can't bow your head and say a simple prayer at a luncheon in a public school," Wallace stated.

What about youth? "I would advise young people to reflect upon the fact that even though we have our kinks under this system in which we live, it still provides the average citizen, the little man, with more opportunity than any other country. I would also advise a young person to involve himself politically, if such is his desire. It's a tough game, but we have people running for office and I would like to see more young people involved. But I wouldn't recommend that they got into it before they got established in the sense of making a living for their family. I think you can serve mankind and people better in a political position, and most people want to serve who are there. I always wanted to see in my state such things as a junior-college program, so low-income people could go. If I wanted to go to college I would work my way through. But there were so few people in my day who could go at all because they had to work, make a living. I wanted a program within traveling distance and technical-school training for these rural boys where I lived. So they wouldn't have to go to the big cities to live but industry could be enticed to come there. One of the great problems we face is the fast growth, overgrowth of certain areas, such as the eastern seaboard, the Great Lake region, and Los Angeles—regions without proper planning. And if we could have had industry, thirty-five, forty, fifty years ago dispersed and gone to the broad expansions of Ohio and Alabama, we wouldn't be facing some of the social and economic problems we now face in the inner cities of our country," he continued.

"Even if I do not win the nomination, I will influence the convention to turn back toward the middle of the road. I will push for an antibusing plank in the platform. I did push for such a plank in 1972 and it was not adopted. That was one reason the Democrats were beaten so badly, I believe. People would not vote for a ticket which did not support an issue common to the average man. It is essential that the Democrats move now. If they don't, they will suffer another great loss," he predicted.

Wallace sat stiffly in the aluminum wheelchair. He gripped the armrests tightly. His biceps bulged. He stared straight ahead toward the future. He did not look behind. He wanted no one else to look into his past, which he talked about in symbolic terms. But to the people who lived through those times when he was fighting his way to the top, his actions were not simple symbols. His personal rebellion had been very real in their lives, and they remembered clearly.

WHERE IT ALL STARTED

"GEORGE WALLACE WAS BORN thinking about politics. That's the first thing that enters his head in the morning. It's what he's thinking about at night. And I believe he dreams about politics. He couldn't have been knee-high to a June bug when he knew he was going to spend his life as a politician."

The man who summed up Wallace's life is his best friend, Oscar M. Harper, a lanky, prematurely gray-haired fellow whose flat nasal drawl and sleepy-looking eyes give the impression that he's a slow country bumpkin. Harper, like Wallace, is anything but a bumpkin. While Wallace has made a name for himself in the political world, Harper has done better than OK on the financial side of the street.

"I guess I've known George Wallace almost all his life. I really got in with him during the 1958 governor's campaign," Harper explained.

"He wanted somebody to drive him around the state, take care of him, get some money somehow or another. He wanted my brother, Henry, to do it. Henry was in law school at the University of Alabama. He knew George better than I did, but I didn't want Henry to drop out of school to run the campaign.

I wanted him to stay in school. I had had to drop out early. I was working and making some money and sending him to school.

"I took George Wallace to Scottsboro on first-Monday trade day when all the people come into town with all their goods to sell and trade. The streets are just crowded with folks. We went up there and he did real good, and we worked our way down the state. He talked to people in every crossroads.

"I've never seen anybody push like he pushed. He'd be up early and go until after midnight. It really wore him down to a frazzle. I know it about got the best of me. I think it really about got him. He lost the race, but he never stopped running for the office. He kept on going.

"I pitched in some money with some more folks to get him over the hump of the three years or so after his judgeship ran out and the 1962 race started.

"It never was any doubt in his mind that he was going to win the 1962 election. I took off into it headlong, never looking back. When he started running this time he had more money than back in 1958, when he was always about broke except for the money me and a few others took out of our pockets and gave him. I mean, he didn't have money to pay for little sidewinding bands from Birmingham to play at rallies. But in 1962 he had more going for him. And he was in better shape physically. He had gotten himself ready to run. Like I said, he had been running all the time. He didn't really stop. He proved himself a natural-born campaigner, but he had been doing that all his life," Harper continued.

Prior to Wallace's first inauguration, Harper stated, "He [Wallace] has the least regard for money of any man I have ever known. He spends all his time worrying about other people, people who are sick, or down and out. When you ask him about how he is making out, he always tries to pass it off, when you know dern well he's not much better off financially than the people he's worrying about."

Harper, owner of National Services, Inc., a printing, publishing, and office-supply company in Montgomery, was given the first concession of the new administration. Before Wallace even took control of the government, Harper's company printed a 296-page official inaugural program. More than ten thousand copies were sold at two dollars each, plus hundreds of advertisements congratulating the new governor. Everybody who was anybody bought the ads.

It was obvious that Harper would have substantial influence in the Wallace administration. He and Wallace's youngest brother, Gerald, a lawyer, formed several partnerships designed to do business with the state. The most profitable were asphalt companies. Harper's shrewdness and cunning ability were abundantly apparent by the fact that the business operations never became public knowledge until well after Wallace's first term.

Harper denied that he ever called the shots in a Wallace campaign. "Let me tell you something, George Wallace is his own strategist, if you want to call it strategy. I don't think there was any strategy to it [in 1962]. I mean, Wallace ran the show. Oh, he'd listen to advisers, all right, but then he'd go right out and speak just as he pleased. He would say, 'It might not be smart, I don't know, but I've got to tell the people what I think and what is in my heart, win or lose. . . . I've got to be honest with them.' And he did it, just like that. No, there weren't any strategists or sharpies, and I doubt there was any planned strategy at all, just old-fashioned speaking ability and conviction," the Geneva, Alabama, native said.

Harper demonstrated his closeness to Wallace by naming his son, born in 1961, George Wallace Harper. "I want him to grow up half as smart as his namesake," Harper said good-naturedly.

Speaking of the governor, Harper said, "I've known a lot of people in my life. I've known hundreds of thousands. But I don't believe I've ever known anybody who has the total belief in himself that George Wallace has. He's the most remarkable individual I've ever had the pleasure of being around."

Wallace was born and grew up on the main street of a sleepy little town on the edge of Alabama's Black Belt. Clio was no different from hundreds of other towns that dotted the southland, monuments to the antebellum days when cotton was king. When Wallace was growing up during the twenties the town had a dozen businesses including the cotton gin, which was located on the road to Texasville.

The Wallace house was a three-bedroom frame house that was torn down and replaced by a three-bedroom brick in 1933. The archways of the new home showed off some rather fancy brickwork. It sat catty-cornered on the half-acre lot. It faced downtown.

The barbershop, located no more than a hundred yards from the front door, was the center of his boyhood universe. It was his favorite spot. And it was where he sold his first subscription to *Grit*, a national newspaper that specialized in human-interest tidbits. It was as American as apple pie and Norman Rockwell.

During the blistering summers the sweating traveling salesmen sat in front of the fans in the barbershop and talked about what they had seen in Montgomery. Every odd year the legislature met through the summertime, and the talk was about the battles representatives and senators were having over particular bills pending before them. Shortly before Wallace's tenth birthday, in 1929, Governor Bibb Graves asked the legislature to pass an antimask law to make it illegal for the Ku Klux Klan to parade under their hoods. The prevailing thought among the barbershop sitters was that the law was too liberal. The Ku Klux, people of the Black Belt thought, should have the right to cover their faces. And sure enough, the legislators failed to pass the bill into law.

Wallace was not a wanderer. Whenever his mother wanted him, she knew that he would be either in the barbershop or hardware store. He had a corner next to the shoeshine stand where he sat and listened to the men talking. If a stranger came to town, Wallace was one of the first to meet him, shake his hand like a grown-up, and ask if there was anything he could do to help. He noticed how the strangers showed enjoyment when they were approached with friendliness.

When he was twelve years old he bought a small black notebook from the hardware store. In it he kept the names and addresses of all the people who bought subscriptions to *Grit* and other publications that he sold. At night he would read the newspaper. Once, he said, he read about a man who had tattoos on every inch of his body. Wallace asked his mother about the man. She explained that he was a freak and apparently chose to be different from the rest of the world. Wallace said he hoped he would never have to be tattooed. His mother said if he worked hard he would not be tattooed. The next day he sold a dozen new subscriptions to people who came into town on Saturdays.

Saturday was the most exciting day in Clio. The farmers in bib overalls and BVD's rode in on their wagons and parked along the main street. With them came their families: towheaded children, boys wearing overalls like their papas and girls wearing flour-sack dresses like their mamas. All the country children went barefooted until first frost, which usually came in late October.

On Saturdays Wallace learned the art of politicking on the crowded narrow sidewalks of the town. During elections the politicians would be out in force. The best of the lot shook hands, talked about the weather, asked people how their crops were doing, and showed interest in the individuals. Those who were not so good just shook hands and exchanged pleasantries and went on down the road to another town.

When he was thirteen Wallace took on his first political chore. Fred Gibson was running for secretary of state. Wallace heard him speak and asked to work for him. The candidate jokingly told the youth he'd be glad to have such a fine worker. Young Wallace knocked on every door in Clio, asked everybody to vote for Gibson, and although he lost the statewide race he carried Clio.

Wallace's grandfather, Dr. G. O. Wallace, was a fair county politician. He had been probate judge of the county and was loved by a great many. He was a country doctor who drove his buggy into the hinterlands to tend to sick farm people. He always had time to talk or listen, whichever the other person needed. And young George was the favorite gleam in his grandfather's eye. Doubtless young Wallace learned much about politicking by watching the older man practice the art.

Wallace's father, also named George, was a mediocre county politician. He had served one term as chairman of the Barbour County Commission. He expressed a desire to run for probate judge, but his health failed him when his oldest son was a young teen-ager. Stricken with a respiratory disease, he spent his last few years bedridden.

Wallace was not the finest student at Barbour County High School and he was not the best athlete, but he made respectable B's and C's and played quarterback on the football team. He took care of his body with exercise and read voraciously, usually Civil War and southern history. This habit was to remain with him throughout his adult life. He enjoyed reading about J. E. B. Stuart or Stonewall Jackson or—his favorite—Robert E. Lee engaged in battle with the northern enemy.

The church, too, was a place of politics in the small town, he learned. He was saved in the Presbyterian Church of Clio.

Sunday school was an extension of his everyday life when his mother read him dramatic bedtime Bible stories. The worship service fascinated him. He liked to hear the preacher hold a word as though on a silver platter, then lean forward and rip through hellfire-and-damnation phrases which would tear his very heart loose from its arteries. He enjoyed the springtime revivals best, when the out-of-town evangelists were even more powerful in their talk than the regular minister. Sometimes they sounded like the radio missionaries who moaned and groaned and cried out over the air for the Lord. Wallace watched how people reacted, how they might actually shiver and close their eyes, and how they might reach into their pockets and give hard-earned money to keep alive heaven's works on earth.

One of his classmates from Barbour County High said that Wallace was a contradiction among his peers. "George was really pretty much of an introvert around his classmates. It's hard to believe now, but he never did the glad-handing bit back in those high-school days. That's not to say he wasn't popular. Everybody liked him. He just didn't seem to be that much of a politician with us. He was really liked more by the adults. I think they saw a potential in him. He wasn't as shy with them as he was with us. He'd go right up to some older person and grab their hand and shake it and start talking. I wouldn't have done that for anything back then. But it was like George had already grown up when he was fourteen or fifteen years old. And he knew everybody. It wouldn't surprise me if he could call the name of every living soul in Barbour County. Even then he had that phenomenal memory for names. There'd be people who'd come over from Troy or Luverne or from down in Dothan and wouldn't come back for two or three years. If he met them the first time, he'd know their names when he saw them again. I wouldn't call him a real smart kid when he was growing up, but he sure wasn't dumb. We always knew George would make out all right in the world beyond Barbour County."

But Wallace was not entirely a child prodigy. He had a good time like most other teenagers. Another classmate remembered, "We used to go out to Blue Springs, now a state park, and swim in that ice-cold water. We'd usually go in naked, skinny-dipping, and it was real nice between long, hot afternoons picking blackberries alongside the dirt roads. We'd pick the berries and sell them for ten cents a gallon. We'd give the money to our parents, who'd buy us clothes with the money. George was a good boy. He'd get into regular boylike mischief, like stealing a watermelon from somebody's patch. When he played quarterback for Barbour County he weighed ninety-eight pounds. He was always a little scrapper. He was kind of scrawny, but he was tough as nails."

In the spring of his fifteenth year he made arrangements to work as a page in the state senate. His father drove him to Montgomery and let him out in front of the capitol. "I stood on that bottom step and looked up at the dome," he said later. "It seemed so huge. I wasn't sure I'd be able to walk in the shoes of some of those people who had been here before. On the top step I stood next to the bronze star where Jefferson Davis stood when he took the oath as president of the Confederate States. I felt chill bumps all over my body. I stood there with my feet on the star and looked out down Dexter Avenue. In my mind I could see myself in the future. I knew I would return to that spot. I knew I would be governor of the people of this great state," he added. Before the end of the day he was elected page. He lived that summer in a boardinghouse near Goat Hill, the former pasture on which the capitol stood. He spent long days listening to the lawmakers in action and watching the events that unfolded almost surrealistically on the floor of the upper chambers.

In the hallways of the capitol he discovered the portraits of two men his Clio teachers had told him about. Both were Barbour County men. One was John Gill Shorter, governor from 1861 to 1863 and a member of the Provisional Confederate Congress in Richmond. The teachers had praised Shorter's immense loyalty to the South and its causes. But the teachers failed to point out that Shorter was defeated in a bid for a second term by a vote of almost four to one. The other was Braxton Bragg Comer, a successful businessman who served as governor from 1907 to 1911. He established Avondale Mills, which grew into a multimillion-dollar textile industry. Later he was appointed to serve the unexpired term of U. S. Senator John H. Bankhead, who died in office in 1920.

That summer was not filled entirely with politics. He practiced prizefighting, a sport in which he had become interested. It was a sport that suited his fiery temperament. He loved to fight then just as he loves to fight politically today. In the fall of his fifteenth year he fought an eighteen-year-old competitor in Montgomery's Cramton Bowl in the South Alabama Tournament. During early rounds he looked beaten to a pulp, but he came back and punished his opponent with battering right hooks and left jabs. Afterward Wallace said, "You couldn't tell I had won by looking at me. My face was such a mess that when I went downtown later a Montgomery policeman stopped and questioned me. He thought somebody ought to be arrested." He lost in the semifinals that year. But in 1936 and 1937 he won back-to-back State Bantamweight Boxing Championships.

In his last years of high school his father's health began to wane more and more. Wallace continued selling *Grit* and other publications, sometimes receiving a mess of collard greens or a basket of black-eyed peas as payment. Anything he could get, his mother appreciated. When he was a senior he was president of his class, and he worked after school as rabies inspector for the Barbour County Health Department. "Later when he ran for office and those people from out in the country saw him coming around, they recognized him as that fine young man who'd taken care of their dogs for 'em. They knew he'd been good with the dogs, and the dogs loved him. They called him 'The Dog Man,' and they figured that anybody who loved dogs and vice versa had to be good for the legislature, and they voted for him," related Joe Azbell.

He went on to the University of Alabama in the fall of 1937 with a cardboard suitcase in which he carried a few odds and ends, including one extra shirt. He owned only the suit he was wearing.

The school in Tuscaloosa was not overcrowded that fall. The Great Depression was still in progress. People in the South were not as hungry as those who lived in the cities, but a good job was hard to come by. Most college-aged youngsters had to go to work as soon as they finished high school.

He worked out a deal with a woman who ran a boarding-house near the school. He waited tables and did busboy chores for his keep. He scrubbed the floors and cleaned the kitchen regularly.

About one month after he started school he received a call that sent shock waves through his body. His father had died of Brill's disease, a respiratory ailment.

After traveling home to Clio by bus for the funeral, he experienced a second emotional jolt. His father had mortgaged the farms outside of town. The holders foreclosed on everything but the family house. Wallace was the oldest child and felt a responsibility toward the family. He told his mother that he had decided to give up school and return home to make a living for them.

His mother, Mozelle, a tough little mite of a woman with thin lips and thick skin, shook her head. She told him he was going back to school. There was no question about that in her mind. She had already made arrangements about how the family would survive. She would take the job as sewing-room supervisor for the National Youth Administration in Clio. He would return to school.

He did not argue. He returned to his classes in Tuscaloosa. He took a nighttime job driving a taxi, which he did after he finished his chores at the boardinghouse.

"All he did was work and study. I don't think he ever got any sleep, unless it was in the classroom," recalled one classmate. "I'd be sitting in English class and George'd come in and sit down. He had a way of sitting straight up with his eyes closed. Sometimes he'd snore and wake himself up and look around quickly, embarrassed. Everybody who had classes with him liked him. After classes he'd go around and talk to everybody. You might not realize it until much later, but he'd be mixing and mingling, politicking the way he always did, but he'd also be finding out what the professor said in class. He did all that work, was elected president of the freshman class, and made pretty good grades. He didn't make the dean's list, but he wasn't far from it."

It didn't take him long to become thoroughly immersed in campus politics. He was already displaying his phenomenal memory, and he put it to work when election time got close. He talked to everybody, knew everybody's names, and he decided to run for president of the prestigious Cotillion Club during his second year.

Already he had been captain of the freshman baseball team, a member of the boxing squad, and president of the Spirit Committee.

"George Wallace campaigned like you've never seen anybody campaign at the University of Alabama," said the classmate. "There always were politics on the campus, but he really put on a show. It seemed like he was everywhere. He shook hands all day and all night. He table-hopped in the Sup Store [University Supply Store] coffee shop. I don't believe

97

there was anybody left who didn't know him by election time. His opponent was Conrad 'Bully' Fowler, a fraternity man and a pretty sharp politician himself. When it came down to the election, the fraternity machine was able to get more people to the polls. Wallace had scared them so bad, the fraternities had their pledges carrying people to the booths and the sororities turned out everybody they had to vote for Fowler. But even then it was a close vote. Fowler won, but Wallace had scared the bejesus out of the fraternity boys who liked to think they ran everything."

In 1939, when he was a junior, Wallace was captain of the prizefighting team, and the next year the sport was dropped. But that was okay with Wallace. He had other things to occupy his mind and time.

Law school was made for him. He got another job as a part-time truck driver when he moved again, this time with Glen Curlee from Elmore County. Wallace liked Curlee immediately, and vice versa, because they were about the same height. Curlee was a heavy-set chain smoker who also loved to talk politics. The two moved in with a third friend, Ralph Adams, who owned an old boardinghouse near the football stadium. Another young man to play a vital part in twentieth-century Alabama politics was Frank Mims Johnson, Jr., who visited the Adams house on frequent occasions to talk politics. "People came and went in that place. It was a magnificent time, reminiscent of the bawdy ages when people drank their ale out of great pewter mugs and ate turkey with their bare hands," said Curlee, who was named Elmore County circuit judge and later district attorney by Wallace.

"How in God's world George Wallace made it through school, I'll never know. It's beyond me. But he always surprises me in the accomplishments that he gains. I don't think he ever owned a law textbook while he was going to school. He studied mostly in class or borrowed books. He'd

98

read over some treatise once, and he'd know it better than most people who studied it for hours. Hell, he just wanted it to pass the exam. He knew even then he'd never be a lawyer, not really. He was a born politician," Curlee said in his deep, rich voice.

"We had some wonderful fun when we were in school. We had a great time. We considered ourselves fully grown, mature adults. After all, we were the lawyers of tomorrow, the politicians who would have dominion over the legislative bodies of the land, the judges who would pontificate the complex issues of the time . . . And of course George Wallace was no mere student. He *was* the future governor of the state of Alabama. And he damn well knew it," Curlee stated.

On one occasion Curlee and Wallace attended an Alabama-Tennessee football game in Birmingham, and Wallace was to prove his true friendship. With the Volunteers leading, and less than a minute to go, the Crimson Tide drove down the field and scored. As the Alabama player crossed the goal, Curlee, wild with enthusiasm, rapped a policeman over the head with a folded newspaper. Without a word, the policeman and his partner took the protesting Curlee into custody.

After Curlee was shoved into the back of the paddy wagon, appropriately referred to by students as the Black Maria, his friend Frank Johnson appeared at the grill in the rear of the wagon. Johnson asked if Curlee was all right. After a stream of profanity, Curlee said he was not injured. He also insisted that he was not drunk and had not been drinking.

By this time Wallace was at Johnson's side, and the two law students assured Curlee they would follow him to the South-side Police Station.

At the station Johnson and Wallace demanded that a physician check their arrested friend's condition. They wanted proof. But the police turned down their request.

Within an hour Johnson walked before the night-court

99

judge. He presented himself as a University of Alabama law student originally from Haleyville who would be defending Curlee, the president of the law school student body.

When Wallace took the stand, he swore under oath that Curlee had not taken a drink in his presence that afternoon. But Wallace did not leave well enough alone. He testified that he had known Curlee for many years and that Curlee was a "fine, upstanding citizen who has never drunk alcoholic beverages."

The judge found Curlee innocent of the charges, after which he leaned across the bench and shook Johnson's hand. "I'm from Haleyville too," the judge said.

"Yes, your honor, I know," Johnson said.

The judge asked if the young men would like to visit his home and have a beer.

They followed the judge to his home, where all but Curlee drank beer into the wee hours. Wallace had been such a good witness that Curlee, who enjoyed a stiff drink of whiskey or a can of beer as well as any man, was offered only coffee or Coke.

This was not the last time George Wallace and Frank Johnson were to meet in a courtroom.

During his last year in school, Wallace frequently dropped by the Johnson apartment. He seemed to always appear at dinner. Ruth Jenkins Johnson, a native of Winston County, was a fine cook who prepared vegetables exactly the way Wallace liked them. After Wallace graduated and took a job driving a dump truck in rural Tuscaloosa County for the State Highway Department, he used part of his first paycheck to buy meat and vegetables and paid a cook to prepare the meal. He invited Ruth and Frank Johnson to dinner, his own sentimental way of paying them back for the meals he had taken with them.

In later years Johnson was to become Wallace's number-one opposition, although they never met in a political race.

Johnson, who was as country cunning as Wallace, was from the opposite corner of the state from Barbour County. He was born in the eastern hills of Walker County, where moonshiners, coal miners, and Republicans made up ninety-five percent of the meager population. His mother and father were teachers in a two-room schoolhouse at Old Jagger until the family moved to Haleyville, where the patriarch of the family became mayor.

Johnson was raised on courthouse politics, just like Wallace. But this was a maverick brand of politics. Winston County had attempted to secede from Alabama when the state separated from the Union in 1860. When it was not allowed to legally remain with the Union, the place determinedly called itself The Free State of Winston. Thus it was not altogether unusual when Frank Johnson, Sr., was elected to the state House of Representatives and served a full term as the only Republican among more than a hundred members.

Back home, the elder Johnson was elected probate judge of Winston County, and his son enjoyed the activity of the courthouse. The boy would sit on the hard wooden pews and listen to the lawyers argue toward an ultimate justice.

As a teen-ager, Johnson was sent to Gulf States Military Academy in Gulfport, Mississippi, and after graduation he worked as a surveyor and attended Massey Business College in Birmingham. When he was nineteen he married a pretty farm girl, Ruth Jenkins, and they worked their way through the University of Alabama, where they first met Wallace. After Mrs. Johnson finished school she taught speech at Tuscaloosa County High School in Northport, across the Black Warrior River from the college town, and one of her students was Lurleen Burns, who was to marry George Wallace and become governor of the state.

During World War II, Ruth Johnson stayed in Washington as a WAVE lieutenant editing secret papers for an admiral on the Joint Chiefs of Staff. He became an infantry lieutenant in General George Patton's army and won a Bronze Star in the Normandy invasion. He was wounded twice and sent back to England as a legal officer.

When the husband and wife were reunited in Alabama, he found his niche in the courtroom. He worked in Jasper, the county seat of Walker, and was respected by peers in the legal profession. In 1952 he served as one of Dwight Eisenhower's nine state campaign managers, holding to the Republican image which had been started by his great-grandfather James Wallace "Straight Edge" Johnson, the first GOP sheriff of Fayette County. When the new president took office, Johnson was appointed U. S. attorney for the northern district of Alabama. He was thirty-four years old.

Within the next two years he compiled an impressive record. He prosecuted a case against two Alabama planters who had paid Mississippi jailers to bind Negro prisoners over to them. He won a conviction.

In 1955 the U. S. judge for the middle district of the state died. Johnson was appointed to the job one week after his thirty-seventh birthday, and he moved into offices in the federal building in Montgomery only a half dozen blocks from the state capitol.

It didn't take the young judge long to become the center of controversy. Montgomery's bus boycott had generated a suit that ultimately wound up in the lap of the federal court. The public buses in the city had always been segregated. Rosa Parks, a modest seamstress, sat down in the front section of a bus, after which she was arrested for her move. The Montgomery Improvement Association, led by Dr. Martin Luther King, Jr., inaugurated the boycott and sued to break the segregation barrier. Sitting on a three-judge panel hearing the case in 1956,

Johnson joined with Circuit Judge Richard T. Rives, also of Montgomery, to hand down a majority vote in favor of desegregation. The effect of this decision spread rapidly throughout the South, and it wasn't long before the segregationists came out of their separate-but-equal outhouses and swore Johnson was in the same "Communist" nest with the Earl Warren Supreme Court.

Johnson, who made up for youth with a stern veneer, did nothing to dispel such talk. He didn't believe in judges making speeches to ease their opinions with the general public. "Judges make decrees. They can't sell 'em," he stated.

Inevitably, he and Wallace had a confrontation. Wallace was spending his last days as circuit judge after being defeated in the 1958 gubernatorial election, when the U. S. Civil Rights Commission, headed by A. H. Rosenfeld, asked for the voter registration records of Bullock and Barbour counties. As judge, Wallace took possession of the records and refused to turn them over. After he promised several intimates, "I'll never be out-niggered again," he decided to milk the situation for all the antiblack publicity he could squeeze from it.

When Wallace persisted, Johnson ordered that Wallace turn over the records to the commission and show cause why he should not be held in contempt of court. Wallace ballyhooed. He called the hearings "Roman holiday investigations," and he insisted for the television cameras, "The time has come when we must stand up and defend the rights of the people of Alabama regardless of the personal sacrifices." This was his first stand.

On the night before he was to appear in Johnson's courtroom, the mutual friend from college days, Glen Curlee, telephoned the federal judge at his suburban Montgomery home. He asked if Johnson would talk to Wallace. Johnson said he would listen.

After eleven o'clock Wallace rang the doorbell of the

judge's brick ranch-style house in a fashionable area of the town. When Wallace walked inside, he said, "You've got my ass in a crack, Johnson."

The two went into Johnson's paneled den, had coffee, and Wallace said, "If you'll give me a light sentence, you can find me in contempt. I know I wouldn't be able to spend more than a week in jail."

Without blinking, Johnson said, "If you don't hand over those records, I'll throw the book at you, George."

Wallace, pacing the floor, asked, "What if I turn them over to the grand juries and let them give them to the commission?"

"If you can do that by morning . . ."

Wallace walked out and the next morning both Barbour and Bullock grand juries were assembled and had the records in their possession. To each, Wallace said, "When I turn the records over to you, I realize I no longer have control over them. The grand jury is the supreme inquisitional body of this county. The records are yours to do with as you see fit. I am willing to accept whatever consequences there are for my action in impounding the voting records and in turning them over to you." The juries then gave the records to the commission.

When Wallace arrived at the courtroom he was followed by a barrage of attorneys, his wife, and the press.

On the stroke of ten the solemn-faced judge stepped through the door in the royal blue, gold-star-dotted wall behind his bench. After hearing testimony, he stared over half-moon glasses with deep brown, piercing eyes. His thin lips drawn tight, he said in his flat nasal drawl, "This court further finds that, even though it was accomplished through a means of subterfuge, George C. Wallace did comply with the order of this court concerning the production of the records in question. As to why the devious means were used, this court will not judicially determine. In this connection, the court feels it sufficient to observe that if these devious means were in good faith considered by Wallace to be essential to the proper exercise of his state judicial functions, then this court will not and should not comment upon these methods. However, if these devious means were for political purposes, then this court refuses to allow its authority and dignity to be bent or swayed by such politically generated whirlwinds." He then found Wallace not guilty.

Afterward Wallace held an impromptu press conference on the steps of the courthouse. As outraged as he had ever been, Wallace ranted, "Since there was a grave constitutional question involved, I had hoped to take it to a higher authority; but now I have been acquitted, I believe this justifies my militant stand against the efforts of the Civil Rights Commission to take over the courts of Alabama." He continued, "I was willing to risk my freedom in order to test the question at this time as I felt an opinion should be rendered on this important question. The whole matter arose as a result of my doing my duty, and plead guilty to the failure to bow to the wishes of the court, and if the judge holds this is not contempt, then I have no control over such conclusion."

A group of Wallace's friends were with him afterward at a downtown Montgomery hotel when he was "tossing down whiskey right and left, hitting his head against the wall of the room, and saying, 'He's a no-good goddamn lying son-of-a-bitching race-mixing bastard.'" Later, for public consumption, Wallace called Johnson "an integrating, carpetbagging, scala-wagging, race-mixing, bald-faced liar."

Frank Johnson never flinched. He kept going down the path he had blazed for himself.

In 1963 he broadened the Supreme Court's famous Gideon decision, which gave all defendants the right to adequate counsel. Johnson ruled that court-appointed attorneys must be paid for their services because the Constitution requires "effective" counsel. Soon after his decision Congress passed a law requiring payment to attorneys in federal courts everywhere.

He sat on the three-judge panel that struck down Alabama's poll-tax law, which unfairly burdened poor people by not allowing them to vote unless they had money to pay for the privilege.

Early in 1965 civil-rights demonstrations flared up in Selma, the seat of Dallas County, and confrontation after confrontation occurred. At the same time Dr. King was organizing the Selma-to-Montgomery march. On Sunday, March 7, some six hundred and fifty blacks walked over the Edmond Pettus Bridge east of Selma. They were met by Sheriff Jim Clark's mounted posse, hundreds of state troopers, electric-shock cattle prods, tear gas, and billy clubs.

Judge Johnson enjoined both Governor Wallace and Dr. King from further action. He pondered the case: whether to allow the blacks to march down U. S. 80 to Montgomery to petition Wallace for their voting rights.

He permitted the march and held that "the right to assemble, demonstrate, and march peaceably along the highways and streets in an orderly manner should be commensurate with the enormity of the wrongs that are being protested against. In this case, the wrongs are enormous."

The night after the Selma-to-Montgomery march climaxed with a congregation of thousands gathered in front of the capitol, a Detroit housewife named Viola Liuzzo was gunned down in Lowndes County on U. S. 80. After three Klansmen were acquitted in state court, they were tried for the crime in Johnson's courtroom. After the jury heard the evidence, the judge read a thirty-page charge which discussed the American trial system as "a beacon of hope and last resort for the protection of individual citizens." He called for a verdict that "rests completely upon the proposition of justice rendered by

an impartial court and rendered by twelve impartial jurors."
The jury reported back after deliberating twenty-four hours.
Hearing the jury was "hopelessly deadlocked," Johnson leaned
over the bench and stared into their eyes. "There is no reason
to assume that the case will ever be submitted to twelve more
intelligent, more impartial, or more competent men to decide
it, or that more or clearer evidence will be produced on one
side or the other," he said. Three hours later they reached a
guilty verdict. Johnson sentenced all three defendants to the
maximum ten years in prison.

After hearing evidence in an unprecedented case asking
that patients in state mental hospitals have a constitutional
right to adequate care, Johnson issued an order from the bench
that immediate steps be taken to relieve horrible conditions
existing in the state hospital for the mentally retarded. He
followed this with a complex, detailed guideline stating exact
criteria for adequate care. In his order, which was later upheld
by the Fifth Circuit Court of Appeals, Johnson threatened
judicial funding if the legislature did not provide necessary
funds. In Governor Lurleen Wallace's first year in office she
had asked for better conditions for mental patients, but
following her death her husband never provided the necessary
leadership to push such a program through the legislature.
After Johnson's order, however, Wallace and the State Department of Mental Health immediately went to work with the
legislature to find the needed money.

Throughout the terms of Wallace and his wife, Johnson has
watched over the schools of the middle district with a careful
eye. Under Lee vs. Macon, which originally desegregated the
schools of Alabama in the 1950s, Johnson became the guardian
of the school systems. After he ordered twelve black students
admitted to the all-white Tuskegee High School, white students were given $185 a year by the state to provide tuition in
private schools. Wallace sent 216 state troopers to keep the

black children from entering the high school. Johnson then ordered the black students into other white schools and requested that a five-judge court convene to order Wallace to quit sabotaging desegregation.

In 1967 Johnson sat on a three-judge panel which ordered the state to "take affirmative action to disestablish state-enforced" segregation. At that time Alabama's state-controlled schools had the lowest percentage of black integration, 2.4 percent; more than 25 percent of the black high schools were unaccredited, while 3.4 percent of the white high schools were unaccredited. The state was spending $607 for each white student and $295 for each black student. Of the 28,000 teachers, only 76 taught students of another race.

Johnson ordered "affirmative" desegregation. He gave the students their freedom of choice. If overcrowding occurred, they would be assigned to schools nearest their homes without regard to race or color. All aspects of school life were ordered desegregated.

Wallace screamed about it. He said he and the legislature would not give money to the school system to operate under such rules. But after his initial outburst the schools were quietly opened and integration occurred.

During the years Johnson was also called on to examine the State Department of Public Safety. The director of the state troopers in Wallace's second administration, Walter Allen, testified that Wallace ordered him to disregard court-ordered desegregation of the state troopers. Johnson then ordered that black troopers be hired by the department until it had at least twenty-five percent black.

Throughout the Wallace years Johnson has lived a quiet, unassuming life. He has chosen to play golf on the links of Maxwell Air Force Base. He and his wife have kept their social life down to include only a tightly knit group of close friends. The solitude of fishing in freshwater lakes or the Gulf of

Mexico has appealed to his sporting nature. Tall, trim, and handsome, he has continued to believe in a toughly acquired set of strict rules.

Every May 1, Law Day, he has spoken to a group of newly naturalized citizens. One year in the midsixties he told them:

"It is necessary, now more than ever, that the responsible American citizen realize and discharge his obligation constantly to support and defend the proposition that our law is supreme and must be obeyed. This means that irresponsible criticism—by those who can hardly read the Constitution, much less study it and interpret it—must not be allowed to stand unchallenged.

"When those who frustrate the law, who undermine judicial decisions, run riot and provide uncurbed leadership for a return to nothing more than medieval savagery, for the responsible American citizen to remain silent is tantamount to cowardice; it is a grievous injustice to the proposition that in America the law is supreme."

And it was not too difficult to imagine these words ringing in the ears of Wallace.

"SEGREGATION FOREVER"

ALTHOUGH HE WAS CIRCUIT judge when he ran for governor in 1958, Wallace's campaign treasury was dirt poor. He had been personally campaigning for more than four years. He had spoken in every small town from one end of the state to the other. He had addressed civic clubs, police fraternal organizations, labor-union meetings, and had stopped in more barbershops than he could remember.

Alabama was virtually a one-party state. In gubernatorial elections the Democratic primary was the main event. If one of the candidates did not get a clear majority, there was a six-week period between the primary and the runoff election. During this time the top two candidates ran for the nomination. The general election in November was a mere formality. If the Republicans put up a candidate, he was usually a stick figure attempting to gain state-wide exposure.

It was unusual in 1964 when a fairly high percentage of local, county, and congressional offices went to the Republican candidates. Alabama went strongly for Barry Goldwater in that presidential year, after Wallace had dropped out of the picture, and the local Republicans received the benefit of being listed under the elephant emblem.

Also in Alabama politics, the runner-up in one year's governor's race usually wins four years later. And in 1958 Wallace began his campaign for the nomination to win state-wide recognition. Prior to that time he was known only in pockets here and there. Even where he had made speeches he was known only to those people who had been in his audience.

His kickoff rally was held in Ozark, the southernmost town in his judicial district, where the people knew him well. His headline entertainer, whom Alabama politicians have historically hired out of Nashville to draw crowds, was Minnie Pearl, the comedienne who was a South-wide radio favorite from the Grand Ole Opry.

More than a thousand persons were gathered in the Dale County High School football field, and when Wallace took the microphone he told them about the programs that he had planned to help all the people after he became governor. The speech was lukewarm to the cold February gathering, and the words were less than memorable.

McDowell Lee, a state representative from Barbour County, handled the money that was raised from the rally and remembered that barely enough was taken in to pay the entertainers.

At the end of the rally a group from nearby Troy approached Wallace and asked if he would speak at the town's trade day the following Saturday. Wallace replied, "Sure, I'll speak." Then the spokesman for the group asked if he would bring Minnie Pearl. "I'll bring her," Wallace promised. Wallace never thought twice about how he would pay for Minnie Pearl's services. She was among the highest paid of the Nashville people. At that time one performance cost three thousand dollars plus expenses.

When she appeared the following Saturday at Troy's trade day, her husband-manager, Henry Cannon, went to McDowell Lee and asked for Minnie Pearl's pay. Lee grabbed Wallace, who was shaking hands, and pulled him aside. "How are we going to pay?" Lee asked. "You take care of it," Wallace said, and went about his business of politicking.

A check was made out to the entertainer, and it was later covered by the board of directors of the People's Bank of Clio.

The home-town people were making sure their boy was financed.

In the meantime some semblance of organization was rounded up by Barbour County people. Lee, who had been mayor of Clio and had known Wallace since they were both boys, took the job as campaign manager. All political advertisements listed his name and his function. A bachelor known to most of the home-county people, Oscar Harper, was recruited to drive Wallace from town to town. And Sim Thomas, another legislator from Barbour County, worked at raising funds to pay the bills. "The amazing thing was, after everything was paid for at the end of the campaign, we had about one thousand dollars left, and that was given to his wife, Lurleen," one organizer stated.

When the race started Alabama newspapers picked Jimmy Faulkner, a Bay Minette publisher and businessman who had run second to "Big Jim" Folsom four years earlier, as the man to beat. Far down the scale in second place was John Patterson, the young attorney general. Patterson's father had been elected attorney general in 1954 on promises to clean up corruption in Mafia-type gambling-infested Phenix City, known as the wickedest city in the South. But the elder Patterson never lived to take office. After winning the Democratic nomination he was killed in a gangland-style murder. His son, John, a lawyer in the town, was later credited with cleaning up much of the corruption. He was appointed to run in the vacancy created by his father's death. Although it did not register on the polls at the beginning of the race, there was still much sentiment in the state for young Patterson, whose mostly fictionalized dramatic cleanup had been told in a B-grade movie entitled *The Phenix City Story*. Wallace was listed by most papers as being the choice for third place in the field of fourteen. Some of the others in the group included

A. W. Todd, a one-armed Franklin County poultry farmer nicknamed "Nub"; Shearen Elebash, a Yale-educated song-and-dance vaudeville-style entertainer; Ralph "Shorty" Price, a five foot five inch carrot-headed perennial candidate for state-wide office; and retired Admiral John Cromlin, a bona fide John Bircher who shouted about fluoride in drinking water being a project of the Communist-Jewish conspiracy.

With every day of his town-to-town stumping Wallace gained more and more strength. Toward the end of his first month of campaigning he went into Mobile to appear before the annual convention of the Alabama League of Municipalities.

All candidates had been invited to the league's program, but Wallace was the odds-on favorite to carry the weight of the politics there. He had long been the league's fair-haired boy. When he was in the legislature he had been groomed by Ed E. Reid, executive director of the league, and became a floor leader for the group.

When Wallace rose to speak, the mayors and other city personnel applauded. He was the only candidate to be welcomed with immediate clapping. He was interrupted once by applause and after he finished speaking the crowd stood and continued clapping.

Faulkner's lead continued to slip, and it looked to most politicos that Patterson had to be discounted. Early on in the race it was discovered that Patterson owned stock in a loan company that had been criticized for unethical business dealings. When his stock was disclosed Patterson commented, "I thought it was a bank." Several candidates attempted to make the attorney general the laughingstock of the crowd by talking about his statement. One told an audience, "I don't go around buying up loan companies and then call myself a banker."

On the night of the first primary Wallace sat with his friend, Grover Cleveland Hall, Jr., editor of the Montgomery *Advertiser*, in Hall's office and watched the returns filter in.

Patterson took an early lead and held. It was obvious that he was controlling the urban vote. Faulkner was in second place but was soon inched out by Wallace when the rural south Alabama vote trickled in during the late-night hours. Wallace was never to relinquish his firm hold on second place. But he could not catch Patterson. The two were destined for a runoff.

Among his closest cronies, Wallace listened to Hall more than to any of the others. And at this turning point in his career Wallace asked Hall for advice.

Together the two worked out speeches in which Wallace could thrust his positive programs forward dramatically. In the early hours of the morning after the election they planned an itinerary of speeches.

At that time television, except for the larger cities, was not a viable political tool in Alabama. Most of the rural voters did not own sets. Even in urban areas it was regarded as strictly an entertaining object, although Patterson did use it effectively.

During the first week of his campaign Wallace stuck to his schedule. He talked about building more trade schools, a system of junior colleges, more and better highways. He said he wanted to raise the old-age pensions, a ploy that always won votes for Folsom.

Throughout the first week Patterson did not utter a word. He was not seen. He was not heard. In the cities, where Patterson had drawn the bulk of his strength, television stations played film clips from *The Phenix City Story* with an appeal for votes for Patterson. In newspapers, ads were run showing Patterson as the clean-cut young protector of law and order.

Wallace ran to Grover Hall. Wallace talked and Hall listened. Then Wallace picked Hall's brain. By the time they had finished the session Wallace had a visual gimmick with which to attack Patterson.

The next day Wallace went out on the stump. In the bed of a pickup truck he had a four poster with a patchwork quilt spread over the top.

Wallace made his usual speech, and everybody in the audience wondered why in the world he had a bed on stage with him.

At the end of his speech, he asked rhetorically, "Where is John Patterson?" He looked throughout the crowd. The people looked from person to person. "Where is John Patterson?" he asked louder.

"You know what they say?" he asked the people. "They say politics makes strange bedfellows." He lifted the edge of the quilt. He peeked between the covers. "Is that you down there, John Patterson? Why don't you come out and face the people? What do you have to hide, John?"

The people chattered. They laughed. He was making fun of John Patterson. The people were laughing at Patterson. Surely, Wallace thought, this will bring Patterson out in the open.

But Patterson didn't appear. His radio advertisements doubled, but he made no personal appearances.

In the third week of the runoff the Ku Klux Klan publicly endorsed Patterson. When Wallace heard about it, he was on the phone to Grover Hall, who added to Wallace's bed speech.

The next time Wallace raised the covers, he said, "Who's down there between the sheets with you, John? Are you in bed with the Ku Klux Klan?" And the people howled.

In the last week of the campaign Wallace asked, "Why doesn't John Patterson show himself and debate the issues? He's afraid. He's afraid of the issues because he knows nothing about the issues. He has given no one a possible program. What will he do for you? Nothing! He's a do-nothing, know-nothing, invisible candidate."

But when the tally was counted, Patterson had about sixty thousand more votes than Wallace. After slightly more than ninety percent of the votes were in, Wallace raised a toast with Hall and several other close friends and swore that he would be elected in 1962.

Hall was the flamboyant, debonair son of the Pulitzer Prize-winning editor of the Montgomery *Advertiser*. He became editor of the same newspaper and won many writing awards himself. He was introduced to Wallace in 1946 by Ed Reid, whom both admired for his vast knowledge of local politics. An erudite dandy with a constant rosebud in his tailored lapel, Hall was a sometimes supporter and permanent friend of Wallace. Although Hall fed Wallace information, and often guided him through rough times, Wallace was many times taken aback by Hall's twist of humor. At one of Hall's irregular Saturday-morning stag brunches, Hall turned loose his parrots from their cage. One perched on Wallace's shoulder and commenced to jabber away some high-pitched nonsense. For better than a quarter hour Wallace stood rigid in the middle of the living room and stared speechless at the multicolored bird. He was obviously frightened of the animal. Finally Hall, with a snicker, extended an arm to the bird and relieved Wallace's obvious predicament.

In 1958 Hall talked his publisher into allowing him to support Wallace. Other than the bed gimmick, Hall wrote anti-Klan speeches for the runoff. Hall's father, a good friend of H. L. Mencken, had won the Pulitzer for his hard-hitting editorials criticizing Klan activities in the 1920s.

During the four years between races Wallace spent much time with Hall. Hall traveled with Wallace from one end of Alabama to the other. Hall became more enamored with Wallace's belief that he had to be the spokesman for the South. "You and I together will be able to make this nation see that it's not just the South that's so terrible," Wallace would tell him. "We know that the North commits the same sins against its people. But who chastises the North?" Hall saw in Wallace an embodiment of the great southern childhood myth of the warrior astride a great white charger doing battle for the love of his people. Hall had been born into a grand family, seeped in tradition and clothed in style and grace. Hall was realistic enough to know that political knights did not come from aristocratic background. Wallace was the knight: emotional, energetic, single-minded, and appealing to the masses.

When Wallace suggested to Hall in 1963 that he was planning to enter some presidential primaries, the editor's first reaction was, "Wallace, you're out of your mind." But later he thought it was a good idea that Wallace carry the Alabama story to the nation. Not only did Hall accompany Wallace to his first appearance on *Meet The Press*, he joined the governor on many trips into Yankee land.

Wallace thought Hall "one of the most fascinating people I knew, that's why I called him almost incessantly; sometimes I asked for advice, sometimes we fussed at each other. He was compassionate, he was concerned about black people, he was against big government, he was an individual, he influenced me in many ways."

Hall wrote of Wallace's "daring, dauntlessness, and imagination." Analyzing his own feelings, the editor wrote in a letter to a friend, "Part of my feeling [for Wallace] derives from love of Alabama and pride in the Kickapoo juice in the breed's blood. I can feel the same way about Hugh Black." And he continued, "I have sometimes been cowardly about Wallace, but I hope on balance it can be said I refused to deny him in Montgomery or Richmond, costly as it was."

He was fired as editor of the *Advertiser* because he went against the policy of new management. He fought his own battle in his own private world. Afterward he went with the

Richmond *News-Leader* as editorial-page editor, and immediately began writing and talking about Wallace. He arranged for Wallace to be interviewed by a panel of executives from the *News-Leader* prior to the primaries of 1968, and he urged the candidate to tone down his rhetoric for the Virginians. Wallace later told Tom Wicker of *The New York Times* that the group was "the most cultured, polite, well-dressed crowd I ever saw in my life and I gave 'em a real cultured talk. . . . And then I forgot and called the Supreme Court a 'sorry, lousy, no-count outfit,' and you ought to have heard that cultured crowd stand up and cheer. People are about the same everywhere, but ol' Grover here keeps trying to polish me up."

Although he was the ultimate of southern gentleman with manners and bloodline to prove it, Hall quickly tired of Richmond. Also, Richmond quickly tired of his writings about the virtues of Wallace and Alabama.

After a stint writing from Washington for Publishers-Hall Syndicate, during which he called himself "an Alabamian exuding Alabama nationalism" and nicknamed Wallace "Beelzebub Alabammus" in many columns featuring the governor, Hall was offered the job as "resident intellectual" with the Wallace for President forces. His duties were to include being editor of "The Wallace Letter," writing a book extolling Wallace, doing a syndicated column, and developing radio and television material.

Troubled by fainting spells and nervous seizures, he prepared to leave Washington. His final column, entitled "Peck's Bad Boy," linked South Vietnamese Vice-President Ky and the Reverend Carl McIntyre. Hall delivered it to Western Union on the night of September 9, 1970, but Teletype operators found it impossible to decipher. At least three typewritten pages were badly garbled. He attempted to correct the copy after the telegraph company returned it, but the column was never sent.

He left Washington by car, but he did not arrive in Montgomery when he was scheduled to make a Kiwanis Club return-home-victorious speech. Wallace, worried about his friend's disappearance, had state troopers put out a missing-persons report, notifying all states between Alabama and the District of Columbia.

For two weeks he did not turn up. The first week was apparently spent traveling very slowly southward. On the eighth day of his journey he was stopped by a Mecklenburg County, North Carolina, policeman at 2:45 A.M. near Charlotte. With half a fifth of Scotch next to him and alcohol on his breath, the patrolman arrested Hall and charged him with driving while under the influence of alcohol. He was given a breath test when he was jailed, and it showed he was sober. He was also charged with driving without a license.

During the next seven days the fifty-year-old journalist remained in the county jail, until a supervisor notified a medical officer that he thought Hall needed treatment. The officer, trained in first aid, examined Hall and told the jail attendant to watch for symptoms of alcoholic withdrawal. On the seventh day, after he had not complained once of feeling badly, a jailer said Hall claimed to be a newspaper writer. An editor at the Charlotte *Observer* was notified, recognized Hall, and Hall was taken to Memorial Hospital. Diagnosis showed he had suffered a brain tumor, and his condition worsened quickly. He was transferred by special ambulance-airplane to Birmingham's University Hospital, where he underwent surgery for a cystic tumor in the right frontal area of the brain. It was highly malignant, and he remained in the Birmingham hospital afterward to undergo cobalt treatment.

Wheelchair-ridden, he came home to Montgomery to a quaint tree-smothered home in the gracious Old Cloverdale district. As wryly humorous as ever, he made the best of a bad physical situation, and among his most frequent callers were

Wallace and his new bride, Cornelia, whom he proposed to be the cover girl of a Wallace brochure. He suggested she pose in a red velvet gown for the photograph. Whenever the Wallaces visited he asked them to hurry with this project. It was never finalized.

Exactly one year after he had been found in the jail, Hall died. *The New York Times* eulogized the 1957 Headliner Award winner as "probing, wry, and capable of great courage." Wallace said, "We have lost one of the finest journalists Alabama has ever produced."

In 1962 Hall for the second time endorsed Wallace's candidacy for governor.

For almost four years Wallace had been pounding home the anti-integration stand which had made him famous. After he was defeated by Patterson, several intimates said they overheard him swear, "I'll never be out-niggered again." During his final year as circuit judge he made more news than he had created during any other period of his life. Sometimes twice weekly he held press conferences in Clayton, and the news media came to him. He withheld the voting records from the U. S. Civil Rights Commission and came within an inch of being held in contempt. All the while, he made news.

After he became a private citizen in 1959 Wallace began running as hard as possible for governor. By the time the race came around in 1962, nobody was surprised to hear him promise to "stand in the schoolhouse door and keep the Negroes out."

He said, "They talk about civil rights up North, but they don't know what civil rights are. Those lily-livered liberals, they talk real sweet about the Negro people they have living in Harlem or some slum section of Chicago. They talk about us down here. We've got Negroes living in our backyards. We take care of 'em. We clothe 'em. We feed 'em. We don't let our people go hungry, starve on the streets, beg for their bread. . . . Southern people have soft hearts. They don't like to see their fellow man get stomped on. If we see somebody down and out, we'll pick him up, give him food, put a roof over his head. That's our kind of civil rights."

His rhetoric was disjointed, an uneven emotional appeal to the hearts of his audience. When he spoke in Warrior, a coal-miner and steelworker suburb north of Birmingham, he touched on what he called "the worst thing that's happening to our chillun is this integration mess." When he said "in-te-gra-tion" he strung it out and twisted it around like it was the ugliest four-letter noun in all of creation. In fact the word was downright filthy before he got it out of his curled lips, and when he finished saying it his face looked like he had been eating rotten persimmons. The people listening to him would stomp their feet and clap their hands and literally shout with joy when he told them he was going to stop in-te-gra-tion. "I'll stand in the schoolhouse door to keep them out!" he swore, and the folks went mad with admiration. He was their kind of man, and he knew how to speak to them. He was a little fellow who carried his head high. He stood up there on the back of a pickup with that microphone in his hand. He pointed his finger toward Washington, D. C., and he said, "It's about time somebody told those big shots up there where to get off!" By damn, these good folks had been saying that around Ned's Grocery and Bill's Texaco Station for years. The federal government was eating 'em alive with income taxes every year, and what were they getting out of it? They weren't getting anything, the way they saw it, except more misery. It was the federal government that was telling 'em they were going to have to send their children to school with black children. If they were going to eat in a restaurant, black people could eat there too. Before you know it, they said, the federal government would force black people and white people to live next door to each other. It just didn't make any sense to them, and now they had a fellow telling them exactly what they had been saying to themselves.

At each stop Wallace would try something new. If it worked, he kept it. If it didn't, he acted as though he never even said it in the first place. He stood flatfooted on the back of the truck. He hollered into the microphone about the outside evils encroaching on these good peoples' everyday lives, and when he got that bait planted real good and solid, he'd jerk the old fishing pole. "First thing you know, the federal courts'll be telling you who you can invite over for Sunday dinner and who you can't," he allowed. They whistled and clapped. They liked that. They'd punch each other in the sides with their elbows and nod and grin. "Ol' George'll tell 'em," they said. He would rock forward on his toes and back on his heels. "The federal government up in Washington is breathin' down our backs, and we got to fight 'em off! You elect me yo' governor and I'll fight 'em!" And they knew he would. Why else did everybody call him "The Fightin' Little Judge"?

When he stood before the hillbillies in Albertville on Sand Mountain in mid-April, it suddenly came to him in the middle of his speech. He was telling them what he had told many other audiences. The high-school band had already played "Dixie," and he'd sung it louder than anybody. Now he was standing on the makeshift stage in the new gymnasium and nearly two thousand people had come out of the coves and were waiting for his great pronouncements. They had heard him four years ago, and most of them had voted for him then. But he had grown in four years. My, how he'd grown! He was taking on the big boys now. He was no longer talking about "Programs For People," he was getting down to the nitty-gritty. He was saying what they all wanted from a politician: Stop the Negroes! And he kept saying it, grinding down with promise after promise. At the end of the speech, he tacked it on like the afterthought it was. "And if I'm elected," he said, "I promise I'll not serve one drop of alcohol in the governor's mansion!" With the last word, they exploded. Even the women jumped up from their bleacher seats and clapped and shouted.

He had thought about it while he was talking about something else. This was north Alabama hill country. Twice before they had gone overwhelmingly for "Big Jim" Folsom. Now Folsom was running for a third term. During his second term he had been embarrassing to some people, drinking whiskey on the front porch of the mansion and inviting Adam Clayton Powell, the black congressman from Harlem, to the mansion. These people up here didn't understand things like that. But George Wallace made 'em understand it in one simple sentence. When he said he wouldn't serve liquor in the mansion, they knew he meant he wouldn't be leaning back and drinking and wouldn't be inviting niggers for cocktails and conversaton.

On his next stop Wallace kept the promise not to serve alcohol and he added that he would stop the whiskey-agent business in the state, which had been a system of patronage since Prohibition was repealed in the thirties. The jobs as agents or middlemen between wholesale companies and the Alcohol Beverage Control Board, which operated all legal sales of beverages in Alabama, were given to friends of winning politicians. In rural counties agents made from one thousand to five thousand dollars a year for little or no actual work. They also received a handsome supply of gratuitous whiskey. In urban areas such as Birmingham or Mobile agents could make as high as seventy thousand dollars annually; they too did very little work. The agents were primarily public-relations people, keeping sales transactions on a friendly basis. They received accounts of all liquor sold to the state in their district. They received a percentage of the sales. Any time a liquor company issued a commemorative souvenir bottle, agents would be given a complimentary case. At Christmas agents were bombarded with cases of whiskey.

For the many who had been seeing the few receiving so much for so little work Wallace's latest promise was wonderful. They hated to see their neighbor get rich just because he supported the right candidate for governor.

By the day of the first primary Wallace was in front of all other candidates. Jim Folsom had been in second place before his nonsensical "Cuckoo Speech" on television the night before election day. A young legislator from Tuscaloosa, Ryan deGraffenried, gained on Folsom in the final stretch and overcame him by only a handful of votes.

Although the runoff looked hopeless for deGraffenried, he stayed to the finish against Wallace. The tall, youthful attorney, running on a "Good Government" platform, was making a name for himself. He had his eye on the gubernatorial race four years in the future. When he lost to Wallace, he continued running. Throughout four years he kept an office in Tuscaloosa, out of which campaign literature and solicitations for contributions were sent. Early in 1966 the small plane in which he was traveling on his way from one speech to another crashed. DeGraffenried and his pilot were killed.

Wallace was inaugurated governor on January 14, 1963, and every county in the state was represented by a float. Some counties spent as much as five thousand dollars and three months building floats. Wallace and his eleven-year-old son wore matching morning coats, silk top hats and carnations in their lapels. More than one hundred marching bands sashayed past the reviewing stand. Hundreds of cars carried dignitaries from each of the state's sixty-seven counties, all of whom saluted the incoming governor. After more than five hours of festivities Wallace stood on the bronze star where Jefferson Davis had stood when he was sworn in as president of the Confederacy. Wallace's brother, Circuit Judge Jack Wallace, administered the oath of office while his wife, Lurleen, held the Holy Bible.

Amid cheers from the more than ten thousand standing in the bleak, colorless, overcast Alabama afternoon, he mounted the platform and spread his arms high above the red, white, and blue streamers surrounding the lectern. He grinned broadly and nodded to county commissioners, probate judges, tax assessors and collectors, farmers and merchants—all the people who had worked to get him elected.

As the cheering calmed, he spread his speech out across the holder with his left hand. It was a speech that had been honed to a fine edge out of the roughness of his campaign speeches. The words were put together by his friend and employee Asa Carter, a Ku Klux Klan leader who was the most literate worker in Wallace's camp. And Carter's words were polished until they shined by Grover Hall, who had burned the midnight oil the night before with the governor-to-be.

In a serious vein, Wallace immediately challenged the federal government. "This nation was never meant to be a unit of one, but a unit of many," he stated, "and so it was meant in our racial lives. Each race, within its own framework, has freedom to teach, to instruct, to develop, to ask for and receive deserved help from others of separate racial station; but if we amalgamate into the one unit as advocated by the Communist philosopher, then the enrichment of our lives, the freedom for our development is gone forever. We become, therefore, a mongrel unit of one under a single all-powerful government. And we stand for everything, and for nothing. . . ." And the crowd cheered as enthusiastically and loudly as they had during his campaign. His words were broadcast state-wide. That evening the national television networks carried much of his outcry for separation.

As loudly and as distinctly as he could speak, he said, "Today I have stood where Jefferson Davis stood, and took an oath to my people. It is very appropriate then that from this Cradle of the Confederacy, this very heart of the great Anglo-Saxon southland, that today we sound the drum for freedom as have our generation of forebears before us time and again down through history. Let us rise to the call of freedom-loving blood that is in us and send our answer to the tyranny that clanks its chains upon the South. In the name of the greatest people that ever trod this earth, I draw the line in the dust and toss the gauntlet before the feet of tyranny. And I say: Segregation now! Segregation tomorrow! Segregation forever!"

STAND IN THE SCHOOLHOUSE DOOR

WHEN JIMMY HOOD and Vivian Malone were less than a year old (Jimmy in Gadsden and Vivian in Monroeville), George Wallace was a buck private in the U. S. Army. In the gleaming, white-hot Texas sun the governor-to-be loaded bombs in the Pantex Ordnance Plant. His governor-to-be wife, Lurleen, worked the day shift in an Amarillo ten-cent store. They lived in a five-dollar-a-week apartment.

James Alexander Hood was the pride of his father Octavia's eye when he was born on November 10, 1942. He was the first of the Hood's six children, and the tractor operator instilled in his son the ambition to grow up to be a good Christian.

He attended Central Elementary School and then went to all-black George Washington Carver High School, where as a well built but rather slight youth he tried over and over to break the American outdoor record for the one-hundred-yard dash, but he was never fast enough. He also played halfback on the football team, but he was never more than average. He knew he would never succeed in athletics as a professional, and that bothered him only enough to make him want to succeed in other fields.

He went to Atlanta, where prior to June of 1963 he took liberal-arts courses at Clark College, doing his best work in English and literature. "Someday," he said, "I want to write a book about Negro life—my life, for example."

Jimmy Hood decided to become a clinical psychologist, but he couldn't major in psychology at Clark. In a University of Alabama bulletin he read that his state school offered courses he needed and wished to take.

When he approached his parents, "They only told me, if that's what I wanted, to go ahead." And when his application form reached the admissions office the blank next to the word *race* had not been filled. University officials returned the application with a red check next to the word. When Jimmy Hood sent it back he wrote *American Negro* next to the red check.

The fourth of eight children, Vivian Malone was an attractive, soft-spoken child. She had been interested in the civil-rights movement, but she had never demonstrated with the other students who staged sit-ins, marches, and picketings in the early sixties. She worked long hours over her homework and brought home excellent grades from Monroeville Elementary School. After the family moved to the city, where her father was a maintenance worker at Brookley Air Force Base, she graduated from Central High School. She entered all-black Alabama A & M in Normal, near Huntsville. In her two years at A & M she was an honor student with a high B average. And in business courses and mathematics she made A's.

She agonized for weeks about the possibilities of attending the University of Alabama. Although the prospects of becoming the center of attention in the press did not appeal to her, she was offered a scholarship through the NAACP if she would become one of the first black students to attend the previously all-white school. She also explored the business school within the university and settled on industrial relations as a major.

Her mother and father had little education, but they encouraged all of their children to attend college. Her mother had worked most of her life as a domestic servant in the homes of whites in the Mobile area, and she wanted a better life for her offspring. "There was no way in this world that we could send them to college without help, and we asked for help through the church and the people in the community," Mrs. Malone said later. The parents thought it was a godsend when the NAACP offered to give assistance to their daughter.

After the two applied and their transcripts were perused, it was brought to the attention of a meeting of top officials that two qualified blacks had applied for admission. At that meeting was the president of the school, Dr. Frank A. Rose, now executive director of the L.Q.C. Lamar Society in Washington, D. C.; Dean of Women Sarah Healey, who later retired to Florida; Dean of Men John L. Blackburn, whose assistant that summer was David Matthews, who was working on his Ph.D. in higher education at Columbia and who later became president of the school and secretary of the U. S. Department of Health, Education, and Welfare. Others included Jeff Bennett, administrative assistant to Rose and later vice-chancellor at the University of the South at Sewanee, Tennessee; and Alex Pow, academic vice-president who later became president of Western Carol University in North Carolina.

There was no panic when they were told. All of the powers knew exactly what they had to do. Dr. Rose immediately telephoned the governor of the state. He knew George Wallace would be interested.

As soon as he got the word, Wallace turned over the information to the chief of his state police force, Director of Public Safety Al Lingo.

"Do with these what y'all did with that Autherine Lucy," Wallace gave his terse demand.

Although Lingo, a short, fat, popeyed man with huge red and blue veins running visibly through his large nose, had not been director of the Department of Public Safety when Miss Lucy had been the first black to enter the school in February of 1956, he knew what the governor meant.

At the time of Wallace's call to Lingo, Miss Lucy was living quietly in Texas with her Baptist preacher husband, H. L. Foster. She spent most of her days talking with the ladies of the church about the goings-on around the community. She seldom spoke of her miserable three days on the oak-studded campus in Tuscaloosa where riots broke out and she was frightened constantly. She seldom mentioned that day when she walked next to her adviser, attorney Thurgood Marshall, and enrolled. Nor did she speak of the day when the car in which she and Marshall were riding was stoned and almost turned over. At the office of the registrar that day she was handed a telegram from the trustees: "For your safety and the safety of the students and faculty members of the university you are hereby suspended from classes until further notice." Marshall took it to court and she was ordered back to class. That night the trustees met and accused the twenty-six-year-old woman of making "false, defamatory, impertinent, and scandalous charges" against school authorities, and she was permanently expelled.

Al Lingo called in two Public Safety investigators, and he dispatched them in separate directions. One went to Gadsden, the other to Mobile. Within a few days both reported to the home base in Montgomery that there was absolutely nothing in the backgrounds of Hood and Malone that would keep them from being perfectly fine students. When Lingo heard the words he exploded. He unleashed a tirade of profanity and slammed the phone onto the hook. He paced the floor of his office with his hands clasped behind his back. He told an investigator sitting in his office, "The governor's going to have my ass if those boys don't find something on those two niggers. He's going to have mine, and I'm going to have theirs [the two field investigators]."

After another day passed the two reported again, after which Lingo telephoned Wallace, whose immediate response was to summon Lingo to Capitol Hill to his office. Wallace was as emphatic as he could be. After raging for more than fifteen minutes about the incompetency of some of the state troopers, Wallace said, "If you can't get something on them, dig up something on their daddies and mamas." Lingo trudged across Bainbridge Street to his office in the Public Safety Building. When the two investigators checked in, they were ordered to continue looking and not to call again until they found something.

Two days later the investigators were still empty-handed. They were reluctantly called back to Montgomery.

Shortly afterward, when the university officials maintained a neutral silence, it became certain to the NAACP what would have to be done. A suit was brought before Chief U. S. Judge Seybourn H. Lynne of the Northern District of Alabama in Birmingham. After one relatively succinct hearing, Lynne ordered the university desegregated. He also issued an order enjoining Wallace from interfering with the admission.

Wallace had promised that he would defy the courts. While campaigning for governor he swore in his kickoff speech in

Ozark before a cheering crowd that he would "stand in the schoolhouse door." And he repeated the promise time and again. He had challenged the court, "The federal government is not going to jail the constitutional officers of a sovereign state if they but have the insides to stand up for Alabama." He cocked his head and smirked his lips and pointed his finger northward and called the federal courts "lousy and irresponsible."

So now he began to make plans for the great moment of confrontation. He would speak out against that power which he saw as the symbol that stood against everything he had ever believed. If they would only put him in jail for standing up against the federal power . . . Even Patrick Henry had not had nationwide television watching when he spoke against the tyranny of England's monarchy. Wallace truly believed that he had now arrived, and he spent hours working on his presentation.

Although the Wallace people deny it, U. S. Attorney General Robert Kennedy spoke several times via telephone with Wallace and aides. The attorney general traveled to Montgomery, and in a tape-recording for posterity, Kennedy and Wallace play their respective roles to the hilt.

"You think it would be so horrifying to have a Negro attend the University of Alabama, Governor?" Kennedy asked during the conversation.

"Well, eh, I think it's horrifying for the federal courts and the central governments to rewrite all the law and force upon the people that which they don't want, yes. I will never myself submit voluntarily to any integration of any school system in Alabama. And I feel it's in the best interests of the country and Alabama, and everybody concerned, that these matters ought to be—attempts ought to be—at least delayed. In fact, there is no time in my judgment when we will be ready for it—in my lifetime, at least. Certainly not at this time," Wallace retorted.

Youthful Wallace at his first
inauguration in 1963.

Birmingham *News*

Wallace stands in the schoolhouse
door at the University of
Alabama in 1963. Nicholas
Katzenbach, deputy attorney
general, has back to the camera
on right.

Birmingham *News*

Wallace listens to Senator Hubert Humphrey at Montgomery's Dannelly Field with Senator Herman Talmadge of Georgia in background left.

Tommy Giles

Tommy Giles

George and Lurleen Wallace
before her 1967 inauguration.

George and Cornelia Wallace
before the 1971 inauguration.

Tommy Giles

Morris Dees, civil rights attorney, has led suits against the State of Alabama while Wallace was governor. Dees was co-founder of the Southern Poverty Law Center.

Author's collection

U. S. District Judge Frank M. Johnson, Jr., was a Wallace friend when they were University of Alabama students. Later he took many opposing views in legal battles.

Author's collection

Tommy Giles

A happy Wallace after the 1970
gubernatorial election which
he barely won.

Grover Cleveland Hall, Jr., was a
close Wallace friend and editor
of the Montgomery *Advertiser*
and later national syndicated
columnist.

Tommy Giles

Wallace talking in governor's office in 1971.

Tommy Giles

Wallace arrives in Montgomery to resume his position as governor after he was shot in Laurel, Maryland. His wheelchair was placed on Alabama soil shortly before the 1972 Democratic National Convention.

Tommy Giles

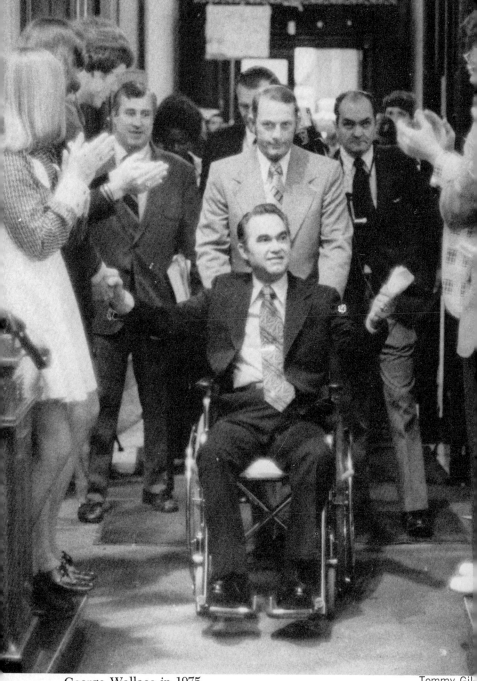

George Wallace in 1975.

Tommy Gil

The two bantered the question back and forth until Kennedy asked, "Would you get angry if your orders were not obeyed? Did you when you were judge? Did you care?"

"Did I care?" Wallace asked.

"Yeah."

"I don't recall any were ever disobeyed."

"Oh? What would your reaction be if they did disobey?" Kennedy said.

"If they did what?"

"Disobeyed your orders."

"Well, of course, you are assuming that my actions as contemplated would be an outright disobedience of a court order."

"Ultimately, after that's litigated, Governor, will you follow the orders of the court?" the attorney general asked.

"I will never submit to an order of the federal court ordering the integration of the school system."

"How would you feel if your orders were not obeyed?"

"It's not an analogous situation."

"But don't you think it's fundamental?"

"We're dealing in great constitutional questions in this matter," Wallace maintained.

After coffee for Wallace and Coke for Kennedy, their exchange flared even hotter.

With a courthouse-square slowness in his speech, Wallace said, "It depresses me and makes me very sad to think that we have these strained relations between the states and the federal government, but it's that way, and we feel very strongly about this matter. In fact, according to y'all's attitude, of course, it's: 'We may have to send troops and jail you as governor of the state.' "

"We never said that, Governor," Kennedy stated.

After a short discussion about whether Kennedy should speak to the press, which had crowded the outer offices,

Kennedy said, "Why don't we just leave it; I'd speak for what I said and not get into what you said, and you could get into what you said and what your position is, without getting into what I said."

Wallace said with a country superiority, "I agree. I can speak for myself and you can speak for yourself." He had always had a way of getting straight to the point of a matter.

At this point Seymore Trammell, an old Wallace cohort who had been district attorney of Barbour County when Wallace had been judge and was now finance director, became the aggressor. Facing Kennedy, he said, "You don't want the people to be led into thinking maybe that Mr. Kennedy agrees with the governor."

"There's no agreement," stated Wallace flatly.

"Well, I think that the people of Alabama and the South should know."

"Let's get it straight, now," said Wallace. "You will not use . . ."

"I will hope and expect that the orders of the court—there's no plan or idea of using troops. I think as you said, these are going to be resolved in the courts."

Wallace asked why photographs were taken from jets of the University of Alabama, a news story that had broken in the Montgomery *Advertiser* the previous week by political journalist Bob Ingram and later been confirmed by Washington sources. "We'll give y'all a picture of the school if you ever want one. I mean, you won't ever have to, eh . . ."

"I understand that," Kennedy said shortly. "It could have been handled better."

"Well, I'll say this, the governor has made his position very clear," Trammell said. "He's asked what your position would be, whether or not troops would be used. . . ."

"I don't plan to," Kennedy said. "You seem to want me to say that I'm going to use troops. You're pushing it so much, I

134

sort of get that opinion. In any case, so we understand each other, we haven't the use of any force prepared, so I want to make sure that we don't get out of here—I mean, I didn't say anything to the contrary, and I don't want to have any inferences about . . ."

Further, Kennedy said that it was up to the Alabamians whether federal troops would be used to desegregate the University of Alabama. He said he had no plans to use troops. He said he did not want a repeat of the turmoil at the University of Mississippi during the previous September when James Meredith became the first black to enter that school.

After a few more cursory remarks by the governor and the attorney general, Kennedy left.

Between the time of this meeting and Wallace's stand in the doorway, the attorney general attempted to reach Wallace several times. According to most of the governor's aides, Kennedy never reached Wallace. However, at least two have pointed out that Kennedy and Wallace talked at length between Washington and Montgomery. A timetable was read by Kennedy to Wallace. This precise schedule was taken down by the governor's confidential secretary. It was agreed that Wallace would call out all of his state troopers to guard the campus. And President Kennedy would nationalize the Alabama National Guardsmen to keep Wallace from breaking the federal law. Everything would go smoothly, each agreed. There would be no violence. Both Wallace and Kennedy would be able to make a point.

Three days before Hood and Malone were to become students, troopers in Confederate-gray cars began filing onto the campus. Road blocks were set up on every road that led onto the one thousand-plus acres on the banks of the polluted Black Warrior River.

These were quiet, typically smoldering June days, bright

and lush. Occasional students meandered across the oak-dotted quadrangle where Union troops had burned all buildings but a small octagonal brick munitions house when General John T. Croxton's raiders stormed the town of Tuscaloosa in March of 1865.

A school that had reveled in the party atmosphere of Old South Day at the Kappa Alpha fraternity and the Fiji Island festivities of the Phi Gams and all the other wild times including the drunkest homecoming weekends anywhere, the University of Alabama was an up-tight place as the day neared. Only those with student or faculty identification cards were allowed on campus—other than police and troopers.

On the night before the day, four students, two boys and two girls, drank beer and listened to the jukebox in the basement of an otherwise-empty fraternity house.

"We're gonna have hot and cold running poontang by September," a Sigma Nu junior from Dallas County said, hoisting his Budweiser. "Here's to poontang," he toasted drunkenly.

The girl and boy from Tuscaloosa stared at him silently.

"What's wrong with y'all?"

The other boy, whose arm was around the waist of his girl, shrugged.

The junior's girl friend, a pretty little coed with ratted blonde hair, grabbed her date's hand. "Let's dance, sugar," she said.

The Dallas County boy, short and stocky, shook away from her. He turned toward his friend, still sitting next to his girl, and said belligerently, "You some kind of nigger-lover?"

The Tuscaloosa student, twenty-three but still an undergraduate, said, "Aw, man, cut it out. Let's drink some beer and forget all this stuff."

The other, younger student held his ground. "I said, you a nigger-lover?"

The older stood up, pulled his girl friend with him, and said, "I enjoyed it, hoss."

The younger shoved the older, who stumbled against the corner of a couch. His girl friend balanced him, but the younger came around with a windmill swing. The older did not have to duck. The swing was off target, and the fist connected solidly with the plaster wall. Something cracked inside the hand. The younger crumbled, mumbling, onto the couch and gripped his right knuckles with his left palm.

The older and his girl friend scampered out the back of the house. From the screened porch of his apartment late that night the two watched across the corner of an ancient cemetery as two troopers shook down four men in a red Buick. The troopers cuffed the men and called for reinforcements when they found a virtual arsenal in the trunk. The young man and woman hugged each other and did not feel safe.

Early on the morning of June 11 James Hood and Vivian Malone met with university officials in downtown Birmingham, about sixty miles east of the school.

She was wearing a plain pink dress, he a dark suit with narrow tie and felt hat. Both appeared calm as they were assured everything was prearranged, the governor would make his speech and they would be registered students by midafternoon.

At the same time they were leaving Birmingham with escort, President John Fitzgerald Kennedy was sitting down to breakfast with congressional leaders in Washington. With House Speaker John W. McCormack and Senate Majority Leader Mike Mansfield the President discussed pending civil-rights legislation. He emphasized that "an effective bill" had to be enacted during the current session of Congress. Also present, GOP Senate Leader Everett M. Dirksen of Illinois said afterward that Kennedy mentioned a proposed "title three" provision to authorize federal intervention in school desegregation cases, extension of the life of the Civil Rights Commission, and desegregation of all facilities, both public and commercial.

Shortly after Hood and Malone arrived in Tuscaloosa, and were taken to the W. W. Brandon Armory between Tenth Street and University Avenue, within a mile of campus, some eight hundred state troopers completely sealed off the university grounds.

Newsmen scampered about Foster Auditorium, television cameramen pushing and shoving for position, and Wallace Press Secretary Bill Jones was a one-man team attempting to keep order among the journalists.

At eleven A.M. eastern daylight time, two hours ahead of Tuscaloosa time, President Kennedy signed a proclamation which had been written and rewritten during the last minutes. Secretary of State Dean Rusk also signed the document.

The paper assailed Wallace's planned action to "oppose and obstruct the orders of the U. S. District Court relating to the enrollment and attendance of Negro students at the University of Alabama." Kennedy said the "unlawful obstruction and combination on the part of the governor and others against the authority of the United States will, if carried out as threatened, make it impracticable to enforce the laws of the United States in the State of Alabama by the ordinary course of judicial proceedings." He added that the stand "threatens to impede the course of justice" under the laws. And he commanded the governor and his cohorts to cease and desist.

Twenty-two minutes later, while his press secretary was standing in the doorway for the television cameramen to get proper light-meter readings, Wallace arrived at Foster Auditorium, where about five years before the moving portrayal of

"John Brown's Body" had stirred the minds of many southerners who experienced it.

Dressed in his usual gray suit and blue shirt, Wallace walked swiftly through the crowd of newsmen, nodding and waving, followed by his entourage, including his two brothers, Jack and Gerald. Inside the front of the building he shook hands and spoke to everyone there, the regular university help, assistant professors, registrar, and others. During the following hour he paced the floor, talked privately with his people, glanced out the windows frequently. He held his prepared speech curled in his hands.

For the second time this day, President Kennedy met with Congressional leaders to discuss the pending civil-rights legislation. Vice-President Lyndon Johnson was also present.

In Tuscaloosa a caravan of dark cars moved west on University Avenue, snaked under the boughs of huge oaks, and stopped within one hundred yards of Foster Auditorium.

Hood and Malone remained in a car with John Doar, director of the civil-rights division of the Justice Department, who more than a decade later became general counsel to the House Judiciary Committee and presented Watergate evidence in the impeachment proceedings against President Richard Nixon.

Walking toward the doorway where Wallace had taken his stance was Nicholas Katzenbach, a forty-one-year-old, poker-faced former law professor who had become deputy attorney general about one year before when his predecessor, Byron R. White, was appointed to the U. S. Supreme Court by Kennedy. Katzenbach was a no-nonsense, six foot two inch, two hundred pound World War II prisoner of war whose soft-spoken voice later privately expressed disgust with George Wallace and his beliefs. When he approached Wallace, it was not difficult to see that disgust behind the Rhodes scholar's cold, dark eyes. As he neared, Wallace held up his left hand. Katzenbach halted.

In his low-volumed baritone Katzenbach said, "Will you move aside?"

Wallace merely stared at him.

"I have here President Kennedy's proclamation. I have come to ask you for unequivocal assurance that you or anyone under your control will not bar these students."

"No," Wallace said.

"If you do not move aside, the consequences of your stand must rest with you," Katzenbach said.

Katzenbach did not move an inch. He stared into Wallace's eyes. His expression did not change.

The forty-three-year-old Wallace straightened the paper in his shaking hands. He began to read.

Time and again in the future Wallace has referred back to his statement as "my one and only principle." With forceful tones he has spoken on national television, "Can't you see that it's not racism that I'm talking about? It's the basic issues on which this country was founded." He has leaned across conference tables and, in pleading tones, has said, "I was talking about the Constitution and the meaning of the document the way it is translated into our lives during this modern day." He has told the National Conference of Black Mayors, "I'm not a racist. When I stood in the schoolhouse door it wasn't to keep you out. I was standing up for a principle, that men and women should be free to choose where they get their education." He failed again to point out that Alabama never provided equal education, that a black person never had the choice to go to the University of Alabama or Auburn University during the days of segregation, and that he was not talking about a black person's choice but a white person's freedom of choice.

He spoke out strongly, and Katzenbach and Malone and Hood and an entire nation listened. Sitting in his rolled-up shirt sleeves in the Justice Department office, Robert Kennedy listened.

"As governor and chief magistrate of the state of Alabama, I deem it to be my solemn obligation and duty to stand before you representing the rights and sovereignty of this state and its peoples.

"The unwelcomed, unwanted, unwarranted, and force-induced intrusion upon the campus of the University of Alabama today of the might of the central government offers a frightful example of the oppression of the rights, privileges, and sovereignty of this state by officers of the federal government. This intrusion results solely from force, or threat of force, undignified by any reasonable application of the principle of law, reason, and justice. It is important that the people of this state and nation understand that this action is in violation of rights reserved to the state by the Constitution of the United States and the Constitution of the state of Alabama. While some few may applaud these acts, millions of Americans will gaze in sorrow upon the situation existing at this great institution of learning.

"Only the Congress makes the law of the United States. To this date no statutory authority can be cited to the people of this country which authorizes the central government to ignore the sovereignty of this state in an attempt to subordinate the rights of Alabama and millions of Americans. There has been no legislative action by Congress justifying this intrusion.

"When the Constitution of the United States was enacted, a government was formed upon the promise that people, as individuals, are endowed with the rights of life, liberty, and property, and with the right of self-government. The people and their local self-governments formed a central government and conferred upon it certain stated and limited powers. All other powers were reserved to the states and the people.

"Strong local government is the foundation of our system and must be continually guarded and maintained. The Tenth Amendment to the Constitution of the United States reads as follows: 'The powers not delegated to the United States by the Constitution, nor prohibited by it to the states, are reserved to the states, respectively, or to the people.'

"This amendment sustains the right of self-determination and grants the state of Alabama the right to enforce its laws and to regulate its internal affairs.

"This nation was never meant to be a unit of one, but a unit of many, this is the exact reason our freedom-loving forefathers established the states, so as to divide the rights and the powers among the many states, insuring that no central power could gain master government control.

"There can be no submission to the theory that the central government is anything but a servant of the people. We are God-fearing people—not government-fearing people. We practice today the free heritage bequested to us by the founding fathers.

"I stand here today as governor of this sovereign state and refuse to willingly submit to the legal usurpation of power by the central government. I claim today for all the people of the state of Alabama those rights reserved to them under the Constitution of the United States.

"Among those powers so reserved and claimed is the right of state authority in the operation of public schools, colleges, and universities. My action does not constitute disobedience to the legislative and constitutional provisions.

"It is not defiance for defiance's sake, but for the purpose of raising basic and fundamental constitutional questions. My action is a call for strict adherence to the Constitution of the

United States as it was written—for a cessation of usurpation and abuses.

"My action seeks to avoid having a state sovereignty sacrificed on the altar of political expediency.

"Further, as the governor of the state of Alabama, I hold the supreme executive power of this state, and it is my duty to see that the laws are faithfully executed. The illegal and unwarranted action of the central government on this day, contrary to the laws, customs, and traditions of this state, is calculated to disturb the peace.

"I stand before you today in place of thousands of other Alabamians whose presence would have confronted you had I been derelict and neglected to fulfill the responsibilities of my office. It is the right of every citizen, however humble he may be, through his chosen officials of representative government to stand courageously against whatever he believes to be the exercise of power beyond the constitutional rights conferred upon our federal government. It is this right which I assert for the people of Alabama by my presence here today.

"Again I state—this is the exercise of the heritage of freedom and liberty under the law—coupled with responsible government.

"Now, therefore, in consideration of the premises, and in my official capacity as governor of the state of Alabama, I do hereby make the following solemn proclamation:

"Whereas, the Constitution of Alabama vests the supreme powers of the state in the governor as chief magistrate, and said Constitution requires of the governor that he take care that the laws be faithfully executed; and,

"Whereas, the Constitution of the United States, Amendment Ten, reserves to the states respectively or to the people those powers not delegated to the United States, nor prohibited to the states; and,

"Whereas, the operation of the public school system is a

power reserved to the state of Alabama under the Constitution of the United States and Amendment Ten thereof; and,

"Whereas, it is the duty of the governor of the state of Alabama to preserve the peace under the circumstances now existing, which power is one reserved to the state of Alabama and the people thereof under the Constitution of the United States and Amendment Ten thereof.

"Now, therefore, I, George C. Wallace, as governor of the state of Alabama, have by my action raised issues between the central government and the sovereign state of Alabama, which said issues should be adjudicated in the manner prescribed by the Constitution of the United States; and now being mindful of my duties and responsibilities under the Constitution of the United States, the Constitution of Alabama, and seeking to preserve and maintain the peace and dignity of this state, and the individual freedoms of the citizens thereof, do hereby denounce and forbid this illegal and unwarranted action by the central government."

Katzenbach did an about-face as soon as the last word was spoken, walked toward his car through the brittle, quiet atmosphere of the eighty-five-degree, humid midday, and rode away.

In Washington, Robert Kennedy was talking to his brother. Everything was going according to schedule. The executive order to federalize the Guard was on its way to the White House.

Thirty minutes later the President signed the order and Secretary of Defense Robert S. McNamara called all seventeen thousand Alabama Guardsmen into active federal service. He also directed the 31st Infantry Division to proceed to Tuscaloosa.

During this time Wallace, who had ordered the doors and windows of the auditorium barred, sat in the air-conditioned office within and ate a lunch hand-delivered by one of his local supporters, who graciously remembered to include the catsup. He devoured a catsup-drenched, medium-rare steak, French-fried potatoes, and lettuce, and drank a tall glass of iced tea.

While he was eating, Hood and Malone were taken to their respective dormitories by U. S. marshals. In Washington a spokesman at the Justice Department said they were considered students of the University of Alabama as soon as they entered the dorms. But in Tuscaloosa the charades continued.

In the middle of the afternoon, after about two hours of virtual silence, state troopers commanded by Al Lingo were lined up in front of the auditorium.

Shortly thereafter federalized guardsmen in six trucks arrived on the scene. Led by several beret-clad Special Forces officers, they stopped ominously about one hundred yards away. Television cameras panned the scene while the nation watched.

Brigadier General Henry V. Graham arrived with Hood and Malone. Wearing a small Confederate flag stitched to his breast pocket, the forty-seven-year-old general marched toward the doorway in which the governor stood.

Before Wallace, Graham snapped to attention. He saluted. With his voice quivering slightly and only the sound of cameras grinding in the background, he said, "It is my sad duty to ask you to step aside."

Wallace, not moving, read from his wrinkled sheet of paper. "But for the unwarranted federalization of the National Guard, I would be your commander in chief. It is a bitter pill to swallow. I am grateful to the people of Alabama for the restraint which they have shown. I ask the people of Alabama to remain calm, to help us in this fight. We must have no violence. The guardsmen are our brothers. The trend toward military dictatorship continues. But this is a constitutional fight and we are winning. God bless all the people of Alabama, white and black."

Wallace saluted Graham quickly and stepped aside.

Hood and Malone were escorted into the building.

Wallace, his brothers, and several aides rushed to an awaiting state-trooper car. They sped away toward Montgomery. As the car slowed to turn a corner on the edge of the campus, a crowd of spectators gave a rousing cheer. Wallace smiled and waved.

Miss Malone breezed through registration in less than ten minutes, Hood took about twelve. They paid their tuition with scholarship checks issued by the Unity Club, Inc.

Less than twelve hours after this beautifully orchestrated political-theatrical presentation, an unplanned anticlimax happened. As he stepped from his car in front of his home in Jackson, Mississippi, thirty-seven-year-old Medgar W. Evers, state field secretary for the National Association for the Advancement of Colored People, was shot in the back. He was returning from an integration rally where he had been planning more demonstrations against racial discrimination in Mississippi's capital. Fifteen minutes after he was shot he died.

While Governor Wallace did not hold the gun himself, he created the atmosphere of hate in order to become a nationally recognized spokesman for ultra-right-wing conservatives. He was at that time looking ahead to the next year when he would run in presidential primaries. Most of his life he had yearned to become a national figure. Now, within five months of his taking office as governor, he led the racist pack.

STAND ON HIS RECORD

TWO DAYS BEFORE his inauguration in 1963 Wallace played host to a miniconvention of think-alike segregationists. Meeting at the Graystone Hotel, Wallace's unofficial headquarters in those days, was the mutual admiration society of Leander Henry Perez of the bayous of Louisiana, Ross Barnett of Mississipppi, Roy Harris of Georgia, and James Gray, who ran as a segregationist candidate for governor of Georgia in 1966. A smattering of aides accompanied each of the men.

"We don't let niggers have their way down in Plaquemines," Perez, a heavyset man with a booming voice and a sweeping white pompadour, broke the ice.

"We're going to show everybody in this country where we stand, Judge," Wallace said.

"I hope you let 'em know loud and clear, Governor," said the man who had served as circuit judge in south Louisiana in the twenties. Since that time he had learned the subtle maneuverings and the possible power of levee-board politics. During the thirties he had taken care of some of Huey Long's business. During the forties and fifties he had helped out Earl Long's quest to become governor. And he always kept his finger in Russell Long's senatorial pie. "I know how to take care of *business*," he explained his behind-the-scene political operations. For decades he had been known as the third house of the Louisiana legislature. His motto was, "Always take the offensive. The defensive ain't worth a damn."

The group put together a plan by which they could run a strong favorite-son southerner in the fall and take votes away from John Kennedy. They agreed on the "free elector" plan, putting uncommitted electors on the Democratic primary ballots throughout the South, running the favorite son to take the votes.

Wallace was playing head-to-head politics as well as he'd ever played on that day. He was shaking hands right and left. He saw himself as the favorite son to emerge in the primaries of 1964 as the great southern vote-getter. In the end, however, only Alabama and Mississippi went through with the plan.

Judge Perez tried desperately to get Wallace on the ballot in Louisiana in 1964, but he was unsuccessful. He sent letters to his constituents telling them that Wallace was an "outstanding independent candidate for president." His States' Righters party attempted to have Wallace's name put up, but it was too late.

In 1966, when Wallace ran his wife, Lurleen, for governor, Perez sent what Wallace later called a "generous" contribution to the campaign.

In late 1967 Perez planned another campaign to capture Louisiana for Wallace. When he found out Governor John McKeithen would not go along with such a move, Perez urged his friends, members of the States' Righters and White Citizens Councils to write the governor "because he's slipping too far to the left. I think we can help him see the light of day." On the other hand, Perez urged support of Wallace on every level of state government, including the Plaquemines courthouse. A man who worked in the courthouse for the parish government wrote in an underground newspaper, the Plaquemines *Voice*, that "if you work for the parish, are you a free man? Ask anybody who works for the parish. You get low pay, and you gotta put up for everything, schools, Wallace, [segregated] swimming pools, and anything Perez wants."

Early in 1968 Wallace wrote Perez, "It is particularly gratifying to know that you are willing to give your time and talents in behalf of our efforts. I am indeed grateful. . . . I hope that you will find time in your busy schedule to follow through in your state in the manner outlined in our discussions. . . . I am confident that as a team our efforts will be successful."

In New Orleans Perez said Wallace would restore "honesty in government. . . . It is time for law and order, and all it takes to get these things is determination, guts, and will power. And George Wallace has the courage to accomplish this." Afterward he traveled throughout the South on Wallace's behalf.

A week before the 1968 election Perez wrote to Wallace, "I enclose check for $30,000 to cover net receipts for our New Orleans Wallace Testimonial Dinner. . . . Best wishes for a successful climax."

With Perez fighting for him all the way, Wallace's American party received the rooster emblem over its slate of candidates in Louisiana. The state supreme court ruled in favor of Perez.

But Wallace still did not win in Louisiana.

In March of the following year Perez died. Wallace, along with the contingent of Perez admirers from Alabama, including Wallace's brother Gerald, attended the funeral.

Afterward, with tear-rimmed eyes, Wallace told newsmen, "I loved the judge personally. He was the noblest Roman of them all." Wallace said that Perez would be a "loss to his state, the southland, and to the entire nation. He served his people well in many positions of leadership and will long be remembered for the contributions he made to the welfare of all of the people of his state and nation."

Stand on His Record

Following his stand in the schoolhouse door, Wallace accepted an invitation from Lester Maddox to speak to a Fourth of July celebration at the Southeast Fairgrounds in Atlanta. Maddox had not yet entered the political arena, but he was well known in all right-wing circles. Maddox stood about the same height as Wallace, although he was bald-headed while Wallace had a head full of dark, slick-backed hair. The two were brothers under the skin. Maddox owned a restaurant in Atlanta from which he handed out hundreds of miniature axe handles, the symbol of his own fight to keep blacks from entering his place of business. He had earned the nickname Axe Handle by wielding such a weapon when civil-rights demonstrations took place in the parking lot of his restaurant.

George Wallace looked like a grinning bantam rooster as he strutted through the anxious crowd. He shook their hands and they screamed and shouted. No matinee idol had ever been more enthusiastically received. His long speech, which was written in part by Asa "Ace" Carter, a card-carrying KKK member from Gadsden, Alabama, was a masterpiece in racist rhetoric.

On the platform with him that day was Georgia Ku Klux Klan Wizard Calvin Graig, who commented later that Wallace's was the "finest speech I've ever heard presented."

Unlike the stand in the schoolhouse door, not many newsmen were present at the fairgrounds. This speech was not broadcast throughout the nation on all three major networks. If it had been, his words, "A politician must stand on his own record," would have echoed endlessly in his background no matter where he went.

When he said it that day, the 188th birthday of the nation, the words rang out and stuck with many, "A politician must stand on his own record." Wallace was making his stand.

Shaking his fists in his own idiosyncratic manner, he said it was a "cruel irony" that President Kennedy was on that day signing the Civil Rights Act into law. He twisted his lips into an angry snarl and called the law "the most monstrous piece of legislation ever enacted by the United States Congress. It is a fraud, a sham, and a hoax."

With his head bobbing and the audience applauding after every phrase, he said that signing the bill into law was "tragic. To do so upon the eve of the celebration of our independence insults the intelligence of the American people. It dishonors the memory of countless thousands of our dead who offered up their very lives in defense of principles which this bill destroys."

Wallace was at his speech-making best. He would later repeat the style and form countless times, but he would never be better. He had his audience humming with him like the best brush-arbor revivalist in south Alabama. He drove like a bull at full speed into the United States Supreme Court, describing the members as "omnipotent black-robed despots.

"There is only one word to describe the federal judiciary today. That word is 'lousy,' " and the mob howled its approval. Fathers held little children in the crooks of their arms and clapped despite the burden. Men who had not moved so spryly in years did jigs in the aisles to the rhythm of his voice. They loved it.

The Supreme Court, he maintained, "asserts more power than claimed by King George III, more than Hitler, Mussolini, or Khrushchev ever had. They assert more power to declare unconstitutional our very thoughts. To create for us a system of moral and ethical values. To outlaw and declare unconstitutional, illegal, and immoral the customs, traditions, and beliefs of the people, and furthermore they assert the authority to enforce their decrees in all these subjects upon the American people without their consent."

It seemed as though every word was a jewel to them,

something to praise, something to "oooh" and "aaah" over, something to be proud of. They had thought the same thing, they had cursed the Supreme Court in the privacy of their homes since the Brown vs. Board decision in 1954, and now somebody had stepped up there on that red, white, and blue-papered wooden platform and was saying it to them loud and clear.

George C. Wallace had found his people. They loved him just as much in Georgia as they did in Alabama. They showed their love by their response. Years before in the poor flatlands of south Georgia peanut-growing country Eugene "Just Call Me Ol' Gene" Talmadge popped his suspenders and said, "They call us Rednecks. Damn right we're Rednecks. We get our necks red from plowing mules under that hateful hot sun."

By the time Wallace became the symbol of segregation the children and grandchildren of Ol' Gene's Rednecks lived in the suburbs in three-bedroom, one-and-a-half bath, kitchen-den combination, twice-mortgaged split-levels. George Wallace caught the emotion of their collective inferiority complex. He told them, "You're just as cultured and refined as anybody. Those liberal Yankees send their chillun to Ivy League universities while yo' chillun go to the state schools. Yo' chillun, whether they go to college or not, are just as educated as theirs—but yours have got manners, say 'Yes, sir' and 'Yes, ma'am' to their elders, and don't demonstrate in the streets like common criminals." The descendents of the dirt farmers had grown up, moved to the city, bought two cars, a color television, washing machine, dryer, and if they were lucky had a boat, motor, and a little place on the lake. Who cared if they owed for eighty percent of what they "owned," they paid their taxes, went to church on Sunday, raised their kids to be "good Christians," and they were damned if they were going to let some federal judge tell them what they could do or couldn't do. You could no longer tell a redneck by his sunburn.

Redneck was now a way of life, country boys and girls fighting the city blues. If the Negroes moved in, they'd move out.

Now they were listening to their man. No one had ever represented the city-billy's point of view, and now there was George C. Wallace, and he wouldn't give in to the Big Boys.

George told these folks what they wanted to hear. He said that it was "perfectly obvious" that the Supreme Court and other so-called left-wingers "don't like our form of government."

He said the left-wingers "think they can establish a better" form of government. "In order to do so it is necessary that they overthrow our existing form; destroy the democratic institutions created by the people; change the outlook, religion, and philosophy; and bring the whole area of human thought, aspiration, action, and organization under the absolute control of the [Supreme] Court. Their decisions reveal this to be the goal of the liberal element on the Court which is in a majority at present," he said.

To find the nature of the opinions, he said, one has only to look in the *Communist Manifesto*. "The Communists are dedicated to the overthrow of our form of government. They are dedicated to the destruction of the concept of private property. They are dedicated to the object of destroying religion as the basis of moral and ethical values. The Communists are determined that all natural resources shall be controlled by the central government, that all productive capacity of the nation shall be under the control of the central government, that the political sovereignty of the people shall be destroyed as an incident to control of local schools. It is their objective to capture the minds of our youth in order to indoctrinate them in what to think and not how to think.

"I do not call the members of the United States Supreme Court Communists. But I do say, and I submit for your judgment the fact that every single decision of the Court in the past ten years which related in any way to each of these objectives has been decided against freedom and in favor of tyranny.

"A politician must stand on his record," he announced, and the crowds cheered even louder. "Let the court stand on its record!" he said loudly, and they applauded and whistled and screamed with delight.

"The record reveals, for the past number of years, that the chief, if not the only beneficiaries of the present court's rulings, have been duly and lawfully convicted criminals, Communists, atheists, and clients of vociferous left-wing minority groups.

"You can't convict a Communist in our federal court system!" Again they shouted.

"Neither can you convict one of being a Communist in Russia, China, or Cuba. The point is that the United States Supreme Court refuses to recognize the Communist conspiracy and their intent to 'bury us.'"

He went on and on and on. He never let up. He pounded away at the Supreme Court for making "our little schoolchildren" be bused across towns, attend school with people they don't want to sit next to, and live through days without hearing prayers in the schools.

He worked on their insecurities like a skilled surgeon slicing open a festered wound. He promised that he would run for the presidency. "I am a conservative," he told them. "I intend to give the American people a clear choice. I welcome a fight between our philosophy and the liberal, left-wing dogma which threatens to engulf every man, woman, and child in the United States. I am in this race because I believe the American people have been pushed around long enough and that they, like you and I, are fed up with the continuing trend toward a socialist state which now subjects the individual to the dictates of an all-powerful central government. I am running for

154

President because I was born free. I want to remain free. I want your children and mine and our posterity to be unencumbered by the manipulations of a soulless state. I intend to fight for a positive, affirmative program to restore constitutional government and to stop the senseless bloodletting now being performed on the body of liberty by those who lead us willingly and dangerously close to a totalitarian central government."

As he spoke these words two black men in the back of the audience mumbled something under their breath. Two white factory workers from Decatur, Georgia, were standing nearby. One looked at the other. There was immediate silent communication. They picked up the lightweight metal folding chairs. They swung at the same time. They caught the black men across the backs of their heads and brought them to their knees. They swung again, connecting again, and blood ran down the sides of the faces of the black men. Later they were taken to a nearby hospital. Twelve stitches were taken in the skull of one. The other suffered a minor concussion.

While they were falling to the ground Wallace was screaming, "We must destroy the power to dictate, to forbid, to require, to demand, to distribute, to edict, and to judge what is best and enforce that will of judgment upon free citizens. We must revitalize a government founded in this nation on faith of God!"

The thousands chanted, "George! George! George!"

As he stood mightily before them, a strand of hair drooping limply over one eye, he held up his hands and formed *V*'s with his fingers.

They screamed and clapped and whistled and called for more.

He was on his way. He had delivered one of the greatest racist addresses which had ever crossed the lips of a human. He never uttered the word "nigger." He was too brilliant in his political rhetoric. He knew he did not have to use the word. But he evoked the image through the usage of well-chosen code words: race, creed, or color; the boot of tyranny; the power to dictate; the framework of our priceless freedoms, and others. Whose priceless freedoms? The white people of the world were having their excesses of freedoms diminished, and he cried out for their cause.

The fairgrounds speech was not the first time Wallace had aligned with the KKK, nor would it be the last. A man of many contradictions, Wallace once said in a private talk, "They said I made antisegregation speeches back in 1958. I never did that. Every one of them was prosegregation. I've never been for anything else. They called me a liberal back then. That's just a label. Somebody called me that, probably a newspaper editor who liked to put labels on people. I personally don't like to put labels on people. But I'll tell you, I've always been prosegregation. That was the law of this land, and I've always been a law-abiding citizen. I've never varied from my law-and-order stand. It's part of the basic foundation of this country, of this democracy, and it's something every politician and every person should stand up for."

In 1958 the KKK supported Wallace's opponent John Patterson, who won that election for governor. Afterward Wallace met the Wizard of the United Klan of America, Robert Shelton of Tuscaloosa, and they struck up a friendship which continued for years. "We made him governor in 1963, and we kept him governor, and now we must make him President," Shelton said.

Wallace speechwriter Ace Carter and Shelton traveled together to Indiana in 1964 to campaign among the Klans of that grassroots area. "We found our people throughout the state. They're good people, tired of being shoved around, wanting something different, and seeing what they needed in George Wallace," said Shelton.

Shelton campaigned for Patterson back in 1958 among the factory workers and Klansmen throughout Alabama. Four years later he switched to Wallace because "he was and is the man most responsive to our welfare. He talks our language. We don't care if he says he's not against integration anymore because it's the law of the land now. We know what he means. We've been with him too long, and he's been with us. You ask him if he's against us, he'll tell you."

Wallace stated that he can't help who supports him. "I'm not going to tell people not to vote for me. That would be downright ridiculous. I'm glad to get the support of anyone except gangsters and Communists," he added.

An old-time supporter of the Wallace cause is anti-Semitic and anti-Negro backer of the National States Rights party, J. B. Stoner of Georgia, who has never given up the white-supremacy banner. "We have built George Wallace up from a small-time governor in Alabama to an international figure. In South Africa they speak of him reverently. In England he is admired by those who hate to see the mongrelization of the Anglo-Saxon peoples. Throughout the world people are keeping their eyes on the United States. Millions of people want George Wallace to be President of the United States. They know that he would be the savior of the white race. Without him we might be lost forever." In 1968 Stoner said, "Our slogan is the same as in 1964. Governor George C. Wallace— Last Chance for the White Vote."

Also in 1968 the official KKK newspaper, *The Fiery Cross*, editorialized that Wallace "may never be President, but the psychological impact upon our enemies to this possibility is our greatest word weapon, and we dare not let this great man fade from the national scene."

During the third-party battle in 1968 the Liberty Amendment Committee of Wisconsin, a group that had been fighting for the repeal of the income-tax law, swung its support to Wallace and the White Party of America enthusiastically supported him.

When Wallace made a more or less bland inauguration address in January 1971, still antibusing but moderated to the point of praising freedom of choice, his old ally Ace Carter and a dozen fellow Klansmen pulled out placards and demonstrated. "Wallace Is A Bigot," one sign read. Another announced in red, white, and blue letters: "Free Our White Children." Carter, who was busily publishing an irregular mimeographed pamphlet entitled "The Southerner," saw himself mirrored on history's walls as the Thomas Paine of the Dixiecrats. After all, he had been the author of the "Segregation forever!" speech, and when he spoke those words a fiery gleam appeared in his eyes. On the afternoon of Wallace's 1971 inauguration Carter sat on the back steps of the capitol. His physical build was almost a replica of George Wallace. He was short and chunky. He held his sweating palms clasped, his elbows anchored on his knees. "George Wallace has changed in the last eight years. All the campaigning has taken the fight out of him. He's not the same person he was when he stood on the star [a bronze plaque in front of the capitol's front door, placed there by the United Daughters of the Confederacy] where Jefferson Davis took his oath, and spoke out for the great principles involved in that struggle one hundred years ago. He's not the same man who shook his fist in the face of a possible jail sentence. I think he has found himself getting too close to the White House, and he can't cope with the idea of being a racist who failed to win the presidency. I am a racist. I understand that. I fight for a cause which I hope to win. With George Wallace I had a wonderful spokesman for the cause. Now we have to look somewhere else. We can no longer look at George Wallace." He cast his sad damp eyes downward and rubbed the heel of his shoe against the ancient marble of the step. "He said words out there today that he would never have uttered eight years ago. He would not have thought them. He is being influenced by other people now, people who want to get their feet inside the White House, people who want him to become another turncoat like Lyndon Johnson. He once talked out against Johnson, told the world about the hypocrites, and now he is a hypocrite himself." His voice grew soft. "His problem is, he doesn't really believe. Back then he listened to me. I wrote the words and he said them. We had the liberal no-accounts on the run. They ran with their tails between their legs." Remembering, his face lighted with pure excitement. In his mind's eye he could see them taking off in the opposite direction while he and George Wallace drove them with whips into the bramble bushes. "Now we have to go after him. We have to tell everybody about him. I will write the words in 'The Southerner,' and we will distribute them among the people. It's disturbing to have to write about a man who came so far, but when he turns around you have to point out the faults of his new direction. We have a calling." One of his fellow soldiers called from under the hillside that he had given out all the copies of "The Southerner" from his cardboard box. Carter said he'd meet him at the car. "When I went to Indiana for him six years ago it was like reaching into heaven and actually feeling the soft, magnificent texture of the golden streets. Don't anybody wear shoes in heaven, you know." His eyes were glazed with the thought. "When I went to Indiana for him, we met with the people—and they loved him. Those folks were starved for the truth. They knew it in their hearts. They could see the dragon in Washington breathing down their necks, taking away their very livelihoods, threatening them with the loss of the most precious thing any of us own—freedom. The Supreme Court was stealing from them.

They just wanted back what was rightly theirs, and George Wallace was going to get it back for them." Another of his troupe called out, said he was empty, and suggested they should be heading home. He agreed. He stood. Walking down the steps slowly, he said, "If we keep on the way we're going, with the mixing of the races, destroying God's plan, there won't be an earth on which to live in five years." He passed three people on his way to his car. Each of them turned and stared after him. When he drove away tears were streaming down vein-marked cheeks.

About six months later he published "The Southerner" with photographs of Wallace, whom he called an integrating liar, a hypocrite, and a sellout to the cause of the white people of the world.

Within the following year a two-paragraph Associated Press story from Gadsden reported that the former Wallace aide had been arrested for driving while intoxicated. About one month later another story said he had been arrested for public drunkenness. No more issues of "The Southerner" were forthcoming. He disappeared from public view. His telephone was disconnected. Former associates in his home town said they no longer heard from him.

In the meantime, Carter's former fellow traveler, Bobby Shelton, was gearing up for the national campaign of 1976. There was no doubt in his mind that George Wallace was the strongest candidate in the country. While the Klan itself had been showing signs of moderation (to the point where some Klaverns were admitting Jewish members), the Grand Wizard knew that Wallace was attempting to appeal to more across-the-board votes. If Wallace could get elected with black votes, that was all right. Once in, the position would be secured.

Shelton knew that Wallace was his friend. Back during the first administration Wallace ordered an underling with a construction company doing business with the state docks in

Mobile to hire Shelton's father. In 1964 the U. S. Bureau of Public Roads accused the Wallace administration of forcing an engineering firm to hire the younger Shelton as an "agent" for four thousand dollars. The entire federal matching-funds program was threatened by the move, and Wallace backed off hurriedly. Shelton had also gained notoriety when his Klan Bureau of Investigation was hired with state money to investigate Klan activities within the state. Again Wallace backed off after the deal was made known to the public.

Shelton, who had led seething mobs through downtown Tuscaloosa streets where they overturned automobiles and rallied around the Main Street flagpole when the first Negro, Autherine Lucy, tried to integrate the University of Alabama, was certain in the summer of 1975 that George Wallace would be President of the United States when inauguration time, 1977, rolled around. "I don't see how anybody can stop him," said Shelton, who managed a service station near the university when Miss Lucy came to the school in February 1956. "His strength lies in the little man throughout the country. The little man has had enough from the heavies in Washington who have been ramming it down his throat. He knows that he hasn't had a say-so in government. You tell him all you want about Watergate, and all he knows is that it was started by the big men up there—and to the man on the street George Wallace is not a big man, he's just like them. They're going to vote for him. All the political science in the world is not going to take that away from him.

"George Wallace has been waiting for this day. It's his day. It's got his name written all over it. Everybody's been hollering about the nigger vote, you've got to have the nigger vote; hell, he doesn't have to have the nigger vote. He's got every white vote that'll stand up and call itself white," he stated.

After his career as a filling-station manager ended, Shelton worked at the Goodrich Rubber Plant as a salesman. He sold tires to the Patterson administration until he was discovered and written about in the press. He became friends with George Wallace in 1962. "I went to him and asked him if he wanted our support. That was after he sent somebody to see me, to feel me out about whether or not we would support him. I didn't want to play any behind-the-scenes games. I wanted everything out in the open. As far as I can remember he never did speak at one of our rallies, but Ace Carter came to them and spoke for Wallace. He'd get the crowds all churned up. He was really good at doing that. Then we'd burn the crosses and march around them. There were some beautiful occasions. I remember a particular one in Warrior. We had nearly two thousand people there. Of course they weren't all members of the Klan. They were visitors as well as members. All of 'em believed what we believed, they clapped and whooped it up. Ace spoke to 'em and told 'em George Wallace was the white savior and that he was against no-good Communists on the Supreme Court and no-good scalawags on the local federal benches. Even the people who had been sitting way back in the pine trees on the hoods of their pickups got up and slapped their thighs and hollered 'Hallelujah!' It was like a camp meeting down home."

Bobby Shelton, who made more fund-raising speeches in 1976 than Wallace, said the Klan was on its way toward a new heyday. "People who say the Klan is dead are crazy. They haven't looked to see what we've been doing, where we're going, the membership which is coming out of the suburbs where people are scared. People in this country don't like to be frightened. They don't like to be afraid to walk down a downtown street at night. They want their streets safe for themselves and especially safe for their children."

The Klan today, Shelton said, is attempting to become more sophisticated and urbane. In 1974 the Klan started its first private school in Belton, South Carolina, and studies were being made to find other locations for expansion. "This is all a part of the same fight that George Wallace is the mouthpiece for. We're against the federal courts telling parents they have to bus their little schoolchildren all the way across the cities and counties so they have to go to school with niggers. We don't see any logic in that. The only person who speaks out against it is George Wallace, and we're going to back him all the way down the road that leads to Washington, D. C." Shelton stated emphatically.

AMBUSH AT PETTUS BRIDGE

EVER SINCE WALLACE'S proclamation of "segregation forever," a fevered relationship had been building between the Alabama chief executive and the black community of the state. Black leaders had been working intensely to register their people to vote in such places as Dallas and Lowndes counties in the middle of the Alabama Black Belt, where the Negro population ranged from sixty to seventy-five percent. In late 1964 Dr. Martin Luther King, Jr., leader of the Southern Christian Leadership Conference based in Atlanta, asked Wallace for an extension of the time to register voters. Wallace replied by giving a ten-day moratorium, then registration was cut off.

Spokesmen from right-wing groups such as White Citizens Councils, John Birch Society, and the Alabama Sovereignty Commission (a group formed with state money by a Wallace executive order) visited registrars throughout the state with conservative guidelines about how they could and should legally not register blacks to vote. The governor gave his tacit approval to this practice.

When Wallace stopped all registration of voters, King and other civil-rights leaders planned to congregate in Selma, Alabama, the largest town and seat of Dallas County. The town, located in the heart of the Black Belt, was in the center of the troubled land. Founded long before the Civil War, Selma was a primary port city on the Alabama River, where cotton was stacked on riverboats by slaves. Outside Selma a plantation society stretched for hundreds of miles in all directions. Rich, rolling land gave forth the cotton around which developed a brand of feudal economics. The white people owned the land. They were the only persons who were educated. The black people worked the land; in the beginning they were slaves, and after the Civil War they operated as sharecroppers. Historically the white landowners controlled politics as well as the economy. Very few blacks ever voted. Few blacks could read or write in the Black Belt. They were never educated. No one had ever cared about the poor black farmer who toiled the land, propagated his race, drank corn likker and danced in honky-tonks on Saturday nights, attended church and sang good old-time spirituals on Sunday mornings, and died and was buried in graveyards furnished generously by white landlords. It was a tough system with layers on top of layers of time-worn calluses. The blacks simply did not revolt from within. All of them owed their soul to the proverbial company store. If they dared rebel the boss man would foreclose, or stop all debt, or throw the ingrates off the precious land.

The whites did not realize that the system they kept alive into the twentieth century was self-defeating. The whites patronizingly played father, mother, and caretaker to the black, saying the workers were too poor and uneducated to vote. These same whites nurtured the poverty which they scorned. Out of that poverty-stricken race arose some people, however, who would not bow and scrape and buck-and-wing for the white man. Some went to Detroit to work in automobile factories. Some traveled to Akron to mould tires for the cars their brothers were making. These children of the South spread the word about the dehumanizing treatment in the land of their birth. They didn't wish to stay in the North. They were southerners. They wanted their children to be southerners. But they were damned if they would allow their children and their children's children to grow up being whipped down into a nasty dirt by a system that didn't give a gnat's life for their petty existence. A mere handful also came out of this culture who would stand up against the white boss, who would go off to school, and who would return to fight for education, jobs, housing, and the basic right to choose political representation by the process of voting.

Dr. King had been preaching for voting rights. He had been wanting the rights for his people. And in Alabama, George Wallace would not step into the arena of the Black Belt and ask that blacks be registered to vote. On the contrary, he gave his silent approval that county registrars register as few blacks as necessary. In speeches he stated that people who are illiterate should not vote. In practice he stood in a schoolhouse door to keep blacks from being educated. There were fewer black schools than white schools in Dallas County in 1965, although there were almost twenty percent more black children than white children. And Wallace was still fighting the desegregation of schools throughout the area.

Wallace paid little heed to King's pleas. In fact the only attention the governor gave these pleas were in rabble-rousing speeches before ultra-conservative groups where he heaped sarcasm onto the situation rather than explaining it sensibly. Of course the sarcasm was an integral part of his demagoguery.

Believing that barring his people from the privilege of voting was the most undemocratic sin that a government could commit, King arrived in Selma in mid-January of 1965 to confer with local leaders. Within days, hundreds of other religious and civil-rights leaders poured into the town of about thirty thousand, the population of which was split almost equally between blacks and whites.

King organized demonstrations which took place daily. His people formed lines and picketed the Dallas County Courthouse. Sheriff Jim Clark arrested the first small group, but they were freed on bond almost immediately. The picketing continued. Clark and his deputies always stood nearby, listening for anything which could be construed as a vulgar remark, and watching for a movement which could be interpreted as disorderly conduct. The numbers of demonstrators grew during the first two weeks. The numbers of white bystanders also grew. During the month of February several skirmishes took place. Once a shootout broke loose in the warehouse district near the river. But no one was injured.

During the month Wallace told Lingo to send more state troopers into the town to help Mayor Joe Smitherman, City Public Safety Director Wilson Baker, and Sheriff Clark. Several hundred troopers were appointed to Selma indefinitely. One trooper later remembered, "That town was in the damndest shape you've ever seen. Hell, law enforcement officers were stepping all over each other. In the two or three shootouts, where nobody was really hurt, it turned out to be sheriff's deputies firing at city police, or police shooting at troopers. It was chaos. And in the middle of it all was this bunch of newspaper and television reporters wanting to know everything that was happening, taking pictures of everything, and they got to be a bigger nuisance than the Negroes."

King realized he was making little or no headway. After the first half dozen demonstrations the only news that was generated came from the violence. When the SCLC leader spoke to crowds of sympathizers only a few of his words were ever reported.

Finally he decided the time had come to push ahead in a

gigantic way. He needed to demonstrate to the entire country what was happening in Alabama. With a massive demonstration he would be able to shove Congress into a position where it would pass the pending Voters' Rights Act.

King held a press conference in Selma and announced that he would lead a march from Selma to Montgomery in order to petition Wallace for voter-registration remedies. He said a list of specific grievances would be handed to the governor.

On the night following King's press conference Wallace called together his staff to meet with Colonel Lingo, his chief state policeman. According to one account Wallace asked the general question: Would the troopers stop the march or permit it to proceed?

Press Secretary Bill Jones, in his laudatory biography, *The Wallace Story*, writes that he suggested,

> If the press reported the march would be stopped, the marchers would approach the trooper lines unprepared to march the fifty miles to Montgomery. As soon as the marchers met the troopers, the troopers would stand aside and tell them to proceed. My plan next proposed closing the highway to motorists except those who lived on the highway. All other traffic would be re-routed to Montgomery and points east. The visiting press, if they wished to walk, would be allowed to follow the marchers on foot; no one would be allowed to drive a car, truck, or bus. In short, King wanted to march, I wanted to make sure he marched and didn't ride, nor did I want him to have a comfortable trailer for sleeping. The highway would remain closed to all transportation; if the marchers wanted to return to Selma, they would have to walk back.

After hearing the story Wallace asked, "Why not let them march?" And from that moment until two days later, according to Jones, Wallace was in agreement with the plans.

On Friday morning Jones leaked the news that the troopers would stop the march.

By late Friday afternoon when Wallace summoned legislative leaders, the governor had obviously changed his mind. State Senator Alton Turner, a Wallace floor leader, recalled that he outlined a suggestion similar to the Jones plan. "I wanted the state troopers and the Alabama National Guard to both protect marchers and people who live along the highway," Turner said. But when he finished his remarks, he said, Wallace slammed his fist on his desk and stated, "I'm not going to have a bunch of niggers walking along a highway in this state as long as I'm governor." Turner said that Al Lingo agreed with the governor, who then stated that the troopers would block any marches between Selma and Montgomery. Wallace was hellbent on planned violence.

In a hastily called news conference that afternoon Wallace said he had ordered Lingo "to use whatever measures are necessary to prevent a march." To cover himself he told newsmen, "Any preconceived 'march' along the public highways of this state is not conducive to orderly flow of traffic and commerce within and through the state of Alabama. The additional hazard placed upon the highway travel by any such actions cannot be countenanced. It is clearly obvious to any sensible person that such organized group 'marching' along our highways will only add to existing hazards of traffic such as curves, embankments, bridges, and other normal conditions found along the public ways of this state. Such action would not be allowed on the part of any other group of citizens or noncitizens of the state of Alabama and will not be allowed in this instance. Government must proceed in an orderly manner and lawful and law-abiding citizens must transact their business with the government in such a manner. There will be no march between Selma and Montgomery, and I have so instructed the Department of Public Safety."

At the same time that Saturday night Dr. King was at his home in Atlanta and was making a conference telephone call to his associates in Selma. He had a worship service to conduct Sunday morning at his church in Atlanta. He would not be able to lead the march. He was assured, however, that there was no need for his presence. The troopers would stop the marchers, then the marchers would seek an injunction in federal court to march on the federal highway, thirty-nine-year-old SCLC field coordinator Hosea Williams told King. King warned Williams to be careful and to turn back if the troopers appeared violent, and he added, "May God go with you."

King's chief lieutenant, Andrew Young, later a Congressman from Atlanta, was also in Selma and detailed the route of the march to reporters. He said the demonstrators would never leave the shoulder of the road.

On Sunday morning, March 7, about two hundred marchers stepped spryly into the hot spring sunshine singing a spirited version of "We Shall Overcome," the anthem of the Black Movement.

They moved toward the deserted Edmund Pettus Bridge, a quarter-moon-shaped concrete structure which curved up and over the Alabama River. Beyond the bridge was the four-lane U.S. Highway 80 which led to Montgomery, some fifty-four miles due east.

Although the marchers could not see them, because the bridge rises to a peak over the river, Lingo had positioned his troopers across U. S. 80 to block the highway about one hundred yards east of the bridge. Lingo sat bug-eyed and waiting in an air-conditioned trooper car nearby. The troopers stood shoulder to shoulder with three-foot billy clubs clinched in their grips. Behind them the horses of Sheriff Clark's mounted civilian posse pranced nervously in the dust.

Major John Cloud was saying, "Don't hit anybody unless

they hit first, then only use the tear gas," when the first marcher's face appeared over the crest of the bridge.

The troopers, tense as tightly wound tin soldiers, stood at parade rest. All eyes were straight ahead.

As the marchers cleared the bridge, Hosea Williams walked along the side of the road with his snow-white cowboy hat cocked to one side of his ebony head. Williams's eyes never moved from the solid line of troopers ahead. He did not think about it at the time, but he later reminisced, "The troopers had it planned so beautifully. There we were, knowing they were going to stop us and turn us around, and we weren't thinking that they were letting us get far enough off that bridge where we wouldn't have any place to run and hide or anything. All those old white people's houses along the side of the road, we sure weren't going there."

As they marched, an elderly wrinkle-faced woman ran in jerky fashion to the edge of her lawn and screamed, "What you crazy niggers doing? What y'all looking for? Where y'all going?" until her face was red.

When the marchers got within forty feet of the troopers, Cloud spoke into his bullhorn. "Turn around and go back. You will not be allowed to march any farther."

Williams did not break stride.

Again Cloud stated, "If you disperse, you will be allowed to return freely to town. You have two minutes."

By this time Williams could walk no farther. Troopers blocked the highway and the shoulders. Stopping, the marchers became a circular-formed group.

Troopers looked on like silent pillars of stone.

The seconds ticked away slowly.

Major Cloud stared through his rimless glasses at the crowd.

An Associated Press reporter standing nearby said he heard Williams ask to speak to Cloud.

"You may disperse or go back or we will break it up. There's nothing to talk about," Cloud replied.

Elbows and wrists of troopers twitched. Sweat trickled down their foreheads and ran into their eyes and mouths.

A nervous giggle cracked inside the mob of marchers.

As though a taut cord was suddenly cut, troopers moved like a tidal wave into the marchers. One trooper raised his club and struck a black across the shoulder. His movement was like a signal for the others.

The marchers, stumbling, falling, attempting to guard their heads with arms and hands, were pushed back fifty yards. Tear-gas bombs were blasted into their midst.

Some elementary-school children and some shaky-legged elderly people, demonstrators in the group, moved toward the bridge, trying to escape, with tears streaming from their eyes and whines moaning from trembling lips.

The troopers didn't stop. They didn't even slow down. They plowed into the gas-dazed blacks with clubs swinging wildly.

From behind the troopers rushed Clark's posse, shouting rebel yells and raring to go. The horses waded forward through the yellow smoke of the gas that lay cloudlike on the ground. Mixed with the screams and cries and clicks of irregular hoofbeats on the pavement were the solid thuds of wooden clubs pounding against flesh. Human yelps, like the sound of frightened animals, were heard when Clark's deputies jabbed the marchers with battery-powered electric cattle prods.

When it was over, less than twenty minutes later, not one black person remained standing. The whinny of sweat-soaked horses and the clicking of hooves were still heard as the blacks, one by one, managed to rise and scamper back across the bridge into Selma.

The degrading sounds of the blacks who were again being trapped in bondage were heard around the world. Every responsible press in the United States and the world literally

screamed with indignation. The Boston *Globe* editorialized,
"What words can describe the depravity of the state troopers
and mounted deputies who committed this outrage against
America? And what can be said of Governor Wallace?" *The
New York Times* wrote that Wallace "has written another
shameful page in his own record and in the history of
Alabama."

When he heard what had happened, King was shocked, but
he also was pragmatic enough to know Wallace had played
into his hands. It would not be difficult to arouse sympathy
now. He told the press that he had not been with the marchers
because it was understood previously that the troopers would
stop the march, but "I must confess that I had no idea that the
kind of brutality and tragic expression of man's inhumanity to
man as existed Sunday would take place. Alabama's state
troopers, under the sanction and authorization of Governor
Wallace, allowed themselves to degenerate to the lowest state
of barbarity." He said he would continue his determined
attempt to walk to Montgomery.

According to those close to Wallace, the governor was
furious at Lingo for the action. Wallace too knew that the
violence would generate sympathy for King's cause. Press
Secretary Bill Jones wrote later that Wallace "was not about to
publicly criticize him [Lingo]. Wallace sees police of the
nation as the closest representatives of lawfully constituted
governments to the people. He feels police protection is vital
to the security of the nation, vital to the safety of all its
citizens. Publicly, Wallace defended the troopers."

However, when Lingo was running for sheriff of Jefferson
County some years later, he said, "I had no other choice at
Selma. I was ordered to cause the scene that the troopers
made. Who ordered me? The governor! Governor George C.
Wallace ordered me to stop the marchers even if we had to use
force, to bring this thing to a halt. He said that we'd teach

other niggers to try to march on a public highway in Alabama. He said that he was damned if he would allow such a thing to take place. He said that not only to me but to many other people who were present over a period of several days in his office while plans were being made."

Taking the only course available, King's people asked for an injunction to stop Wallace from interfering with their march. U. S. District Judge Frank Johnson issued a temporary injunction against King and Wallace. He said he wanted both to stop further action until he had time to study and hear testimony on the matter.

In the meantime, Director of the Federal Community Relations Service LeRoy Collins, former governor of Florida, was sent to Selma by President Johnson. Collins met with King, who wanted to march regardless of the injunction. Collins assured King that the President was working diligently on the Voting Rights legislation which he would send to Congress. Collins advised that he did not believe it would be necessary for King to violate the judge's injunction.

But King believed he needed to prove to his people that he would face even federal contempt charges.

When King led the marchers on Tuesday he was intercepted by U. S. Marshal H. Stanley Fountain. King told him, "I am aware of the court order." Fountain stepped aside.

When the marchers topped the crest of Edmund Pettus Bridge on this afternoon, they looked down onto another line of troopers. This time they were led by short, fat Lingo, who screamed through his bullhorn, "You are ordered to stop! Stand where you are! This march will not continue!"

As King drew closer, he stated that he had the right to walk. Then King turned slowly, dramatically, and faced his people. He knelt on the gravel shoulder of the road. He clasped his palms together under his chin and began to pray aloud. His followers also knelt, bowed their heads, and closed their eyes.

Lingo, standing nearby, looked on incredulously. He swept his arms back, ordering his men to part their lines, leaving an opening through which King and followers could pass if they wished to march to Montgomery. If King had marched on, he would obviously have been in contempt of Johnson's order.

But as soon as King finished praying he stood and, without speaking, led his people back across the bridge into Selma.

When they had returned, King proclaimed, "This was the greatest demonstration for freedom, the greatest confrontation we've ever had in the South. We knew we would be stopped by the troopers, but on the basis of conscience we had to march and stand up to the troopers at the place where the brutality took place."

Three days later, speculating that Judge Johnson would order the march to take place, Wallace sent a telegram to President Johnson asking for a private appointment. Wallace wired that "the situation existing in Selma, Alabama, which is not unlike recent occurrences in other states, possesses some of the greatest internal problems ever faced by this nation. Voter registration and voting rights are not the issues involved in these street demonstrations. The voting rights of every person in Alabama are now being considered by litigation pending in federal courts. I have said many times before, and I say again, that any individual who is qualified to vote is entitled to vote."

Johnson replied that he would see Wallace, and an appointment was scheduled for the following day, Saturday.

In his last years, President Johnson remembered that while watching on television the Selma fiasco with the state troopers beating the helpless marchers, "I felt a deep outrage." He said he contemplated sending federal troops into Alabama, that many people wished for him to take such action. But he was a seasoned southern politician himself and surmised, "Such action would play into the hands of those looking for a states'-rights martyr in Governor Wallace. Sending federal troops would turn the growing compassion of the southern moderates into defensive resistance, and would resurrect the bitterness between North and South. We had to have a real victory for the black people, not a psychological victory for the North." He said that he was hurt when his southern heritage was thrown in his face by public protests to his "unbelievable lack of action." He was hoping, he said, that Alabama "would exercise its state's right and assume its constitutional obligation" when Wallace wired requesting a meeting.

In his autobiography, *The Vantage Point*, President Johnson wrote,

> I kept my eyes directly on the Governor's face the entire time. I saw a nervous, aggressive man; a rough, shrewd politician who had managed to touch the deepest chords of pride as well as prejudice among his people.
>
> It was to his pride as an Alabama patriot that I appealed when I asked the Governor to assure me that he would let the marchers proceed in peace and would provide adequate troops to insure the right of peaceful assembly. The Governor's first response was an automatic one. He said the only problems in Alabama were the troublesome demonstrators themselves. They were the ones who were threatening the lives and safety of the people; they were the ones who were defying law and order.
>
> I told him that I believed the only useful way to handle the demonstrators was to respond to their grievances. "The Negro citizens of Alabama who have been systematically denied the right to register and vote have to be given the opportunity to direct national attention to their plight," I said.

The Governor turned then to the questipn of troops. In his view, the state held the responsibility to maintain law and order. I agreed with him at once and told him that was precisely my point. But I made it clear that I intended no such misunderstanding to occur as that which arose between Governor Orval Faubus of Arkansas and President Eisenhower during the 1957 Little Rock episode, when the Governor actually used the National Guard to prevent integration. I told him I had seven hundred troops on alert. If the state and local authorities were unwilling or unable to function, I would not hesitate one moment to send in federal troops.

The Governor said he understood, and we parted in a mood of cordiality. In fact, the Governor was later reported to have said: "If I hadn't left when I did, he'd have had me coming out *for* civil rights."

The meeting with Wallace proved to be the critical turning point in the voting rights struggle. Several days later I received word from the Governor that the State of Alabama was unable to bear the financial burdens of mobilizing the National Guard. The state could not protect the marchers on its own. It needed federal assistance. I gave such assistance immediately. I signed an executive order federalizing the Alabama National Guard.

So the troops went in after all. They went in by order of the President, because the Governor said Alabama couldn't afford them financially. But they were not intruders forcing their way in; they were citizens of Alabama. That made all the difference in the world.

When it was reported later that Johnson attempted to get Wallace "to change his stripes altogether and join The Great Society," Press Secretary Jones wrote that actually the President suggested Wallace register Negroes to vote and gain their support; the number would increase greatly and that Wallace would win more black votes than the number of white votes he would lose. "Wallace turned the President down cold. Wallace believes in realism and he believes that one cannot forget one's heritage," according to Jones.

In the meantime Attorney General Nicholas Katzenbach and John Doar, chief of the civil-rights division of the Justice Department, both of whom had been present during the stand in the schoolhouse door, joined King's demonstrators in Judge Frank Johnson's U. S. District Court. Katzenbach asked the judge to enjoin Wallace and other state officials from interfering with demonstrations and from using force to break up demonstrations or marches.

On that day Johnson found that Dr. King was not in contempt of court by his demonstration. The leader never actually made an attempt to march to Montgomery. He only led his people to the troopers, where he prayed.

On the following Monday, President Johnson addressed the joint session of Congress as he presented his revised voting-rights legislation. In one of his most powerful orations, the tall Texan read the words of his speechwriter Richard Goodwin, who had worked for John Kennedy and was later to work for Robert Kennedy.

"I speak tonight for the dignity of man and the destiny of democracy. At times history and fate meet at a single time in a single place to shape a turning point in man's unending search for freedom. So it was at Lexington and Concord. So it was a century ago at Appomattox. So it was last week in Selma, Alabama.

"There is no constitutional issue here. The command of the Constitution is plain. There is no moral issue. It is wrong— deadly wrong—to deny any of your fellow Americans the right to vote in this country. There is no issue of states' rights or national rights. There is only the struggle for human rights. This time, on this issue, there must be no delay, no hesitation, and no compromise with our purpose.

"But even if we pass this bill, the battle will not be over. What happened in Selma is part of a far larger movement which reaches into every section and state of America. It is the effort of American Negroes to secure for themselves the full blessings of American life.

"Their cause must be our cause too. Because it is not just Negroes, but really it is all of us who must overcome the crippling legacy of bigotry and injustice. And . . . we . . . shall . . . overcome."

He later recalled, "For a few seconds the entire chamber was quiet. Then the applause started and kept coming. One by one the representatives and senators stood up. They were joined by the cabinet, the justices, and the ambassadors. Soon most of the chamber was on its feet with a shouting ovation that I shall never forget as long as I live."

In Montgomery, after the hearing, Judge Johnson ruled that the planned march could take place. Wallace responded by calling together the joint session of the Alabama Legislature.

Holding a paper curled in his grip, he shook it toward the lawmakers. "We see a most unprecedented order, unprecedented in the annals of American history, having been rendered by a federal court here in Montgomery, Alabama. We stopped the so-called march from Selma to Montgomery, Alabama, because we understood ourselves at that time what a colossal undertaking it would be to provide safety and security, not only to the marchers but the vehicular traffic of the other citizens of this state and nation who customarily use that highway.

"To show you that we understood when others did not, and

evidently the federal court did not, I have a telegram from one of the leaders of the march that says, 'We expect you to meet health and safety needs of five thousand marchers.'

"Great and dedicated men of the past worked diligently and honestly to establish the integrity and the justice of our court system. From their work has come a faith by people in the courts and a dignity and respect accorded the courts that has been the rock upon which our house of freedom has rested, but that integrity and faith has been shaken!

"Now they say our courts are too slow. We must, therefore, submit to the speedier expedience of mob rule. That a federal judge concurs and prostitutes our law in favor of mob rule while hypocritically wearing the robes and clothed in the respect built by great and honest men is a tragedy and a sorrow beyond any words."

Wallace immediately appealed the decision to the Fifth Circuit Court of Appeals, which upheld Frank Johnson's ruling.

On the Sunday of the march Dr. King stood high atop the concrete steps of Selma's Brown Chapel AME Church and told about five thousand persons gathered in the street outside that "this is America's cause. We know we can work within the framework of our democracy for human rights in history. We have waited for freedom. We are tired of waiting. Now is the time!"

All of the people had come to Selma to march, but only a few were to be permitted to make the trek from Selma to Montgomery. Because of the logistics Judge Johnson had ruled that the thousands could walk only on the four-lane portion of the highway. When they got to two lanes only a few miles outside Selma, the group had to be cut to three hundred.

After he spoke, King led the great throng of people through the town, across Edmund Pettus Bridge, and down the highway. At King's side walked Ralph Bunche, a staff member with the United Nations; Dick Gregory, the famed comedian who frequently spoke out for civil rights, and John Lewis, a 25-year-old Selma native who had become a Student Non-Violent Coordinating Committee leader, and many others.

After seven and a half miles, the march halted. The thousands who had to return to Selma were driven back in trucks. Among those returning was King, who had speaking engagements during the week. The group remaining stayed in tents, one for men and the other for women. Hot oatmeal was cooked for the marchers' breakfast. Hundreds of sandwiches were prepared in the basement of the Negro First Baptist Church in Selma and delivered for lunch. The marchers weathered three chilly nights. Even the tents did not keep out the cold that crept over the flatlands when the sun went down. The days of marching were hot and muggy. The heat rose from the asphalt pavement in steamy, smokelike ripples.

One of the marchers later remembered, "There was some hugging up, some gathering together, and some song-singing. But there wasn't wholesale orgies the way some people stated it. The sex thing was all blown out of proportion by Wallace and his people." About a week after the march, U. S. Representative William L. Dickinson of Montgomery, a fresh-man conservative Republican who had ridden Goldwater's coattails into office, charged on the floor of the House, "There were many, not just a few, instances of sexual intercourse in public between Negroes and whites. News reporters saw this and, Mr. Speaker, photographs were taken of this, I am told." Wallace had hired professional photographers to make a film of the march. He spent about thirty-five thousand dollars of state money for this purpose. But not one foot of the film showed sexual intercourse between blacks and whites, nor between people of the same race. When the film was shown that summer to right-wing groups, the people were bored because there was no sex as Dickinson had strongly implied.

Four days after the march had started the group reached Dannelly Air Field, about eight miles south of Montgomery. They looked like the last stragglers of a lost battalion. Sunburned and windburned, Jim Letherer, a one-legged white man from Saginaw, Michigan, made each step with painstaking pride. A short black man who had been born and raised in the feudal society of Selma, his face a dark moon, carried a flag haughtily over his shoulder, keeping it high and clean. The others followed behind, two by two.

Dr. King had returned from Cincinnati, where he had aroused support for the Voting Rights Act, and awaited the marching three hundred at the beginning of the four-lane road leading into Montgomery. When the fifteen hundred persons with King saw the smaller group approaching, the crowd broke into applause, whistles, and yells. When the three hundred joined the others there was hugging and kissing and hearty greetings. King walked with the three hundred in front of the others. As they started out together on the last leg of the journey, they began to sing. At first it was almost a whisper, then it grew to rejoicing, full tones. "Deep in my heart, I do believe, we will overcome some day. . . ." And the sound echoed through the hollows.

They walked north on Mobile Road, passing a three-by-three-foot stone plaque to The Cradle of the Confederacy and did not even pause to take note. At the City of St. Jude, a Catholic complex of hospital, school, and church built and operated through charity to serve the black community, some marchers camped in tents. Other marchers went to homes of friends and people who cared in Montgomery.

That night a show was produced on a makeshift stage on the baseball diamond behind St. Jude School. More than twenty thousand turned out to hear Sammy Davis, Jr., Tony Bennett, Harry Belafonte, Joan Baez, and Peter, Paul, and Mary. Others on stage included Leonard Bernstein, Dick Gregory, Shelley Winters, Alan King, Nipsey Russell, and George Kirby. Mike Nichols and Elaine May lampooned Wallace with a parody of the governor's telegram to President Johnson.

After more than four hours of entertainment the people retired to rest for the next day's completion of the march to the capitol.

Wallace, who had declared the Thursday a holiday for female employees at the capitol, decided he would not meet with any of the marchers, including Dr. King.

During the week the Alabama Legislature had passed dozens of resolutions, all critical of the march. One took note of the alleged fornication in the tents at night and stated that the "young women will return to their home states as unwed expectant mothers."

On the Thursday morning before the marchers arrived in front of the capitol, state troopers formed a line across the steps of the capitol. They stood alone, still at parade rest, throughout the day.

Beginning at St. Jude, on the edge of town, the thousands of marchers wound their way behind Dr. King through the streets of Montgomery.

Dr. King led the multitude around the ancient fountain at Court Square, where pre-Civil War slaves had watered their masters' horses. As he walked up six-lane Dexter Avenue toward the sun-drenched, silver-white capitol with its majestic dome, atop of which flew only the state and Confederate flags, King held his wife Coretta's hand. By their sides walked Ralph Bunche; Whitney Young of the National Urban League; Roy Wilkins, executive director of the NAACP; James Farmer, director of CORE; and others.

When he passed the small, red-brick Dexter Avenue Baptist

Church, only a block from the capitol, King looked up the concrete steps and closed his eyes momentarily. He had preached many sermons inside the church in his younger days. From the pulpit he had generated the enthusiasm which kept alive Montgomery's bus boycott during difficult times.

On the platform in front of the capitol, Harry Belafonte, Joan Baez, Leon Bibb, and Peter Yarrow and Mary Travers of Peter, Paul, and Mary sang "Go Tell It on the Mountain," while the tens of thousands congregated below.

Inside the capitol, Wallace ate lunch in the basement cafeteria and went back to his office to watch three television sets, each tuned to a different network showing the activities taking place outside.

On the platform Coretta King remembered all the problems of the long fight for integration. While she sat there she realized, "There was more national awareness of our problems than there ever had been in the whole history of the black struggle. When I looked over the big crowd, I saw many white people and church people. There were more church people involved than in any demonstration we had ever had, and I said to Martin later that it was perhaps the greatest witness by the church since the days of the early Christians. I still believe that.

"I felt that this whole experience was another unique moment in American history, a great moment of truth. People like Jim Clark had said, 'If you march, you do so over my dead body'; and Wallace had said, 'They shall not pass.' But here we were. Ten years ago we had talked about dignity, but we really felt it now."

When Martin Luther King, Jr., spoke, he began slowly. His words came out in an echoing whisper. "I stand before you this afternoon with the conviction that segregation in Alabama is on its deathbed," he stated. He said that it was time Congress passed a Voting Rights Act. "Selma became a shining moment in the conscience of man. There never was a moment in American history more honorable and more inspiring than the pilgrimage of clergymen and laymen of every race and faith pouring into Selma to face danger by the side of its embattled Negroes. Confrontation of good and evil, compressed in the tiny community of Selma, generated the massive power to turn the nation to a new course." As his voice rose to a finely toned baritone pitch, a slight drizzle began to fall. "Segregation is on its deathbed, and the only thing uncertain about it is how costly the segregationists and Wallace will make the funeral." he said. With rivulets of rain streaming down his brown cheeks like tears from his dark eyes, his voice quivered only slightly as he said, "We are on the move now and no wave of racism can stop us. Let us march on to the realization of the American dream. The road ahead is not altogether a smooth one. . . . We are still in for a season of suffering. I know you are asking today, 'How long will it take?' I come to say to you this afternoon, however difficult the moment, however frustrating the hours, it will not be long, because truth pressed to earth will rise again. How long? Not long, because no lie can live forever. How long? Not long, because you still reap what you sow. How long? Not long, because the arm of the moral universe is long, but it bends toward justice. How long? Not long, because mine eyes have seen the coming of the Lord. Our God is marching on."

After the lengthy applause died, the marchers filed away as orderly as more than twenty thousand persons could leave a downtown area. Twenty-one persons stayed behind at the Dexter Avenue Baptist Church with the petition to present to the governor. Wallace's Executive Secretary Cecil Jackson met the Reverend J. A. Lowery and his group inside the door of the capitol. Jackson said the governor had designated him to receive the petition. Lowery hesitated, refused to give the petition to Jackson, then said he would ask for an audience with Wallace at another time. Wallace did meet with Lowery the following week and accepted the petition.

After all was quiet that evening, the sound of gunfire was heard on a lonely stretch of U. S. 80 in Lowndes County. Mrs. Viola Gregg Liuzzo, the wife of a Detroit Teamsters Union official, had been murdered. A part-time student, Mrs. Liuzzo had come to Alabama to help the marchers. She had been assigned to the transportation committee, and was returning to Montgomery for a second carload of demonstrators when gunshots came from a car that had been following her. A companion, nineteen-year-old Leroy Moton, a Selma barber, later recounted the events. When the car pulled up beside Mrs. Liuzzo, several shots were fired. She slumped over the steering wheel. The car plunged into a ditch, and Moton played dead when the other car returned to make sure the job was done.

Three Ku Klux Klansmen were later identified by Moton and an FBI undercover agent who had infiltrated the Klan. The first to be brought to trial, Collie Leroy Wilkins, was acquitted by a Lowndes County jury even though the FBI informant testified that he saw Wilkins murder Mrs. Liuzzo. In a later trial in federal court, where the three were charged with violating Mrs. Liuzzo's civil rights, they were convicted by a jury and sentenced to the maximum of ten years in prison by Judge Frank Johnson.

The Voting Rights Act was passed overwhelmingly by Congress that summer, and LBJ signed it into law in August. New black voters were registered by the droves in every rural county across the South throughout the years afterward. Previously there had been a special time of the year for registering. With the new law people could be registered at any time.

Living up to his reputation as the inveterate politician, Wallace used the Voting Rights Act to his advantage in his race for governor in 1970. After he fell into second place in the first primary, his people developed a massive voter-registration drive during the six-week runoff period. More than thirty thousand Wallace supporters were registered between elections. In the runoff Wallace barely won, a victory largely due to the new voters who could not have been registered so quickly under the old system for which Wallace had fought.

HIS WIFE, THE GOVERNOR

SITTING NEXT TO HER husband in the back seat of the black Ford LTD, the handsome strawberry blonde gazed occasionally out the window at the flat south Alabama countryside covered with golden sage grass shining in the white-hot August sunshine.

They looked like a well-dressed couple being chauffeured to an outing.

When the car pulled slowly into the small village, suddenly a massive crowd of people appeared on the sidewalks and in the streets. It was obvious that a festival was being held, and it soon became obvious that the couple was the object of their mass affection.

The event was the Blessing of the Fleet in Bayou la Batre, a predominantly Catholic seacoast town of slightly more than two thousand inhabitants whose principal income centered around the fishing industry.

The woman, wearing her campaign uniform of crimson blazer and off-white pleated skirt, had already broken records in the political world of Alabama where her husband ruled supreme. In the Democratic primary she had defeated a field of eight male and one female opponents with a runaway majority. She was now running in the general election, a mere formality.

The year was 1966, and Wallace was running his wife, Lurleen, for governor.

As the crowd closed like a blanket of humanity around the car, Wallace said, "Roll your window down, sugar. Shake their hands."

Lurleen gave him a questioning sidelong glance, but she followed his instructions. She grasped the hands that poked through the open window. She smiled weakly, spoke welcomes, and kept it up throughout the long afternoon.

On a shrimp boat decorated with red, yellow, green, and blue crepe paper she sank into a chair. She breathed deeply, heavily.

After a few minutes Wallace, puffing on a cigar, beckoned for her to come and pose for photos with the gowned priest at the stern of the boat. She went to him.

Lurleen Burns Wallace had never heard of women's liberation. The phrase had not been invented during her day. Even if it had been, she would not have been a member. She was of the old school who believed that a woman's duty was to pay heed to her husband's wishes—like Ruth, whither thou goest I will go. She had put up only a perfunctory fight against George's wish for her to run for the governor's chair. Earlier that year she had undergone extensive uterine surgery, which included a complete hysterectomy, appendectomy, and a thorough abdominal exploration.

She had been born of poor hill-country people near Gordo in west Alabama, and she had met the hyperactive George Wallace, who had talked incessantly of becoming a great politician, when she worked as a clerk in Tuscaloosa's Kress's Five-and-Ten-Cents Store. She had given birth to four children, had watched from a ringside seat while the feisty little fighter made his dreams come true, and had waited up until past midnight on more than a hundred occasions when he was driving home from a far end of the state in a broken-down Chevrolet after long days of speechmaking.

When he'd asked her to run she had been a little apprehensive and a little proud, she said later. "I doubted whether I would really be governor, whether George was just playing some kind of political trick just to see whether it would work or not, or whether it was the way he explained it: To keep 'our' power base 'we' had to keep running and winning. I figured that he knew more about politics than anybody else I had ever seen or heard in the world. When I was a little girl I used to listen to Franklin Delano Roosevelt on the radio; he had the most pleasant voice, and he was the most wonderful man to me. Somehow I figured George knew about as much about politics as Franklin Delano Roosevelt. I figured he knew I could win or he wouldn't want me to run. If I lost, I thought, it'd be just like him losing. He never liked to lose. The worst I ever saw him act was after he lost the governor's election in 1958. He went sour all over. I thought we were going to have to split up. It came almost to that. He just wasn't himself for nearly a year. Finally he came back around and started running for governor again, and he was all right. When I took on the job of running, I decided he knew exactly what he was doing." As she spoke, Governor Lurleen Wallace was sitting in the leather high-backed chair behind her desk in the capitol in Montgomery. She was enjoying a long, quiet afternoon. Three or four times a day she met with groups of schoolchildren who were touring the historical building. She smiled publicly, but privately she worried because she did not feel like she was accomplishing much in the executive office.

On that August Sunday afternoon during her campaign, Lurleen Wallace stood beneath the blazing sun and squinted her eyes and said, "I'm proud to be running as governor of Alabama. I want y'all to know I'd like to be your governor. I'll do a good job, if you elect me." The sweating two thousand-plus screamed and whistled and clapped. Then Wallace stood on that wooden platform like the thousands of other wooden platforms he had spoken from in his life, and gave 'em hell. Like a stumpy Vulcan, he pointed his knobby forefinger, still scarred from prizefights in his youthful career, in the direction of Washington, D. C., where he said the "powers of an almighty bureaucracy is ruining the world for me and you and our children," and the crowd went temporarily insane with shouting, screaming, whistling, and clapping. He recounted his stand in the schoolhouse door, his battles in the Democratic primaries in the Yankee states during 1964, and he promised he'd carry the word from Alabama across the land in 1968, if they wanted him. And they let it be known loudly that they did indeed want him.

After the speech, people crowded around them again. They pushed close to both. Governor and Mrs. Wallace shook every person's hand, smiled for them beneath the layer of dust and sweat, and spoke about their family in a down-home personal way.

As the sun went down over the inlet, George and Lurleen Wallace got into the back seat of the Ford LTD again and started to pull away. Lurleen was already sighing when an overall-clad figure loped from a service station. The heavyset driver, an officer with the State Department of Public Safety, visibly flinched as the man hollered, "Hey, Governor!" and Wallace tapped the trooper on the shoulder and said, "Stop a minute."

His brogans clopping against the street, the man approached and extended a photograph of a smiling Wallace. "You put your autograph on this here, Governor?" the man asked.

Wallace eagerly obliged him, then handed the picture on to Lurleen, who also signed. Giving it back, Wallace said, "You vote for us now, you hear?"

The man grinned and nodded. "Governor, I'd do anything for you. You just ask." The man's face had turned to an expression of absolute and dead seriousness.

Wallace pumped his hand again and said, "I know you would, friend."

Down the road about a mile, Wallace said, "You know, he meant what he said. He'd do anything for us." He slapped Lurleen on the knee.

"What do you want him to do, George?" she asked, half jokingly.

"Aw, honey, it's the principle of the thing," he said.

Using a mean-sounding oratorical style, shaking his fists, snarling, gritting his teeth, and biting like a bulldog after a snake, Wallace had worked many crowds into frenzies. Every year the crowds got bigger. Every year his speeches became more polished.

"I don't have to learn to make a speech, I don't guess," Lurleen reflected on the state plane on the way home. Her voice was girlish with youthful teasing.

"I had to work mighty hard," he said without a trace of humor. "I had to stay up a lot of nights working, preparing, getting ready to run."

He talked on and on about politics. Finally he said he knew he was going to make it because "I've got too good a candidate here." Grinning, he hugged his wife.

She smiled too. "This is my first time out, and I've already made a pretty good showing. Maybe I grew up quicker than George did politically." She laughed.

All the smile was gone from the governor's face. He stared solemnly out the window of the plane into the darkness, his attitude suddenly stricken with stark seriousness. "I don't believe I'll lose," he said. "I believe I'll win. I've got to win. Y'all saw 'em. Y'all saw their faces. They love me. All of 'em love me."

While he spoke Lurleen was staring at him as though she had just seen a flash of what other people had called Wallace fanaticism.

After she became governor, winning by a landslide, her husband was her dollar-a-year assistant. It was understood that he would run the state and she would sign what he told her to sign. Her first speech to the joint session of the legislature was, of course, written by him. Stern-faced, with lips quivering, she asked the legislators to hire more state troopers. Not only must all Alabamians resist desegregation "in every way possible," she cried out, but "the entire nation is the battlefield! This is what Hitler did in Germany!" she said of the federal court order which demanded desegregation of schools and all public facilities.

She had been a petite teen-ager when George Wallace met her in the ten-cents store. She was pretty, with shoulder-length, light brown hair and sparkling green eyes. After almost a year of courtship, during which Wallace graduated from law school and campaigned on campus and in Tuscaloosa for fellow Barbour Countian Chauncey Sparks for governor, Wallace entered the armed services. After his basic training the couple was married by a justice of the peace in downtown Tuscaloosa on May 22, 1943. She was sixteen years old, he was twenty-three. They rode a bus south to Montgomery, where they spent their honeymoon night in a run-down boarding-house across the street from the Jefferson Davis Hotel. The next day they took another bus to Barbour County and spent the remainder of his leave at his mother's home. They were honeymooning, but he was also politicking. Every available moment was spent on the street shaking hands, visiting friends, telling them it wouldn't be long before he'd be back home, and introducing his pretty and shy little wife.

They rode across the countryside in a bus, and he constantly talked about the career back home which he could see for himself. To Lurleen, he was the most exciting person in the world. He knew what he wanted to do with his life. There was no question in her mind that he would not have exactly what he wanted.

She didn't complain about the converted chicken coop where they lived in Alamogordo, New Mexico, where he was training as a flight engineer. And she was very happy the next year when she became pregnant. While he moved to a new home in Amarillo, Texas, she went home to Alabama to have their first child, Bobbie Jo. With baby in arms, she returned a few months later to the cheap walk-up apartment he had rented for them.

About one year later Wallace was discharged, and Lurleen was happy to be moving back to Alabama. In January of 1946 he secured a job as assistant attorney general from Governor Sparks at a salary of one hundred and seventy-five dollars a month. They set up housekeeping in a one-room apartment with kitchen privileges in the same boardinghouse where they had spent their honeymoon night.

"When I look back on those days it seems nice and romantic. I know it was a lot of trouble. I had diapers piled all around everywhere. I had to hang them out on a little porch in the hallway of the place. George was getting everything fixed up where we could go back to his home town and he could run for the legislature. About the only time I saw him was late at night or at breakfast. He'd come in late and get up early. He told me he wanted to have everything perfect for me. He'd always talked about politics. Even when he was in the service he'd talk about what he was someday going to do, run for the legislature, build up a good record, and maybe run for the United States Congress. He couldn't wait to get back home and get started on his ambitions," she recalled.

After only a few months in Montgomery, Wallace drove his

wife and daughter eighty miles south in a rented truck. They settled into another small apartment in Clayton and he ran for the legislature.

"There wasn't any doubt about it. He was a natural-born handshaker. He had been born and raised in this country, and he knew the people. I remember one Saturday in front of the old courthouse, he must have shook five hundred hands. That man was something. He started at about seven in the morning and didn't stop until up in the night. All the time he was talking about what he was going to do for everybody when he got up there in Montgomery," a retired railroad engineer, Calvin Ethridge, remembered.

Another Barbour Countian remembered that Wallace sent Christmas cards to the people back home every year while he was away with the Army. "All through the war people around here had been gettin' these Christmas cards from all kinda places—Denver one year, then the next year it'd be Guam or someplace like that—and openin' them up, they'd read, 'Merry Christmas, George C. Wallace.' I got 'em too, and I couldn't quite figger them out. I thought it was real nice of this young fella, so far away and all and yet being so thoughtful, but I wasn't quite sure I knew who this George C. Wallace was, and why he was writin' me. It seemed kinda strange. Anyway, when the war was over with and the local political races had done got started over the county, I was out in my field one fine spring afternoon plowin', and I happen to look up and see this young fella comin' across the plowed field from the road, like he had just popped out of nowhere, steppin' real smart and lively across those furrows, already grinnin' and his hand already stretched out, and all of a sudden I knew why I'd been gettin' them nice cards every Christmas."

In the Democratic primary that spring Wallace's wife was too young to vote, but he won anyway. They remained living in Clayton, where he opened a law office, and every two years he traveled to Montgomery for the legislative session. Four years later he won a second term in the legislature. Halfway through that term, in 1952, he decided to run for the circuit judgeship of Barbour and Bullock counties.

During this time Lurleen was having babies. Peggy Sue was born in 1950 and George, Jr., in 1951. And when Wallace ran against an incumbent whose ancestors had originally settled Clayton, Preston C. Clayton, she did her duties by walking the children through the downtown area as often as possible. Wallace told the people he needed the job as judge worse than Clayton, and it was obvious by the look of his young wife and their three children. She wore clothes she had made for herself or her mother mailed her from Greene County, where the Burns had moved. She had not thrown away Bobbie Jo's toddling clothes, and Peggy Sue made good use of them.

Wallace won the judgeship, and he decided it was time they owned a home. Lurleen said later that she was as excited as a child at Christmas time. They picked out a three-bedroom frame house about one block from the courthouse. The price was eighty-five hundred dollars, and it took him nine years to pay off the mortgage.

While he was sitting on the bench or out campaigning for a state-wide race in the future, Lurleen Wallace was enjoying the quiet life of Clayton. She was a natural homebody. Almost daily she had morning coffee with her friend Mary Jo Ventress, who taught home economics at Clayton High School across the street from the Wallace home. When she could leave the children with her mother-in-law or another kinfolk, she would steal away to the bank of Pea River or Big Creek for an afternoon of fishing. She enjoyed the solitude of being alone and watching the subtle ripples of the dark water. But the fishing wasn't all pure enjoyment. She'd catch bream and cook them for the family. When Wallace came in from a long night's campaigning in a far-off town, she'd warm up fish and he'd smother it with catsup before eating.

Throughout these years she was very much aware that her husband was making a name for himself. He talked to her about some of his decisions. He told her constantly about how the people in other towns in Alabama liked what he was doing. She read the headlines in the Montgomery *Advertiser*. A year after he became judge he issued an injunction against the removal of segregation signs in railroad terminals in his district. He was the first judge in the South to make such a decree, and he bragged so much about that decision that he became known as "The Fightin' Little Judge," a nickname he used when he was talking to civic clubs and other organizations.

In the 1958 governor's race she went with him on only a few campaign trips. Bobbie Jo was fourteen, but Peggy Sue and George, Jr., were in the second and third grades. And even at this time she did not have outside help to care for the children. Most of his salary went back into the campaigning. Every week for more than four years he traveled to two and three speeches in all corners of the state, driving in the rattletrap old green Chevrolet until his closest friends and supporters urged him to buy a new brown-and-white Chevy for the gubernatorial campaign. All the family's efforts were selflessly aimed toward his career, the politics that would eventually get them out of Clayton and Barbour County and put them on top of the world. Lurleen Wallace sacrificed luxuries which she might otherwise have had for his ambitions. But she said she never regretted their life together until 1959 when they moved back to Montgomery and into another apartment, after he lost the election for governor.

Wallace had a few solid backers, including Oscar Harper, Seymore Trammell, and C. F. Halstead, who supported his family while he covered the state collecting votes for the next gubernatorial election. He had a law office in the new brick Washington Building across the street from the county courthouse, but he seldom handled run-of-the-mill legal work. He was too busy politicking.

Lurleen Wallace remembered that period as the most dismal of their marriage. "The days were long. There was nothing to do. I mean, there was nothing exciting happening. I couldn't go fishing. I had very few friends in Montgomery. George was running from one end of the state to the other. I didn't know when he was coming home and when he'd be stuck with people."

After several confrontations with Wallace, she took the children to her parents' home in Greene County. While there, her depression deepened. She tried to telephone Wallace at their apartment in Montgomery and at his law office. She also tried to find him at his mother's home in Barbour County. She went to Eutaw, the seat of Green County, and filed divorce papers with the probate judge.

One of Wallace's closest friends, Seymore Trammell, then circuit solicitor of Wallace's district, traveled to Greene County. He went directly to Lurleen, pleaded with her to withdraw the divorce papers, and later took her to Eutaw where she signed documents to cancel her previous actions.

From 1959 until her last child, Janie Lee, was born in 1961, Lurleen Wallace was under tremendous strain. Wallace drank almost daily, according to some of his closest friends, and he could not handle the whiskey. "One drink would set him off on a drunk. He wasn't a very pleasant drunk either. He became belligerent, wanting to fight anything that moved," said a former associate. "He didn't have a real law practice. He had an office. That was about it. He was always campaigning. He must have had a speech every day. He'd take off to Florence in north Alabama one day, then would go to Mobile the next. He never stopped talking about being governor. He knew he'd be governor, but he wanted you to tell him, reassure him, like every person's opinion really did matter to him. And there were always women. They'd throw themselves at him. He liked to have them just before he left a town where he'd spoken, like it was a final conquest. And he had women stashed all over Montgomery. They adored him. They worshiped him. It was like they were given some kind of merit badge for sleeping with George Wallace. They could wear it around the rest of their life and be proud," the man continued.

When Lurleen had Lee in April 1961 at St. Margaret's Hospital in Montgomery, her physician called Wallace into his office after the cesarean birth. The doctor told Wallace that the mother and daughter were healthy, but he added that he had discovered suspicious tissue implanted on the inside wall of the mother's abdomen. He removed the tissue, he said, but warned that it could be malignant. He sent the tissue to several other doctors. They had varying opinions as to its malignancy. Wallace chose not to tell his wife about the discovery of the tissue.

In the 1962 campaign she hit the trail for her husband, becoming more active than she had ever been. She spoke to luncheons in Mobile, attended teas in Birmingham, and when the votes were counted she was by her husband's side.

"Moving into the governor's mansion was the biggest thrill of my life," she said in a private interview. "We had been cramped up for so long it was like moving into a castle or something. All of a sudden I had people to help with the children. I had someone to cook for me, but I still liked to do that. It was a thrill and a shock. We had not had very much. Oh, it wasn't like we were dirt poor. We had enough to live on. But sometimes now I think back to how it was like before. It would be so difficult to go back to that life. I don't think I really understood what it would mean when we stood up there on the platform in front of the capitol and watched the floats and the bands and the cars filled with people go by. It meant that our entire lives were changed just like that. And for the better!"

She was an excited person, filled with youthful enthusiasm, and very aware of her position as first lady. "I knew as soon as he won the governor's race that it was only the beginning. Almost instantly George started talking about what was happening in Washington with the Kennedy clan. It was almost as though he sensed a destiny which he had to fulfill. He had always read and talked about southern heroes. He saw himself in the shoes of Robert E. Lee or Jefferson Davis. He had to speak out for the South, not just for Alabama, and he had to be a hero himself. Sure, he was from Barbour County, Alabama, but that didn't matter to him. He said more than once that Abraham Lincoln came from the backwoods just like him, but he never compared himself to Lincoln in a speech," she said, laughing.

After the senate failed to vote through his succession bill, Wallace asked his wife to run in his place. "You know, he kind of talked around it. I knew what he was getting at, but I just let him talk himself out. Finally I said, 'George, you want me to run?' He said, 'You'd make a fine candidate, sweetie.' But then he dropped it. I knew he'd bring it back up. I waited. He did say something else about it, but not much more than the first time," she said.

Between Christmas 1965 and mid-January 1966 Wallace wrestled with the idea of asking his brother Jack, who had taken over the judicial circuit he had left behind, to run for governor. Wallace talked over the various possibilities with several of his closest friends. The consensus among that group was that Lurleen was the best choice.

In mid-January she underwent surgery. Although she had a complete hysterectomy, which was found malignant, Wallace still did not tell her about the mysterious tissue discovered in her abdomen five years earlier. Nor did he tell the public that this was the second occurrence. When she was released from the hospital and recuperating in the mansion, one day Wallace told her he had decided "we're not going to run. We're going back to Clayton when my term is up." And she said, "Yes, George, we will run. I want to run. And I'll be disappointed if I can't run." Apparently that was the last discussion the two had about whether or not to run. Wallace made preparations for her announcement.

Overnight Lurleen Burns Wallace was not only a statewide figure, but she became a nationwide news figure. Only two other women had been governors: Ma Ferguson in Texas and Nellie T. Ross in Wyoming. "She's going to carry the banner. I'll serve as her dollar-a-year assistant. And we'll continue to tell the South's story to the nation," Wallace said for network television.

At her kickoff rally in March she stated, "I am delighted to have the opportunity to be a candidate for governor. The decision to run was reached not reluctantly, but with enthusiasm and determination. While I am humbled by the wonderful response you have given us, I am at the same time grateful to be the instrument whereby you, the people of Alabama, have an opportunity to express yourselves. . . ."

"I enjoyed the campaigning," she said later. "At first it was terrible. I was very nervous. I was always thinking that I looked too blah, or too childish in the blazer with the Alabama emblem, which I picked out, but George said I looked just fine. He wrote the short speech for me. I added to it and cut some of it. He told me just to leave it alone, but I couldn't do that. I wanted to feel like I was saying what I wanted to say. After all, I was going to be governor."

She beat the entire field of Democrats and trounced the Republican in the November general election.

One of her closest friends later complained, "I don't care what George Wallace says, he made her run, and he caused her death. If she had not run, maybe she could have relaxed and enjoyed her last year on earth. That kind of strenuous work—getting up early, traveling all over the state, speaking four and five times a day, ending late at night in some little town God knows where—it had to use up her energy. I was her friend up to the end, but I don't care about seeing George Wallace again. It's just awful, the way he put her up to politics to further his own career. And that's exactly what he did. I don't understand how people could go on voting for him after they saw what he did to her."

But others, including George and Lurleen Wallace's own children, claimed that she never spent a more enjoyable time in her life than when she was campaigning and serving in office. George Wallace, Jr., writing in his book, *The Wallaces of Alabama*, stated she worked hard, enjoyed it, but added, "Mother found the campaign exhausting, and she would come back to the mansion very tired."

In the beginning, she said, she laid ground rules by which she would serve as governor. She would not take orders or even suggestions from Wallace's youngest brother, Gerald. She would not have other Wallace cronies telling her what to do.

One of the first things on her agenda after the January 26, 1967, inauguration and a speech to the joint session of the legislature, was a trip to Tuscaloosa's Partlow School and Hospital for the mentally retarded. She had been told by concerned parents that the place was deplorable. She did not believe it could possibly be as bad as the conditions that had been described to her.

Accompanied by a troupe of mothers, newsmen, and state troopers, the governor traveled one hundred miles northwest of the capitol and entered the attractive, oak-surrounded iron

gates to the state institution. The superintendent gave a verbal
overview of the place, then led a guided tour.

The first two dormitories were spotless. The residents were
ambulatory. The beds were made. Colorful spreads and
pillowcases and toys gave the place a friendly, even loving
atmosphere.

The third dormitory was more like a hospital. Some of the
residents were bedridden. A slight odor of stale urine and
medicine was detectable.

The governor ambled slowly through the buildings, zigzag-
ging back and forth across the wards to speak to the residents
and the attendants.

As she was about to leave the third building she heard the
desperate shriek. She turned to meet the onrush of a frail
blonde-haired girl who threw her arms around the governor
and cried, "Mama! Mama!"

Tears flowed from the governor's eyes as she leaned down
and hugged the girl, patting her back and kissing her cheek.

When an attendant pulled the girl from the governor's
grasp, Lurleen Wallace looked up and shook her head. She
comforted the girl for almost a full minute before the little girl
went back to her bed.

Outside in the harsh sunlight, the governor had to excuse
herself to dry the tears.

When the tour began anew, she demanded to be taken into
every residency hall.

The superintendent warned that some were in terrible
condition.

The governor said she wanted to see everything.

Each hall became worse, until she was finally taken into a
place that literally reeked of feces, urine, and age-old body
smells. Pitiful twisted bodies lay tied in high-sided beds. She
was told that these creatures could not tend for themselves.

There was one attendant and one orderly on duty to care for more than forty residents. There was no air conditioning in the eighty-degree heat.

From one corner the big dark eyes of a girl with shriveled legs and arms twisted into a straitjacket followed the governor in and out of the maze of beds. When the governor came close to her bed, she kicked her heels against the mattress. The governor reached out and touched the girl's cheek softly. The girl laughed loudly and smiled. It was not long before the tour had to be halted again.

Before she left the complex the governor promised that she would push a massive program through the legislature to completely revamp the facilities for the mentally retarded.

About two weeks later, sitting in her office, she reflected on that all-day view into the world which she had not known existed. "If every person in the state could go through there and see for themselves, feel that baby's smile, touch their little bodies . . . I don't think I've ever been so touched. I've been talking to my own children about it. I want them to be aware that they're lucky. I feel so personally lucky. All of us are lucky who were born with all of our brains intact," she said.

Her husband apparently talked her into submitting only a partial mental-health program to the legislature. She asked for only eight million dollars. She said privately that she planned to personally watch over the bill to see that it was passed.

In June, however, she entered Montgomery's St. Margaret's Hospital, where tissue was again taken from her lower abdomen. After a laboratory examination it was determined to be malignant.

Her second major cancer surgery in little more than one year was scheduled in M. D. Anderson Hospital in Houston, Texas. Afterward, she was told the operation had been successful.

About six months after the surgery she walked out of the

physician's office at the Anderson Hospital with the news that she had another malignant tumor. It had to be removed. For the next few months she traveled back and forth from Alabama to Texas and home again. Throughout this time she was given periodic radiation treatments.

Although suffering excruciating pain while awaiting her third major operation, she accompanied her husband to the opening of the Harris County Wallace-For-President Headquarters in Houston on the night of January 11, 1968. Wearing a white wool dress and a mink stole, she smiled broadly and grabbed one hand after the other as they made their way through the crowd of about six hundred supporters who had gathered at the invitation of the American Independent party in Texas. He made a short speech, and they worked their way out again. She said later that she had almost fainted from the suffocating heat in the small house that was used as campaign headquarters.

She went home to Montgomery on February 4, 1968, and was scheduled to return to Texas for another checkup three weeks later. But she was stricken with complications and had to have emergency surgery in Montgomery.

While his wife was hospitalized Wallace stayed awake with her several nights. Often he slept on a cot in her room. She told a reporter for the Birmingham *News*, Anita Smith, that he was a "wonderful nurse."

After fifty-one days of hospitalization the governor was released from St. Margaret's on April 13, her youngest daughter's seventh birthday.

The following twenty-five days were spent quietly. Most of the time she stayed inside the mansion. She took several automobile rides, once about forty miles to Troy and back. Her friend from Clayton High School, Mary Jo Ventress, remained with her full-time during the day. The two talked, worked jigsaw puzzles, knitted, and embroidered. Miss Ventress drove her to south Montgomery, where they'd tour the house Wallace had bought for her little more than a year before.

Shortly before the end of his term, Lurleen sat down with her husband for a serious conversation. She remembered how it had been before he was elected. She had not forgotten the cramped little apartments, the horrendous summertime heat, and she knew she didn't want to experience that living again. She wanted a home. Reluctantly he agreed. She found a four-bedroom brick house in a pleasant surburban neighborhood. She approached him again, told him how much she wanted a fine home of her own, and they purchased the property.

During the last week of Lurleen's life, George Wallace said, "I had an urge to go and just say, 'Well, honey, you're not going to be here but a few more days. Couldn't we talk about old times? About the time I met you in the dime store, about the times we lived in Amarillo and Alamagordo, about when you came back home to wait for Bobbi to be born, about our campaigns together,' but I would never have done that, even though I wanted to. That would have been selfish of me. I couldn't have done something selfish like that for my own satisfaction, and let it have alarmed her and destroyed any hope she might have had." At another time in private conversation Wallace said, "I do wish I had talked to her, had felt closer to her, had let her get close to me. I never did that. I wish I had."

Late on the night of May 7 Wallace called the doctors to her side. The governor was sleeping. The doctor had his stethoscope to her chest.

Wallace, holding her hand, said, "Lurleen, honey, we're all here with you; we love you." He named the children, who were standing nearby, and her mother and father and her brother and sister-in-law. "Lurleen, I love you," he said. "If you hear me, sweetie, squeeze my hand."

The hand tightened.

Wallace looked up at the doctors.

"She's tuned in to you," a doctor said.

Almost an hour later her hand relaxed. She breathed in short gasps. And at 12:34 A.M. the physicians pronounced her dead.

Unbeknownst to the family, the governor had talked to her minister about dying. She had even made detailed plans for her funeral and told them to the Reverend John Vickers of the St. James Methodist Church. He carried out her wishes. Her body lay in state in the rotunda of the capitol, where a severe-looking statue of her now stands, and the procession was carried through the streets of Montgomery to the church, where a very simple ceremony was performed. No cameras were allowed inside during services. And afterward she was buried on Governors' Circle on a knoll in Greenwood Cemetery.

When Wallace ran and won the governor's chair again in 1970, he never pushed through the program that Lurleen wanted for mental health. As a result a suit was brought in U. S. District Court in Montgomery. Wallace's old adversary, Judge Frank Johnson, ruled that mental patients have the constitutional right to minimum adequate treatment. The judge defined such treatment and set up guidelines which state hospitals would have to follow. He also threatened judicial funding if the legislature did not appropriate money for the institutions. As a result of Judge Johnson's order Wallace urged the legislature to appropriate funds.

But Lurleen Wallace's interest and concern in mental health impressed her middle daughter, Peggy Sue, who graduated in special education and later taught mentally retarded children in a Montgomery school.

DICTATOR
IN DIXIE

THE RUNOFF IN THE gubernatorial race of 1970 was by far the dirtiest in recent Alabama history. Wallace pulled all the stoppers and let go with a leading right and a racist uppercut to the glass jaw of Albert Preston Brewer.

Brewer was a seasoned in-state politician, but a mere amateur compared to Wallace. A slender, clean-cut, blond, slick-haired thirty-nine-year-old when he became governor on May 7, 1968, following the death of Lurleen Wallace, Brewer had been speaker of the House of Representatives and in 1966 became lieutenant governor. A nervous fellow with a pleasant, quick smile, he entered the office of governor without an hour's notice. One week before Governor Lurleen Wallace died Brewer told a group of Montgomery newsmen meeting in the Alabama Room of the Albert Pick Motel, "I haven't been kept informed of the governor's illness." With a wry smile he said, "Her dollar-a-year assistant has not told me one word about her condition. As far as I know, she is recovering from cancer. I have been making no preparations whatsoever to move to Montgomery. I am confident everything is okay or I'm sure those close to her would tell me. Of course, the dollar-a-year assistant is running for the presidency of the United States, and he doesn't seem to have much time for me or the state."

When Brewer suddenly became governor he turned to his able friend Alton Turner, a state senator from Luverne in the Black Belt south of Montgomery. Turner, chairman of the

Senate Finance Committee, was already one of the most powerful individuals in the legislature. While Brewer was projecting the freshly washed appearance to the public, Turner was efficiently calling the shots behind the scenes. He was not only a Brewer lieutenant, but Turner also played the role of Wallace confidant and worker. Every week he flew to different states attempting to get George Wallace's name on the ballot under a third-party emblem. In retrospect this appears to be a separation of loyalties. In reality, almost all the legislators were working out of state for the Wallace for President campaign. Brewer even publicly sanctioned the movement. At the time he had no other political choice. He was the pretender to the throne in Wallace country.

Alton Turner was a ramrod straight, tall, sandy-haired, handsome man with a deep drawl which seemed to start somewhere deep in his stomach and work its way up through the esophagus into the pharynx and out the mouth. Today he practices law in Luverne, cooks gourmet Chinese meals in his chef-equipped kitchen, fishes for carp in the pond in his back yard, and tends to his organic garden. Sporting a narrow, snowy Scandinavian-style beard, he speaks of George Wallace with sarcastic reverence. "He's the best damned demagogue in existence. He can out-demagogue anybody. I've never seen anybody like him. The first thing you have to realize about George Wallace when you go up against him in a campaign is that if you'll let him he'll outsmart you, even if you've got an IQ of one hundred and sixty. It's not that he's that smart, but he'll stay up later than you. He'll get up earlier than you. He'll be thinking about ways to beat you every time you turn around. He'll mainly out-long you, staying in there fighting after you've given plumb out. He doesn't have a political conscience. He doesn't know the meaning of principle. He believes in the old adage, 'The end justifies the means.'

"Albert called me early the morning Governor Lurleen

died. I came straight to Montgomery, got some rooms in the Governor's House [a swank motel on the outskirts of the capital city], and we operated out of those rooms for thirty days. Albert met me out there that morning at about six o'clock, and the first thing I said to him was, 'Well, old buddy, you're governor now, but you better start preparing this minute to run against George Wallace in 1970.' He said, 'No, I don't have to worry about that, when George called me and told me Lurleen had died he said I didn't have to worry at all, he wouldn't run.' And I said, 'You wait and see.' I knew damn well George Wallace wasn't going to stay out of a race if he was still living. He couldn't! A political campaign draws him like sugar draws flies. There's no way he could stay out of it. But Albert believed him. Apparently Albert told him he'd keep Wallace's cabinet members, or most of them, especially since George had promised not to run."

When Governor Lurleen died, Alton Turner was already chairman of the Senate Finance and Taxation Committee. He was a George Wallace man. His law partner, Billy King of Luverne, had traveled thousands of miles researching the ways and means of getting Wallace on the ballot of the third-party ticket. Turner, who had been in the legislature for nine years in 1968, had been to nearly every major city in the United States drumming up support for Wallace. With only two colleagues, Drexell Cook and Hubert Gilmore, he entered Chicago to prepare the Windy City for the arrival of the candidate. "The Chicago police chief looked at us like we were the tin man, the lion, and the scarecrow in *The Wizard of Oz.* 'Y'all only got three?' he asked. 'Nixon had more'n forty in his bunch,' the chief said. We told him we were it, and we went to work. We arranged a ticker-tape parade down State Street and a speech later in Cicero. Of course there was a bunch with Wallace when he came in, including Secret Service men," Turner said.

After General LeMay entered the campaign, Turner, Joe Fine, and John DeCarlo accompanied the vice-presidential candidate for nineteen days. Fine later became president pro tem of the state senate, another powerful local position, and DeCarlo was named by Wallace to the State Criminal Court of Appeals. "That was the biggest merry-go-round you've ever seen," Turner drawled. "I've seen plenty of big fools in my life, but not many ever topped Curtis LeMay. He had to have everything just right, had to be everywhere exactly on time. We were running around all over the country in a damned old Electra-Prop jet, and I told him if we got into a place the day we were scheduled we ought to feel lucky. He'd just huff and turn away. He was the second most egotistical man I've ever met. The most egotistical is George Wallace. But to make things even better for us," Turner allowed sarcastically, "he didn't know one hoot in hell about politics. As soon as we got into Montgomery at the end of that nineteen days, after we'd taken the general out to California for him to vote, I didn't even go to the celebration; I went home to Luverne."

When Turner started directing the Brewer campaign, LeMay was only two years in the past. "Up until the day Wallace qualified, Brewer told me not to worry, he won't run. But I knew he'd run. I'd known George Wallace too well. I'd known he was going to run from the first," Turner said.

In Wallace's opening speech in Mobile he revitalized the old tactic he used in the 1958 runoff. On the stage with him was the bed covered with a patchwork quilt. His speech was filled with as much demagoguery as ever. He brought his audience to a pitch with the same racist cries they had heard in 1962. Mobile was a hotbed of racial trouble. As late as 1970 the Mobile school system was still having its internal problems over desegregation. After he used the same old Wallace-style clichés, he raised the quilt. He peeked beneath the covers. As though in a replay from twelve years earlier, he said, "Politics make strange bedfellows! Look at the people in this bed. There's old Albert Brewer under there hiding in the darkness. I'll be doggoned if it's not the U. S. Department of Health, Education, and Welfare—old HEW snuggled down there with him. Why, it's the Alabama Power Company down there with them. Look here, it's the telephone company." He found all the so-called "big mules" in bed with Brewer.

The gimmick worked for about two weeks, until the state's political cartoonists began to depict Wallace in a bed with a nightshirt and cap with all the "big mules" with him instead of Brewer. Included with them were the Ku Klux Klan, the White Citizens Council, and other right-wing groups. Wallace dropped the bed gimmick like a hot potato and went back to his old tried racist techniques and just plain giving Brewer hell.

At the end of the 1968 presidential campaign Wallace had more than $3 million left over. Several politicians who worked closely with Wallace's 1968 effort and the 1970 race estimated between $3 million and $3.6 million remained in the kitty after 1968. "That money was never touched because Gerald and some of the others were fussing about it so furiously that nobody else could get close to it," said a Wallace adviser from that period. However, another source said much of the money was put to use in the 1970 governor's race.

Wallace not only ranted and raved about racist issues. He also talked about how much he had helped the people of the state. He looked back at his accomplishments: the trade schools and the junior colleges, all the miles of interstate highways that had been built, and the progress of the navigable waterway system throughout the state. When he said massive industry had come into the state because of his efforts and had created jobs for the previously unemployed, he was always half correct. His figures, however, were always inflated.

He described himself as a champion of tax reform when in fact he had been a primary pusher behind one of the most regressive tax structures in the United States. He bragged about the low property tax in Alabama but said nothing about the high consumer taxes.

According to one state labor-union leader in 1970, "They [the new industry] are real cats and dogs, a lot of them, and they only locate in Alabama because of the low pay scales." During the decade from 1960 to 1970, the wages of the average production worker in the state rose from $1.92 an hour to $2.86, while in the same period the national rate rose from $2.26 to $3.36 an hour.

The property taxes in Alabama were the lowest in the nation, averaging about $40 a year on a $10,000 home. But then property taxes helped to pay for schools and education. According to the U. S. Department of Health, Education, and Welfare, Alabama was fiftieth among the states in money spent per pupil in the public schools in 1970. HEW stated that Alabama spent $489 per pupil, based on average daily attendance, while such states as Vermont, New York, New Jersey, and Minnesota spent more than $1,000 per pupil. In that year the average teacher's salary in Alabama was $7,376, almost $2,000 a year less than the national average of $9,265.

HEW figures also showed that the situation in health and welfare services was similar. Alabama ranked forty-ninth among the states in general welfare assistance, paying destitute families $13 a month compared to a national average of $112 a month. In 1970 the state ranked forty-sixth in doctors per 100,000 population. The national average was 163, while Alabama had 86.

In per capita income, Alabama was forty-eighth in 1970,

with a total of $2,828. It had also been forty-eighth in 1960 when the average person earned $1,489. Only the residents of Arkansas and Mississippi had lower incomes. But the people of Alabama paid a higher percentage of their income in taxes than the people in twenty-nine other states. The average state and local tax per $1,000 income nationally in fiscal year 1970 was $64.73; in Alabama the average man paid $72.11 in taxes from each $1,000 of income.

Wallace-backed legislatures heaped consumer taxes on the individuals. Between 1963 and 1967, the years of his first administration, consumer taxes were raised by a total of $70.5 million. Major taxes in Alabama in 1970 were a 4 percent state sales tax, a 2 percent city sales tax, a twelve-cent-per-package cigarette tax, a seven-cent-per-gallon gasoline tax, and a graduated personal and corporate income tax ranging from 1.5 percent to 5 percent.

Throughout the first primary Brewer campaigned fourteen and fifteen hours a day, promising the people more of what he had given them during the past two years. He had run an efficient government, had kept the people informed with regular Wednesday press conferences, and had initiated steps toward a more stable economy. For the first time in the decade of the sixties, race was not highlighted by the Alabama governor's office. Brewer had insisted on what he called "quality education for all people."

Turner and other Brewer lieutenants were busy in the shadows. A twenty-five-thousand-dollar contribution had been made to the Brewer campaign by the steelworkers. Other large contributions were made by other labor union organizations. An executive with CREEP, the Committee to Re-Elect the President, contacted Brewer's campaign office. A deal was worked out whereby the Nixon people would put four hundred thousand dollars into the hands of the Brewer people.

One of Brewer's top financial advisers went to New York, met the representative from CREEP in the lounge of the Sherry Netherlands Hotel, and accepted a suitcase full of cash. A Brewer worker later said, "Every dime of the money was used in the campaign. It was the cleanest money we could get. It came from the Nixon people, who had only one thing in mind: Beat George Wallace. That's the same thing we wanted to do. We didn't have to promise a thing to get it."

The climax of the first primary occurred on the night after the ballots had been marked. The votes came in, and for the first time since 1958 Wallace was trailing in an Alabama election. The Brewer people were exuberant. The Wallace people were depressed.

But Wallace went to work quickly. He combed the state making speeches. Money was poured into the campaign. A squad of Wallace workers rounded up every person who would swear support to their leader. These people, who had not been registered to vote, were taken to the registrars. They were registered. The Wallace workers patterned their registration drives after similar work of the civil-rights campaigns of the midsixties. They also used the Voter Registration Act of 1965, passed after the Selma-to-Montgomery march, which allowed people to be registered at any time.

A Wallace committee in Selma printed racist smear sheets. One showed Brewer shaking hands with Elijah Muhammad, the leader of the Black Muslims; under the photograph was the caption: Do We Want To Turn Over Our State To Black Muslims? Another smear sheet showed Brewer's wife, obviously pregnant, standing amid a group of black men leering at her. A third showed Brewer's two teen-aged daughters lying in bikinis on a beach; all the other sunbathers were black males. All three photographs were actually doctored photographs with the Brewers superimposed on other pictures. The sheets were distributed in country stores, service stations, and suburbs bordering predominantly black residential areas. When an Alabama newspaper printed one of the sheets, Wallace disclaimed any knowledge of the smear campaign. "All I can say," said one of his former aides, "is that George Wallace always knew everything about all of his campaigns when I worked for him. Nobody ever did anything that he did not know about."

Brewer kept a low profile during the runoff. His aides later said it was the governor's decision to avoid confrontation with Wallace. Apparently Brewer thought he would play the John Patterson game of silence, which had worked in the runoff of 1958.

In the meantime Wallace demanded that Brewer fire Alabama State Docks Director Houston H. Feaster, who was being charged by State Auditor Melba Till Allen with wrongdoings. Brewer balked. Wallace screamed louder. Actually Wallace had originally appointed Feaster to the docks post, but Brewer did not even swing back with that accusation. Before Wallace was finished, he had verbally linked Brewer closely to Feaster. Shortly before the runoff election Mrs. Allen, who held considerable state-wide strength on her own, came out publicly in support of Wallace.

About one month after the runoff election Brewer fired Feaster, who was later charged with evading income taxes on eighty-six thousand dollars in bribes and kickbacks from 1965 through 1968. Talk among political observers suggested that Brewer peaked a month too late.

When the votes were counted, it was a neck-and-neck battle. Wallace's younger brother Gerald told newsmen that he was sure his brother would win. "It all depends on whether Alton Turner hates to return to Luverne worse than I hate to go home to Clio. And I'll tell you, I don't want to go back to Clio. I like the good life too much," Gerald said.

He was correct. Wallace squeezed into first place by less

than one percent. But it wasn't long before Wallace started talking about the election as though it were an overwhelming mandate in favor of his national cause.

Four years later, after he had made inroads on the national scene and had been shot by an assassin, Wallace won in a landslide. He defeated Eugene McLain, a wealthy Huntsville businessman and former state senator. Wallace polled more than seventy percent of the vote in the first primary. Again Wallace described his victory as a mandate to go forth into the nation and fight for the presidency.

Never before had a governor succeeded himself. Never before had one man won the Alabama governorship three times. Within six months after his third inauguration Wallace singlehandedly controlled the more than five thousand appointed positions in the state—a power greatly exceeding that of any other individual in Alabama's past.

Younger brother Gerald was from the beginning the number-one behind-the-scenes operator of the Wallace administrations. A weasel-like, underweight man with sunken cheeks and a cadaverous complexion, Gerald was always the physical weakling of the family.

Born June 11, 1921, in Clio, he graduated from Barbour County High School in 1938. He did nothing in his early years that would distinguish him as a student. He neither showed brilliance nor did he fail every subject.

In the back of his mind, he told reporters, he was always slightly resentful of having to go to work as soon as he graduated from high school. His brothers George and Jack were already attending the University of Alabama. Their mother could not afford to keep three sons in school. He had stayed home with his mother and sister after their father died. "He was a marvelously loyal son. When he went to work for the State Highway Department after he finished high school, he always made sure Marianne and I were doing okay. He even sent us money sometimes just right out of the clear blue," said Mrs. Mozelle Wallace about her youngest son.

For three years he worked as a rodman for the highway department, walking as many as ten miles in a day with a survey crew. After three years in this job he joined the U. S. Navy in 1941 and was assigned to the Seabees in the South Pacific.

When he returned to Alabama he attended the University of Alabama's School of Business Administration under the GI Bill. After three years he dropped out and opened an employment business in Mobile.

However, before the business started making money, Gerald developed tuberculosis. He was confined to several Veterans' Administration hospitals and underwent two major lung operations. After six long years of struggling, he was released with a clean bill of health in 1955.

Armed again with the GI Bill, he returned to the University of Alabama. In law school he was elected vice-president, beating Gene McLain, who later ran against his brother in the 1974 election. In 1959, at thirty-eight years of age, Gerald Wallace was admitted to the Alabama State Bar Association.

"Everybody has always talked about Gerald being the weakest of the Wallaces, but I'm not sure that that's true. Look at what the man did. I'm not so sure George could have pulled himself back up like that, the way Gerald did," said a friend of the family, who also pointed to their mother, whom he called "one of the strongest people the good Lord ever put on the face of the earth."

After serving two years as clerk for Alabama Supreme Court Justice J. Ed Livingston, Gerald opened an office in Montgomery with George. However, the Wallace and Wallace partnership was never to do a great deal of legal business. Another lawyer who had an office at the time in the Washington Building described the practice: "George spent all his time either out of the office or on the telephone calling prospective supporters. Gerald never got in until eleven or twelve o'clock. I remember that once in 1960 one of them was appointed guardian ad litem in a case and they were awarded some kind of fee. It wasn't much, but it was the only legal business I can remember that they did."

In 1961 Gerald went out over the counties and put together an organized effort for his brother's political race. "I enjoyed getting out there and doing that kind of work," the brother said. "I never was much for up-front politics. I like the behind-the-scenes work. I never wanted to get in the middle of the rat race of politics. I never was interested in the subject like George. I guess you could say I was always interested in material things, in security," the younger Wallace pointed out.

When his brother became governor in 1962, Gerald stated, "I won't take a cabinet position. This is not a rerun of the Kennedy administration in Washington. I will not take a political appointment." He was never offered a political appointment, according to others close to Governor Wallace. But he was given a free hand in other ways.

Shortly after George was inaugurated Gerald purchased a plush country home about ten miles southeast of Montgomery. The large, ranch-style home with luxurious swimming pool and two well-stocked fishing ponds cost approximately five hundred thousand dollars, most of which was included in a mortgage with a Montgomery bank. After four years the mortgage was completely paid.

While his brother was governor, Gerald continued to keep the law office open. It was still referred to as Wallace and Wallace, Attorneys At Law.

While Gerald admittedly did not like the center-ring attention of out-front politics, he enjoyed very much his position as behind-the-scenes maneuverer. Nothing suited him better than his brother's announcement that there would be no more liquor agents. That put all the alcohol business into Gerald's back pocket.

According to a massive investigation into the business dealings of Gerald during the first administration by nationally syndicated columnist Jack Anderson, the brother of the governor profited by more than four hundred thousand dollars in his liquor business dealings. "Anybody who wants to do business with the Alabama Beverage Control Board has to pay somebody close to George Wallace," said Carroll Hutton, who had been a liquor agent in Bessemer under Governor John Patterson. "If you don't pay Gerald, you have to pay Oscar," Hutton explained. When he attempted to continue his dealership through Early Times, one of the largest sellers in Jefferson County between 1958 and 1962, he was told the only way was through operations with either of the Wallace cronies. It took him four months to get in touch with Gerald, and by then someone else had been given the Jefferson County dealer's position. "I was told to have fifty thousand dollars ready the next year and the job would be mine again," Hutton said. Since that time he moved to another part of Alabama and went to work with a pharmaceutical company.

In early 1975 a so-called marketing consultant for the Schenley whiskey company in Birmingham was asked how to obtain advice about getting started in the whiskey business in the state. The consultant, Joseph Rookis, told *New York* magazine reporter Steven Brill, "Come see me, I'll put you in touch with Oscar Harper. Oscar's not only in the liquor business, but he and Gerald Wallace work together on this stuff."

"Can I see Gerald directly?" Brill asked.

"Well, I guess you can, but we all work together," Rookis answered.

Later, when Brill identified himself to Gerald Wallace as a

representative of Northeast Liquors and asked if he could get some help in starting business in Alabama, the younger Wallace said, "Oh, yeah. I know just what you mean. . . . You want to get your foot in the door down here."

"Right," said Brill. "Now what's the best way to go about it? Can you help me?"

"Sure I can help you," Gerald said. "You just come down sometime after the first of the year and give me a call and we'll get together. . . . It'll cost you some money, but I can get you in touch with the right people. Just come down and see me."

After Brill's article appeared, Gerald vehemently denied being involved in the liquor business and said, "Anybody who says I am is a damned liar."

But that was not the first time Gerald called a reporter a liar. He was in the habit of denouncing news accounts by Montgomery newspapers, *The Advertiser* and the Alabama *Journal*, both edited and published by Pulitzer Prize-winning journalist Harold E. Martin, whose muckracking spirit was behind exposés of Wallace's government. "Watergate doesn't hold a candle to the way Wallace runs this state. Everything that was done at Watergate except the actual break-in has been done and is being done here," said the Birmingham born and raised editor who won the Pulitzer for special reporting after a year-long series which uncovered wholesale use of Alabama prisoners in a drug-testing program.

In 1970 it was pointed out in the Alabama *Journal* that the state was paying Gerald-owned and Harper-owned asphalt companies from two to four dollars more per ton than others were paying for the same product. Although the state had a public-bid law for bulk merchandise to be purchased by the state, nobody was bidding on the asphalt. The contracts were going directly to the companies in question. The extra money was going to "asphalt agents" in kickbacks or commissions. These agents, designated by the governor's office as official sources with whom the state was authorized to do business, were costing taxpayers approximately two million dollars a year. This system was initiated by Wallace after he became governor in 1963.

Wiregrass Construction Company, one of several asphalt operations owned primarily by Oscar Harper, sold the state $2.4 million worth of asphalt during the first Wallace administration at above-average prices. Another company, one fourth of which was owned by Gerald, was formed about two months after his brother became governor, and it had sold the state some $2.9 million in asphalt averaging between 79 cents and $3.39 per ton above the normal price paid by others, including the federal government.

Also in 1970 it was reported by the Montgomery press that the president of an engineering firm, George Moulton, had lost a state highway contract because he had not anted up enough money to the Wallace campaign in early 1968 before Governor Lurleen Wallace died. A close investigation showed that Finance Director Seymore Trammell had designed a system of "engineering agents" who would be paid consultant fees to tell companies how and how much to contribute to the Wallace financial kitty. Trammell later said he was told to set up the system "at the direction of the governor." However, the system reeked so of impropriety that the U. S. Bureau of Roads threatened to cut off federal funds if the practice was not stopped. Trammell said the system was halted.

In 1971 it was reported that Gerald had received a $30,000 kickback from a $280,000 legal fee received by Birmingham lawyer Alfred Rose for bond work done for the state. Rose was told by Trammell that in order to get state legal work he would have to pay Speaker of the House of Representatives Rankin Fite $60,000 in legal fees. Fite then paid Gerald $30,000. After this transaction was made public, the grievance committee of the Alabama State Bar Association filed ethics charges against Gerald, but he was found innocent of violating any rule because "nothing was proven except that he received a fee," according to a bar association spokesman.

In another instance it was reported that "textbook agents" were named after Wallace forces passed a free textbook law through the legislature. Wallace took great pride in the fact that he was providing all schoolchildren with textbooks. But he never patted himself on the back for costing taxpayers extra money for middlemen who would arrange for contracts between the book publishers and the State Department of Education. One such agent in Birmingham had a multiacre warehouse containing more than one hundred thousand crates of books to be provided to Jefferson County schools. He was said to have averaged more than fifty thousand dollars in distribution fees during one year.

Throughout the years the U. S. Attorney's office in Montgomery has investigated Gerald Wallace's affairs. In 1971 a special investigation team was sent from the Justice Department in Washington to Alabama specifically to pry into the possibilities of income-tax violations. A source high in the legal operations said that an indictment was pending shortly before President Nixon made a trip to Mobile to officially open construction of an interstate inland-waterway system. Nixon and Wallace rode on the same plane from Mobile to Birmingham, a trip of about forty minutes, during which an agreement was supposedly made between the two. Both later denied any discussion took place.

During the trial of another Wallace aide, however, Gerald was implicated in a payoff scheme. The president of Southern Sash Supply Company, Warner Mathis, testified that he was not allowed to sell window shades and other products to the state unless he put Gerald Wallace on his payroll as a lawyer with a five-hundred-dollar-per-month retainer. Mathis said Gerald stayed on the payroll for eight years and received a total of forty-eight thousand dollars. He said Gerald did no legal work whatsoever for the company.

When asked by Gerald and demanded by the governor, the State Highway Department constructed a special paved road to Gerald's fancy cattle-and-horse farm. The road cost the state $125,087, according to official reports.

After all of his close calls with the law Gerald Wallace has been as cocky about his business dealings as his brother about politics. He said he made money because "I've made good business investments." He grinned slyly and stared owl-like from behind his gold-rimmed glasses. "I have been investigated by just about every federal and state agency you can name. I have been investigated by federal and state grand juries, even the state bar investigated me. But I have never been convicted of anything; I have never been indicted for anything," he added.

According to at least three of the first administration leaders in the Wallace camp, the five foot eight inch, one hundred thirty-five pound Gerald Wallace "took everything that wasn't nailed down when the third-party candidacy finally ended." Between the mid-August convention of the American Independent Party and the November General Election, "more than eight million dollars was raised, and about five million dollars was spent." The campaign was left with almost three million dollars in the bank, "and Gerald wanted to put that in his pockets," said a former Wallace aide.

Among the most bitter of the former Wallace allies was Finance Director Seymore Trammell, who served time in the country club of federal prisons at Montgomery's Maxwell Air Force Base after being convicted of evading income tax on political payoffs. The short, red-haired, former district attorney from Barbour County served as Wallace's right-hand man for more than six years. He signed huge notes to cover the cost of the early 1968 campaign before the money started pouring in from nationwide contributors. "Somebody had to stick his neck out if he was going to make a run for the presidency. I put my name on the notes with an understanding that they would be paid off when we started getting the money. We knew we'd get resources as soon as the party nominated the governor," he said. But he claimed he was left holding the bag for more than one hundred thousand dollars, a debt that was dissolved when he went to jail and declared bankruptcy.

According to Bill Jones, Wallace's press secretary who also left after the 1968 presidential try, "It was Gerald who got rid of us. We wanted to take the campaign all the way [he and other former aides claimed the 1968 campaign was diverted after Governor Lurleen's death], but Gerald didn't. I can suspect, but I certainly can't prove, that he convinced George it was time they started thinking about where their money was going to come from. No one ever did find out exactly where the money went."

Jones was no longer around when the three million dollars was put into the gubernatorial campaign in 1970, nor did he still work for the governor when other former aides say that at least four traveling trunks filled with cash contributions disappeared from the campaign headquarters in downtown Montgomery. A former top Wallace aide stated: "We had been through at least eight trunks. We brought back three trunks filled with money from the convention in Dallas. We got another one somewhere. It was filled up. The girls down there counted the money. Gerald got a daily accounting. He watched that money like a hawk watching a chicken grow. Much of the money went for operational expenses. But it just kept coming in. Every day we'd get thousands of envelopes. Most of them had money inside. At the end there were four trunks filled to the brim. I was told by a security guard one morning that the trunks had been loaded onto a pickup truck the night before. I started looking into the situation, but I was told by the governor to leave well enough alone. That's what I did. I left well enough alone," he added.

SUNRISE
AT
MONTGOMERY

A MOST IMPORTANT and tragic day in Wallace's life was May 15, 1972. Since being shot that afternoon he has been confined to the bed or wheelchair. His critics even hint that the assassination attempt not only affected his physical health but also did irreversible damage to his mental stability, which was already questionable. Before 1972 Wallace liked to brag that he was certified ninety percent sane. But since his own brush with death and Tom Eagleton's being replaced as a vice-presidential candidate because he had had mental disorders and shock treatment, Wallace has been quiet about the subject of his own mental problems.

He spoke to a crowd of about four hundred that afternoon in the shopping center at Laurel, Maryland. Sweat poured from his forehead and drenched the collar of his pale blue Arrow shirt. The last words he spoke broke slightly with the heat and the strain of campaigning. As quickly as the last words were out of his mouth, he shed his coat and rolled up the cuffs of his shirt. He reached for hand after anxious hand. He smiled, nodded, said, "How are y'all?" One hand which reached toward him was not a greeting. The hand held a gun which dropped him to the blistering pavement.

Later Wallace remembered five shots being fired from the gun. "I was spun around by one of the shots, possibly the first—I'm not sure. I understood a woman grabbed the hand of the man as he started shooting and he was aiming right at my head, but one bullet grazed my back and then the other four hit me. It came just like a machine gun's bullets, just as fast. But it seemed like forever to me, fast and slow at the same time." As he remembered, he grimaced. He clutched himself slightly in the middle. "Three of the bullets went through my right arm and then into my body. I hit the ground."

His wife, Cornelia, an attractive brunette twenty years his junior, fell on top of him. "All I could think of was: Another bullet's coming. They're trying to kill him. They're not going to kill him if I can protect him. I wanted my body over his to keep them from harming him any more." Her voice quivered as she remembered that steaming hot afternoon.

When Wallace looked down at his own body, "I saw the blood oozing out of my shirt. I tried to move my legs and I couldn't. I felt I was going to die and many things began to pass through my mind—like maybe if I had it to do all over again I would have been a little better man than I had been, like maybe I had some shortcomings that I would overcome. I asked the Lord to let me live, if that was His will. But I said quietly to myself, 'If it's not Your will, then please don't let me suffer.' I looked around then at my wife because I wanted to see her one more time. I always had the impression that when you died, you simply faded away, and I expected that moment to begin—I wanted to see her face once again—but it didn't happen," he added.

He said that he had looked death in the face once before, when he was twenty-three years old and in the U. S. Army Air Corps. He contracted spinal meningitis while stationed in Arkadelphia, Arkansas. For six days he was in a coma. His mother was contacted by medical corps personnel and told that it was doubtful whether he would pull through. Like a miracle, he recovered. He was not allowed to complete pilot training, but did continue to serve in a ground crew. "It was much different that first time," Wallace said. "I wasn't really awake, conscious of the fact that I was dying, but it left me with a profound feeling that I had lived through something very near to moving on into another life."

As he lay on the ground that afternoon in Maryland, he said, "I remember telling my wife, 'I'm paralyzed. I cannot move my legs.' She attempted to reassure me. She said, 'When this is over, I'm going to carry you home.' She was trying to tell me, I think, that she was going to take care of me, that she knew I was going to get well. I was totally conscious all the while. In fact, so conscious that I wanted to be unconscious, because I hurt so severely. I remember saying quite frankly, 'I don't mind dying, but please get me out of this suffering.'

"The man who shot me—I never saw him. But even with all the tumult going on, I could see people looking down at me with agonized expressions, not knowing what to do. There were others trying to help and I remember one of my friends kept saying, 'It's not bad, it's not bad at all. It's very low.' And I remember I looked at him and sort of smiled and said, 'Well, you look again if you think it's not bad.' "

He was rushed to the Holy Cross Hospital in Silver Springs, where emergency surgery was performed.

Perhaps the best medicine for his wounds was the fact that he won both the Maryland and Michigan primaries the day after he was shot. A photograph was sent out over the wire services and printed on page one of almost every major daily in the United States and in many parts of the world. It showed Cornelia at his bedside. Both were smiling and holding up headlines announcing the victory. At that point in the primaries he had won three states. He was leading the field. But he was bedridden and paralyzed. He was very weak, although he was told that both conditions were only temporary. The best surgeons in the world, several of whom had operated on his first wife when she had cancer, were flown in from University Hospital in Birmingham. After examining the patient, at least two told him they believed there was a possibility that he could walk again. Wallace issued such a statement in a bedside press conference.

Before campaign commercials were taped in his room for the upcoming primaries, he was powdered and pampered to make him appear healthier than he was. A Wallace aide said, "The governor looked like he was on the edge of death every morning. He was weak, pale, and saw only gloom until he started talking about politics. All of a sudden he'd perk up and seem to come to life. I'd pat the pillow behind his head and he'd start talking. When Pennsylvania came in and we had the votes he was happy. But when he saw that we had won practically no delegates he was sickened. Maybe he'd talk himself out on those days, but he'd just come to life when we'd talk about politics. Mrs. Wallace said it was good for him. She said he needed to have something to look forward to every day. We had to work with him to keep up his spirits. His mother, who came up the night he was shot, said he had always been prone to moods. His brother Jack said he had had spells of deep depression, especially after the loss of the governor's race in 1958. Cornelia Wallace decided she was going to do everything in her power to keep the governor from falling into another depression like that."

Wallace insisted later that it had been his excellent physical condition and the assistance of the Lord that kept him from dying. He had always kept in good shape since he was a boy shadowboxing on the sidewalks of Clio. "The doctors told me that had I not been in good physical condition, I would not have survived my ordeal in Maryland," Wallace said. He added, "I wanted to live. I had a desire to live. My family stayed very close to me. And then people were so good to me.

There were so many people who came to the hospital—and so many people who wrote, hundreds of thousands. People from all over the world—even the Pope. And of course Holy Cross Hospital was a good hospital, and they went all out to look after me the way they went all out to look after everybody.

"More than that was the fact that so many people prayed for me—and through me, I think, for all afflicted people. Basically, an overwhelming majority of our people are religious, and they believe in God, and they believe prayer helps, and I believe it does, too. I believe all of that helped to bring me to the point where I am alive today," he continued.

He made an amazing recuperation in Holy Cross, according to his physicians. "We never believed he would be able to attend the Democratic National Convention within four months after he was shot. The man was riddled full of holes. His insides were literally torn to shreds," one doctor commented in confidence.

But Wallace showed the professionals that he had a willpower made of steel, and it nearly killed him. He went to Miami to be a part of the Democratic party. He arrived looking very pale and weak. He stayed in his room most of the time, meeting people there, conferring with them about what moves he would make, how they would vote on various aspects of the platform, and other matters. On the night of his sixth day in the Sunshine State, after he became the first candidate ever to speak to a convention prior to the nomination, he developed a high fever from an infection. On the morning of the seventh day he had to be flown to Birmingham for emergency surgery.

He was bedridden for more than a month. Only a few persons outside the family were allowed to visit with him for any length of time. He began the road toward recuperation again. He had to once again learn to sit up and balance himself in bed, slide down a board out of the bed and into the wheelchair, and brace himself steadily in the chair. But the therapy went very slowly.

"He appeared to be only half trying during those days. It seemed like the days were longer and longer for him. Nobody said anything to him without an unfriendly retort. He lay in his bed most of the time, saying nothing and doing nothing. His wife couldn't make him perk up," according to a staff member at Spain Rehabilitation Center, where he had been moved into a suite of rooms and an office had been established.

Through most of August and September he sank deeper and deeper into a state of depression, according to those around him. After he was told he could not run on a third-party ticket and could not face any active politics for at least a year, he appeared to give up. At one point, an aide recalled, he threatened to take a handful of pills "if Cornelia didn't get out of the room and quit bothering him. She had been trying to cheer him up with stories about how the national races were going." And at another time, an aide said, "he actually pushed himself to the window in his wheelchair and threatened to throw himself out."

In October, five months after the shooting, it was reported that he was just beginning to emerge from the shock of the assassin's bullets. His health was stated as relatively stable, although there was still a fear of secondary infection. "It's difficult to accept, but life has to go on. There are still a lot of things I can do and I'm lucky to be alive at all. Naturally there are times when I get despondent, but that's beginning to go away. I don't have these real bad periods of depression any more," he told the press.

One of his physicians, Dr. John M. Miller III, said Wallace could anticipate recovery to the point where he would be independent of people. He would be able to dress and care for himself if necessary. Miller added that mental depression in the convalescent period was normal as the patient struggled to adjust to the limits that his condition had imposed on him.

He was returned to the governor's mansion in Montgomery, where a special second-floor office had been constructed. He did most of his work there, not going to the capitol until afternoons even after he appeared to have become adjusted.

A year after he was shot he started every day with more than three hours of physical therapy, walked between parallel bars, took twenty or more steps on the aluminum crutches, and stood for as long as an hour while strapped in a box. At least twice a week he lifted about one hundred pounds of weight over his head sixty times. His physicians slackened this schedule to about two hours of therapy daily after a year. Otherwise it remained the same.

"But he is able to miss two or three days of therapy without great physical harm to his body now," one doctor said in mid-1975.

However, there was still "a pain in my side and occasionally burning sensations in my legs, although not near as numerous as they were" shortly after he was first hospitalized, he said.

During recuperation he experimented with many devices and individuals. He saw a woman from West Virginia who had waters from a fountain that she claimed had healing powers. He used a "dorsal-column stimulator" which he said helped the pain somewhat. He explained that "they attach a little pad to you and you have a little charger that runs on batteries and you can turn them up and get a little electrical charge that's supposed to send an impulse to the brain before the pain gets there." For more than one year a Chinese acupuncturist commuted weekly from New York to give him treatments. He also thought the acupuncture helped but it was later abandoned.

Wallace's health continued miraculously to improve. Throughout most of 1975 he kept up a vigorous schedule, traveling to Los Angeles to speak to the national convention of the Veterans of Foreign Wars, speaking before the North Carolina, Tennessee, and Louisiana legislatures on the virtues of preferential primaries, and talking irregularly to the joint session of the Alabama Legislature to apply pressure for his own legislative programs. When there was some doubt about his health in the local press, Wallace would invite newsmen into his office for an off-the-cuff news conference to prove that he was in excellent condition. He was tanned. His voice was strong. He covered state-wide issues thoroughly.

But there was still a major question as to whether he could perform the duties of President. Wallace had never enjoyed the administrative functions of governor. He always had to be running for office. "It's a very good thing for Wallace that the Alabama governor's races were halfway between the presidential races. He would have gone absolutely crazy if he had had to sit out four years between elections," commented one veteran political journalist in the state. Even in the middle of the two-year layoffs he became disgruntled, despondent, restless, and more talkative when he could find even a one-man audience. He pointed toward photos of the last election, whichever that might be, and rambled about how the crowds had loved him in Des Moines or Detroit and Syracuse or Dothan. As the 1976 primaries got closer, Wallace became more like his old self, spryly bantering with newsmen, making offhand quips about his opponents, and generally feeling his oats like a fighter who had been retired and was coming back for the last big battle.

His family, friends, and physicians said that the governor was in almost constant pain. Located primarily around his midsection, where the area of feeling lapsed into the area of nonfeeling, it was termed "denervation hyperpathia," caused by the initial trauma dealt to the spinal cord by the bullet which was lodged between vertebrae. The pain, not severe but nearly constant, often attacked without warning.

However, according to one of his physicians, when he looked as though he was flinching, tightening his arms and hands around the aluminum tubes of his wheelchair, he was actually performing a prescribed exercise. This was not a reaction to pain, the doctor said, but a way in which he could momentarily take the pressure from his lower spine.

Wallace was taking about ten milligrams daily of a relatively mild drug called Tegretol, used mostly in Europe to control epileptic seizures in persons who do not respond to more common drugs. Not habit-forming or mind-affecting, it could be taken by Wallace with no dangerous side effects, according to a physician.

When Wallace could not sleep because of pain, doctors prescribed Dalmane, a light hypnotic drug which was described as not as habit-forming as Seconal. One physician said he prescribed the drug for many of his patients.

Since the shooting Wallace has not had control of his bowels or bladder. Among the first losses in his flaccid condition were internal reflexes. Although he has no feeling below his waist, he suffers the discomfort of pressure on his kidneys from sitting in one position too long. Although he still felt sensations in his legs "that feel like they are asleep but about one thousand times worse," he took no medication for this pain.

He has been faced with the possibility of urinary-tract infections. Such infections—caused by germs brought into the bladder by a catheter, or by stagnant urine not forced out of the bladder by voluntary action, or by germs coming in from outside through the urethra—are a worry of all paraplegics.

He no longer has to wear an internal catheter. He underwent surgery to enlarge the urethra in order that the urine could flow from his body unaided. He was also operated on to

235

remove a muscle in order that the urine could flow out more easily into an external bag next to his leg. However, even under these more hygienic conditions, he suffered several urinary-tract infections during the last part of 1974. At that time he had to take antibiotics to combat complications in the bloodstream.

His physicians worried about the possibility of his becoming immune to antibiotics, a condition that could become disastrous to his overall health. But it was also pointed out that he was never given antibiotics unless absolutely necessary.

Among the other medicines, Wallace was given a daily dosage of fifteen hundred milligrams of ascorbic acid or vitamin C to avoid urinary tract infections.

Although it was publicized that the Wallace family had a history of respiratory diseases, his brother having had tuberculosis and his father dying of Brill's Disease, Wallace's Montgomery physician, Dr. Hamilton Hutchinson, said Wallace's respiratory system was in much better shape than other men his age.

When the governor thought that he might be running a fever, his therapist took his temperature.

Hutchinson stated that Wallace was no more susceptible to colds than any other normal person. However, he did say that sometimes Wallace feigned a cold to keep from carrying out some unpleasant duty of his office.

Wallace has become what doctors refer to as "potty trained," able to sustain a bowel movement in the morning. If he feels that he might suffer diarrhea he fits his underside with an absorbent pad which keeps his clothes from staining.

For a short while he suffered from bleeding hemorrhoids, which physicians said were improving.

During his confinement to the wheelchair he worked himself to a certain nimbleness within the privacy of his apartment on the second floor of the governor's mansion. He picked himself up, twisted and turned and worked his way into the car from the wheelchair, and was generally self-sufficient.

At the flick of a wrist he could curl a fifty-pound barbell, grin playfully at reporters, and challenge them to do the same.

Although his right leg was broken in midsummer of 1975 by a simple twist in getting in or out of the automobile, Hutchinson said that Wallace is very healthy and could easily do the job required by the presidency. The doctor pointed out that Presidents Eisenhower, Kennedy, Johnson, and Nixon took potentially harmful drugs during their administrations. Eisenhower and Johnson both died of heart attacks. Nixon had to take anticoagulants to control phlebitis. Wallace has a perfectly healthy arteriovenous system, according to the physician.

During the years since he was shot, he has grown stronger and stronger. His time doing daily physical therapy was cut down because the lengthy exercise was no longer required. He could get all the exercise he needed in a shorter length of time.

According to the medical experts the chances of his living a long life are far greater now than they were in the summer of 1972. "Wallace carries on much of the state business while going through therapy," said a friend and associate. "He has always been attached to the telephone. He will exercise and talk and think at the same time."

One physician stated, "All presidents should be required to spend at least one hour and preferably two every day in the exercise room. Gerald Ford swims every day. He takes exercise. The thing about Wallace is, he wouldn't spend so much time on the golf course or skiing in the mountains. Even today he spends fourteen to sixteen hours a day at his job."

Throughout the first two years following the shooting Wallace lived through days, weeks, and even months of deep, dark depressions. His mental attitudes, according to acquaintances, associates, and doctors, have run from hopeful to suicidal. He has publicly displayed the hopeful side of his struggle. He has continuously compared himself to FDR, attempting to develop the image of a perfectly normal human being who is merely living in a wheelchair.

But his physical inabilities might not be his worst problems. With the added stress and strain of his physical incapacities, his mental state might become as fragile as his bodily functions. He has a history of mental disturbances. He entered military service in the U. S. Army Air Corps on October 20, 1942, and was hospitalized for acute cerebral-spinal meningitis from April 9, 1943, to June 3, 1943. According to the official records, read into the congressional record by Senator Wayne Morse of Oregon in the early sixties, Wallace was also hospitalized "in September 1945 for severe anxiety state, chronic, manifested by tension states, anxiety attacks, anorexia, and loss of weight . . ."

In June of 1946, after reaching the grade of sergeant and serving as flight engineer on nine combat missions, he filed claim for compensation and in December of 1946 he was granted a service-connected disability for "psychoneurosis." He was examined when he was thirty-seven years old by a Veterans' Administration doctor while he was circuit judge. The finding at that time was, "He was tense, restless, and ill at ease, frequently drummed the desk with his fingers, changed position frequently, sighed occasionally, and showed a tendency to stammer, resulting in the diagnosis of anxiety reaction."

When he was honorably discharged from the Army he was given ten percent disability because of his mental disorders. He continued to receive the check from the government.

In answer to Morse's reading the record on the floor of the Senate, Wallace said, "Well, at least I have a paper that certifies I have ninety percent of my faculties, which is more than Wayne Morse can claim."

However, rather than regressing with age, his mental problems have become more acute, and have expanded greatly since being paralyzed.

"He goes in and out of moods so quickly it's hard to tell whether he'll smile and say, 'Good morning,' or snap your head off because he's hurting so," commented a friend of his wife. "He'll be in his office sometimes talking loudly on the phone to somebody at the capitol, but you'd think they could hear him without a telephone. He never says anything in an even tone. Sometimes he rants and raves all over the upstairs, rolling back and forth, in and out of rooms, wheeling his chair all over the place.

"He's got this terrible jealousy of Cornelia. Every time she gets out of his sight he thinks she's running around on him. He's just as apt to holler about that as something else. It's very difficult for her. She keeps trying. She's a real lady," the friend continued.

His physicians have left little doubt that Wallace's injured spine and paralysis have resulted in his total impotency, although his wife insisted in a magazine interview, "We can still have a baby." She said she was hoping that such a pregnancy would take place. However, a Montgomery physician stated, "In cases like his, where the nerve tracts within the spinal cord have been seriously interfered with, or severed, as the case may be, the patient seldom recovers potency. That is not to say that it is not possible, the odds are against it—especially where there is a total lack of sensation in the lower body." This physical situation in itself will "bring about depression, cause the patient to overreact to otherwise normal circumstances, and develop paranoia concerning his closest loved one."

He has also developed a partial paranoia about the attempted assassination. The assassin, Arthur Herman Bremer, a twenty-one-year-old Milwaukee youth with thinning blond hair, was acting alone, according to all public official sources. But Wallace and his wife have their doubts. Both have read Bremer's published diary. Both have talked with FBI agents from Baltimore who investigated the case. "How could he have gotten that kind of money to roam all over the country and Canada keeping up with political candidates? He not only followed me, he stayed in the Waldorf-Astoria in New York, and he came within twenty yards of Nixon more than once. There's a picture of him that shows him even closer than that to Nixon," Wallace said. Wallace wondered aloud why Watergate conspirator E. Howard Hunt, a former CIA agent and employee of the Committee for the Re-Election of the President at that time, went to Bremer's apartment before the FBI found it. Later Hunt testified that he was given the location of the apartment and told to search it for possible left-wing materials by Charles Colson, then a member of President Nixon's White House staff. Hunt had already searched the apartment when the FBI arrived. FBI agents later said they found only right-wing pamphlets and some pornography among the reading material. It was never explained how Colson knew who Bremer was, where his apartment was located, and why it should be searched, since Wallace had been shot only minutes before Colson gave Hunt the order.

No matter what the prognosis, Wallace kept fighting. With more and more frequency he compared himself with Franklin Delano Roosevelt. In the winter of 1972 his wife, Cornelia, told a *Life* reporter, "I wondered if George would come out of the hospital and decide that he'd done enough, that now was the time to turn inward and spend more time with his family, as some have done. He's lost his ability to walk, and if he lost his career too . . . that's what sustains him. I don't really expect George to do that."

Cornelia Ellis Snively, a thirty-two-year-old gypsy-dark woman with smoldering, emberlike eyes and raven hair, took fifty-one-year-old George Corley Wallace to be her lawfully wedded husband only three weeks before he was inaugurated for the second time. She stood next to her new husband in front of the Trinity Presbyterian Church in Montgomery with her two sons, seven-year-old Josh and six-year-old Jim, by her side. Also present were his four children, whom she said "promoted our marriage all the way from courtship to altar."

Cornelia and George had known each other since she was seven years old and lived in the governor's mansion with her Uncle James E. Folsom while her mother, the inimitable Big Ruby, served her brother as first lady. At the time of their meeting Wallace was a young legislator, but he said later that he remembered the little girl was "so vibrant."

Early in 1970 Wallace visited his friend, Tom Johnson, editor of the pro-Wallace weekly newspaper, the Montgomery *Independent*, next door to Cornelia's mother. Cornelia made it her business to be present. "It didn't take much doing to strike up a friendship," she said later. She was a lovely divorcée and he had lost his first wife almost two years before. It wasn't as though they didn't have anything to talk about; she had been involved in politics since she was a tot.

The governor wooed her, she said, in "that old-time kind of courting. He came to the house with his children and we didn't go out much. Frankly, neither of us wanted to be exposed to all the publicity. We just sat around the house, drank coffee, and talked.

"After we'd seen each other several times, he told me his daughter had first mentioned that we should get married. That was little Lee [then eleven years old]. They were at a political rally that spring. Lee was sitting there on the platform looking so lonely, I wanted my boys to speak to her. After the rally was over, George said Lee told him, 'Daddy, I want you to marry the dark-haired girl with the two children.'

"They really were promoting us. He was very depressed after Lurleen's death, and they were worried about him. They had a lot to do with us getting married. But then, George felt comfortable with me. It was like we'd always known each other."

Like her mother, who is known as the most outgoing personality in recent Alabama politics, Cornelia talks incessantly once she gets cranked up. She was a precocious youth who learned classical piano and hillbilly guitar. "I knew she was going to be an outstanding person when I first laid my eyes on her in the hospital," said Big Ruby.

Cornelia finished Sidney Lanier High School in Montgomery in 1957. One of her former high-school classmates remembered, "Cornelia was always a lovely girl, and she always looked older than she was. She was a cheerleader, but she didn't have much to do with the boys at Lanier. Even then she dated older boys. Most of her dates were college boys or even young fellows in town who were out of college."

She teamed with another girl to sing two ballads she had written, "Baby With Barefoot Feet" and "No Summer Love," for MGM Records.

Through the pushing of her mother, who was always promoting her daughter, Cornelia was signed with country-music great Roy Acuff's troubadours. She appeared with him first on the Louisiana Hayride in Shreveport, then toured with his company for three months through western states and the South Pacific. Back in the states, she was a short-lived guest on NBC television's *Dough-Re-Mi* musical quiz show. She ended her whirlwind career as a country entertainer with a guest appearance on the Grand Ole Opry in Nashville.

Less than twenty years old, she was asked by a reporter if

she wanted to follow in the footsteps of another famous Alabama woman, Tallulah Bankhead. She answered, "I admire Miss Bankhead, but I don't want to follow in anyone's footsteps. I mean to walk in my own."

Finally Big Ruby sent her little girl to Rollins College in Florida, where she majored in music. But she didn't stay with school very long. "I love being active and absolutely thrive on being involved," she said. The summer after her first year at Rollins she captured a position as water-skiing queen at the Cypress Gardens resort extravaganza. During the summer she worked behind the speedboats she met John Snively, a wealthy Florida contractor. "We were married, had two children, and were divorced—and that's about it," said Cornelia. She didn't enjoy sitting at home, mending socks, tending to babies, and doing other domestic duties. And she didn't cotton to her husband staying away on extended business trips while she did the wifely and motherly chores.

Back home in Alabama, she played the field of older bachelors and widowers until she met Wallace. Very quickly, she became totally devoted to him. "I love not only the man, George Wallace, but his family. His children are wonderful. His mother is a magnificent person. When you've met Mozelle Wallace you see where George gets all of his energy and his power," she said. And the feeling toward her was mutual. Each of the children expressed their admiration for their stepmother, especially after the ordeal she went through with their father in Maryland.

She has not only been a constant leader of Alabama's ten best-dressed women; she has driven a convertible pace car 110 miles per hour prior to the Winston 500 NASCAR Grand National Race at Talladega. On a special telecast with Dick Cavett, she commented prissily, "They said before I got married to George, 'Cornelia's so fast they had to put a governor on her,'" then giggled like a schoolgirl.

243

She has fun in the governor's mansion. She hosted large parties with favorite entertainers such as hillbilly star Ferlin Husky. And ofttimes she bordered on the tasteless, such as when she sang "Oh, Lonesome Me" for a crowd of legislators.

It has been strongly rumored that she wants to become Alabama's second woman governor. She answered such rumors with a smile and a quip: "What would George do in Washington without me?" But behind her offhand remarks were serious considerations, just in case Wallace did not win the presidency.

Many longtime Wallace-watchers do not believe Wallace would be able to pull off successfully running Cornelia for the governor's chair. One stated, "I don't believe the voters of Alabama are sophisticated enough to take a divorced woman as a gubernatorial candidate. She has all the political background, the family, and George Wallace, but she isn't Lurleen, the wife, the mother, the fine upstanding woman from the poor family; and Cornelia just hasn't taken her place in their hearts."

Whatever might happen to her politically, no one can take away the courageous manner in which she handled tragedy when it struck. She fell to her knees to protect her man. That picture of her tear-streaked face hovering over his body remained alive in the minds of those who saw it on television and in other media. At that moment her image became one of other twentieth-century heroines: Jackie Kennedy, Ethel Kennedy, and Coretta King.

In that winter of 1972 when he came home to the mansion, torn apart physically and emotionally, she was instrumental in getting a copy of the film *Sunrise at Campobello*, the story of FDR's fight to recover from crippling polio. And when he saw it he was impressed to the point of tears. The movie had been sent from Washington at Mrs. Wallace's request by President Nixon. Starring Ralph Bellamy in the magnificent look-alike leading role, the final climactic scene portrayed Roosevelt pushing up and out of his wheelchair, taking the crutches in his grip, and walking out onto the platform alone to receive the thunderous applause and the Democratic nomination.

Wallace not only compared himself physically but ideologically with Roosevelt. "I liked him," he said. "I think the New Deal came along at a time when Mr. Roosevelt did rekindle hope in the hearts and minds of the great mass of people. They felt, well, he is in and things are going to be better. I think that that in itself defused a very volatile situation that was existing and I was old enough to know about it. I was about twelve or thirteen years of age when he first came to the presidency. I could see people in my little town, rural area, who were all dirt poor, black and white, but when Roosevelt was elected they all sang louder in church, they all felt better when they walked up and down the street, they all smiled. That in itself is something that he's not given credit for.

"I do think some of the policies of the New Deal were overreactions that eventually led to much big government that's not desired. But whether or not that was worse than what might have happened had the spirit, and hope, not been rekindled in the great mass of the average little fellow like myself, who could hardly live in those days, I'm not sure. Because had not that hope been rekindled, and that smile come upon their faces, then we might have had a complete change of the form of government of this country."

All of his talk about Roosevelt and his new way of thinking (during a speech in 1968 he said, "Roosevelt did everything he could to take democracy out of the very fiber of this country") came at a time when he was attempting to receive a wider acceptance. "George Wallace never does anything, never says anything, never even remains silent without a reason," commented one of his former allies. "The reason is always political, I don't care what he or anybody else says is the reason. He'll

245

say his piece with all the heartfelt sincerity in the world, but at the very base of it all is political motivation. He is a political creature through and through."

During and after the shooting Wallace experienced what he has called his "second religious conversion." Or according to his press aide, Joe Azbell, "He has had a religious rebirth. The governor is closer to God now than ever before. He has great faith in God and is convinced that God spared his life for a purpose." And Wallace said, "I have walked through the valley of death twice."

He planned to keep up the prayers which he believes have helped him through trying times. He will conquer not only his infirmities but the great barriers that lie ahead between him and the presidency, he believes. With a will of iron, he dreams of his own moment on that platform, shoving aside the wheelchair, reaching for the crutches, handling himself with relative ease, and hearing the roar of applause. He has said that he has had such a dream, and he has faith that it will come true.

THE PROS
AND
THE CONS

EXACTLY TEN YEARS after he shared the platform with
Lester Maddox and the Grand Dragon of the Georgia Ku Klux
Klan in Atlanta, Wallace pulled himself up from his wheelchair and was strapped into the specially made podium after
having been honored with the Audie Murphy Patriotism
Award. On this occasion Wallace shared the speaker's stand
with one of the most liberal politicians in the United States.
On the Fourth of July, 1973, Wallace accepted the guarded
praise of Senator Edward Kennedy.

After accepting the three-hundred-and-seventy-five-dollar
bronze plaque Wallace said tearfully, "This is the finest thing
that has happened to me this year. It's one of the high-water
marks of my career."

The crowd of about ten thousand standing in the muck of
an early afternoon rain cheered happily when they saw that he
had been genuinely moved. The steam of the late afternoon
sun's heavy rays on the flat turf of Point Mallard Park filtered
up and brought uncomfortable perspiration from most of the
guests. But the people stayed to hear Wallace. Some of them
had come from as far away as Michigan and Minnesota. Ray
Wasserman from Grand Rapids brought his wife, Jane, and his
two sons, Ray, Jr., and Mark. All four of them wore huge
red-and-white Wallace buttons. "I voted for him in 1968 and

247

in 1972," said Wasserman. "The only reason I didn't vote for him in 1964 was because I couldn't. I was away in the Army then, before I was married, and I hadn't registered for an absentee ballot. I would have voted for Wallace in the primary and for Goldwater in the general election." In July of 1973 Ray Wasserman was an assistant manager of a large department store in a shopping center. He made more than fourteen thousand dollars a year. Within two years he expected to be made manager of a similar store. "I expect I'll vote for George Wallace as long as he runs for national office. I like the way he stands up to Washington, D. C. We need somebody who will change things. The federal government has gotten too powerful. It takes my tax money. Then it throws the tax money away. Then it tells me it wants to bus my children across town. We saved our money for four years to put a down payment on a place in a suburb where we now live. It's a nice house. It was a nice school, but the federal-court judge ruled that blacks have to be brought from the other side of town. Now, I don't have anything against black children. But they live all the way over in another area. The courts aren't telling me I've got to bus my children yet, but I figure that's next. All the people on our block talk about what we're going to do when September gets here. We're going to have to do something. But we don't know what to do. What can we do? We don't want to go to jail, but for our children we will go to jail. I don't think there's a person on our block who wouldn't vote for George Wallace for President." That July was Ray Wasserman's first trip to Alabama, and he said he thought it was a "real pretty place, what we've seen." He planned to continue his trip to Montgomery to visit the capitol, the governor's mansion, and the First White House of the Confederacy where Jefferson Davis lived. "We've seen it all on television, and now we want to see for ourselves. Governor Wallace has made this state a popular place," he added. And he said he was hoping to get to shake the governor's hand, if he was lucky.

Wallace brushed away the tears. He turned slightly to face Kennedy, who was smiling and leaning toward Wallace. "I'm not able to walk yet, but I hope you won't think I'm immodest when I say you can't keep a good man down," Wallace said. Kennedy nodded. The crowd cheered again.

The appearance of the two men on the stage near Decatur, Alabama, on the Tennessee River, had caused an uproar among Alabama politicians. To quench the thirst for off-election-year controversy nationwide, Democratic Party Chairman Robert Strauss agreed to sit with Wallace and Kennedy on the platform.

Accepting the invitation, Kennedy told the press, "I think it's important to try and sort of bring this country together. There are too many people and voices in this country that are trying to divide the nation, trying to separate this country. I think he [Wallace] has exhibited those qualities in ways in which I perhaps have a unique understanding."

In the week prior to the get-together, Alabama black leaders spoke their differences of opinion. Perhaps the strongest black vote-getter, Alabama Democratic Conference Chairman Joe L. Reed, asked his people to boycott the third annual Spirit of America Festival. No sooner than Reed had spoken, A. J. "Jay" Cooper of Prichard, chairman of the Alabama Conference of Black Mayors, said that he was in favor of black leaders supporting the festivities. Johnny Ford, mayor of Tuskegee and already known as one of the staunchest black supporters of Wallace, backed Cooper.

Reed said, "My black brothers have forgotten those times of struggle when George Wallace stood up against all black people. This is the man who screamed, 'Segregation forever!'

This is the man who did everything in his power to keep us from obtaining our basic human rights. This is the man who lost his battle against us and is now wishing for us to join him."

But Jay Cooper saw the situation differently. "Governor Wallace has expressed a desire to eradicate his racist image of the past, and his recent conduct supports that desire. Whether the governor likes it or not, black people in Alabama are a political force to be reckoned with, and by the same token, whether we like it or not, the governor is a political force in this state and this nation to be reckoned with," Cooper said. If Alabama failed to improve black-white relations, he added, "then let the responsibility for that failure rest on the shoulders of those who were too stubborn to free themselves from the shackles of the past in an effort to create a brighter future." He said he would go to Decatur and take part in the ceremonies.

The meeting became more controversial when well-known author William Bradford Huie, a resident of Hartselle, about ten miles south of Decatur, wrote Kennedy "a few friendly tips." Huie had opposed Wallace fervently during the years and had followed him like a shadow through most of the 1968 primary campaign to tell his own side of the Alabama story. "George Wallace has been and is now a hateful racist who has spawned bitterness in the hearts of good red-blooded, God-fearing, American white folks," Huie told people of Michigan, Minnesota, Wisconsin, and other northern states.

A strong-jawed, physically fit, bald-headed man who was born and reared in the Tennessee River valley of north Alabama, Huie chronicled the account of his boyhood and early manhood in his first novel, *Mud on the Stars*. He became editor of the *American Mercury* and later a free-lance reporter who frequently became the centerpiece of controversy in firsthand accounts published in *Look* and the New York *Herald-Tribune.*

With the publication of his second novel, *The Revolt of Mamie Stover,* he hit the best-seller lists. And his superb, hard-hitting style of muckraking journalism was highlighted in *The Execution of Private Slovik, The Crime of Ruby McCollum,* and *The Hiroshima Pilot.*

He tore the roof from Alabama politics when he exposed "Big Jim" Folsom's illegitimate son in a national article while Folsom was serving his second term as governor. The lead on one of his Wallace articles read: "I hate George Wallace." From that simple declarative sentence to the last statement, Huie told of the many Alabamians who did not believe in the sanctity of Wallace.

As a native of north Alabama, Huie told Kennedy that if he came to Decatur he would meet many persons "who wouldn't give George the time of day."

He wrote: "You can't praise George for his Americanism without praising the Ku Klux Klan. Several hundred red-blooded Klansmen will be in your audience in Decatur. They are the real Wallaceites. They've burned many a barn in support of George, dynamited many a home, poisoned many cattle, murdered a few 'nigger-lovers,' castrated a few black men, and slandered the wives and daughters of men who ran against George for the governorship. George has rewarded them with prompt paroles, and with jobs in firms doing business with the state. For your coming to embrace George, the Klansmen will stand and sing a chorus of 'The Old Rugged Cross' for you. They'll expect you to respond with three cheers for White Supremacy.

"I hope you can sleep well. If I ever embraced George, my sleep would be disturbed by the accusing faces of courageous men and women, white and black, who have risked their jobs, their property, even their lives, to oppose George during the past fifteen years."

However, the sponsors of the program, members of the Junior Chamber of Commerce of Decatur, arranged cleverly to curb much of the controversy.

Prior to the awarding of the main plaque, Mayor Johnny Ford presented the governor with an award from his home town of Tuskegee. With his voice shaking slightly in exaggerated oration, Ford said, "You have stood up for your country. You have been wounded on the battlefield of politics. You have not turned your back on all people."

While Ford spoke, one Alabama reporter turned to another and whispered, "Ford's making him an honorary nigger." The newsmen in the immediate vicinity chuckled.

On stage, Wallace accepted the award with humility and appreciation.

This meeting, more than any other in Alabama's recent history, demonstrated the separation that has grown between black leaders in regard to Wallace's candidacy.

Soon after he returned home to Alabama after being shot, he was visited by Charles Evers, Mayor of Fayette, Mississippi, whose brother Medgar was killed the night after Wallace stood in the schoolhouse door. After they talked, Evers said, "I believe George Wallace is a brave politician. I am convinced that the man has changed. He doesn't have the same racist beliefs that once filled his soul. He now has compassion for his fellow man. When a person has gone through an experience like that of Governor Wallace, he realizes the meaning of his own life. I truly believe that he wants to make a better world for all human beings."

In a subsequent interview Evers said, "I would definitely support a Democratic ticket which included George Wallace. I believe that he is not only one of the finest and most accomplished politicians in the United States, he has the support of a great deal of people. His support is not only in the blue-collar white community, it's in the black community as well. He has much, much support among the black people of our country. Not every black man wants his child to be bused across a mean city out of his own neighborhood. Most black people are as affected by the unfair tax situation in this country today as the middle-class white people. What George Wallace says about crime on the street applies to the good middle-class black man just as it applies to the white man in the same economic situation. Blacks and whites alike need policing."

Both Johnny Ford and A. J. Cooper said they believed in the words stated by Evers. "Other leaders in this country have changed and have gotten away with it. Why can't George Wallace?" asked Cooper. "Furthermore, I don't understand why everybody gets so down on Wallace. There are demagogues in the North. There are terrible leaders in the North. I think a greater number of people, black and white, are coming around to this realization," Cooper stated. As for Ford, he said, "George Wallace has become a statesman rather than a simple politician. He is now paving the way toward the greatest position ever held by any Alabamian. As for myself and most black citizens of Alabama, we are proud of him for making such achievements."

Ford and Cooper reiterated that they have to get along with the governor if they expect to succeed as mayors within the state. "We want local legislation. We want favors now and then from the governor's office. If we bickered and fought all the time, we wouldn't be able to get these favors. It's all a part of our new way: working together," said Cooper, who worked in Robert Kennedy's presidential campaign in 1968.

Both of the young politicians were elected in places that were trouble spots. Prichard, directly north of Mobile, has been a racially divided town with fevers running hot throughout the sixties and early seventies. In his positive approach toward the governor's office, Cooper has done much to cool the tempers on both sides. Likewise with Ford, who has been trying to mend fences among bickering elements of blacks in Tuskegee.

Sitting at a table in Atlanta's Pascall's Café, eternally youthful Julian Bond took the opposite point of view.

> There would be no way in this world that I could support a ticket which included George Wallace. The man has been the equivalent of the devil reincarnate for the modern southland. He has reached to the lowest depths of depravity with an utter disregard for the welfare of mankind. How could the people of the United States—any of us—rest at night knowing that he had his hand on the button in the White House? Before the people of the United States step into the voting booth and pull the lever for him, they should ask themselves: Do we want George Wallace to have the power of universal life or death? Here is the man who used his own wife to keep his power. He changed the name of the Alabama State Highway Patrol to State Troopers by administrative order because the first name didn't sound strong enough during the Civil Rights Movement. He stood on stage after stage around this country speaking out against a segment of the population simply because these people have black skin.

Bond became Georgia's first black representative since Reconstruction in 1966 after a court battle. The state house refused to seat him because he had made an anti-Vietnam War speech. The U. S. Supreme Court ruled in favor of Bond, who became one of the most articulate spokesmen of the black cause. At the Democratic Convention in 1968 Bond seconded the nomination of U. S. Senator Eugene McCarthy. Bond was later nominated for the vice-presidential spot in that same convention; he was disqualified because he was only twenty-eight years old. He continued to serve in the Georgia house, to speak behind podiums throughout the nation, and to act as president of the Southern Poverty Law Center, based in Montgomery, and to be a thorn in Wallace's side. The law center initiated lawsuits that have resulted in desegregation of many areas in Wallace's back yard.

The principal brain behind the law center has been Morris Dees, a country boy with a razor-sharp mind for making money and causing trouble. The owner of a twenty-five-thousand-dollar bank account when he graduated from Montgomery's Sidney Lanier High School, he had been a farm lad with as much savvy at making money as Wallace had at politics. "In fact, I became interested in George Wallace back in 1958 because he was such a go-getter," Dees admitted. In 1958 Dees was a Wallace campaign manager on the University of Alabama campus, placed in that job by his best acquaintance among the Wallaces, brother Gerald.

While attending school Dees discovered the art that put him on an easy financial street. He and a fellow student sent letters to their classmates' parents asking if they might provide the children with personalized cakes on their birthdays. While the normal response to a direct-mail letter is 1.5 percent, Dees' birthday-cake letter drew a 25 percent reply.

After law school he went into the direct-mail business in a big way. He and partner Millard Fuller started Fuller and Dees Marketing Group, and by the time he was twenty-six Dees was a millionaire. After he sold the business to *Times-Mirror*, he and Bond founded the law center. He then brought Joseph J. Levin, Jr., a young Montgomery attorney, into the operation as general counsel.

255

During Wallace's last two administrations the two energetic, modish lawyers have worked overtime to rid Alabama and the South of discrimination. Wallace has spoken out against them on several occasions, and he particularly expressed distaste over their suit in U. S. District Court which claimed Wallace officials were discriminating against blacks in the hiring of state troopers. After Judge Frank Johnson ordered the state to hire qualified blacks until they numbered approximately twenty-five percent of the force, the law center produced the Public Safety director who testified he had been directed by Wallace not to follow the court orders.

The law center spent thousands of dollars and hundreds of hours on another important case which diametrically opposed Wallace. In its redistricting plans, county lines were ruled invalid by a three-judge federal court attempting to determine the fairest way in which to draw lines for legislative districts. After the law center's plans were accepted, the court ignored local government geography, and followed only census tracts to provide equal population distribution for each legislator.

Many other civil-rights-oriented cases have been handled by the center, and in the meantime Dees has become known as the master of direct-mail campaigning. In 1972 his handling of the George McGovern money effort yielded about twenty million dollars from a cost of about three million dollars.

In 1975 he opened an office for Senator Henry Jackson in Washington, D. C., and started a fund drive. And he kept communications open with Richard Viguerie, Wallace's direct-mail king. "I have the utmost respect for Viguerie. He is the leader of the right-wing direct-mail people. He has been with the business a long time, and he is well respected throughout the marketing community," Dees said.

Looking at the overall picture, Dees explained, "I think there are only two mail-donating segments of our society: the right-wing fringe and the left. The average American does not consider himself part of the political process other than going out to vote. The thing that concerns me this time is whether there's an issue to coalesce around—and a candidate that can arouse people. Everybody's upset about the economy, but that's just the problem. Everybody's upset. There's no cause that people can get behind." He discounted Wallace altogether.

Also swearing that Wallace would not have a chance to get close to the Democratic nomination, much less the presidency, was Joe Reed, chairman of the Alabama Democratic Conference. As feisty as an angry bulldog, the Montgomery city councilman stated emphatically, "I still feel like I felt in 1973 when Teddy Kennedy came down here. I wouldn't honor an event like that with my presence. They say people have short memories. Maybe they do. But that's why I'm going to do everything I can to remind them. George Wallace is a fanatic racist. He is without principle. He has been fighting the good things which some people have been pushing in this state ever since he first set foot in the capitol. There's too much politics to play between here and Washington, D. C., and the party bosses will never let George Wallace get any farther than West Virginia. That's too far, but that's the outermost limits. The liberals in the party will make sure somebody else has the inside track. That you can be assured of."

Saying virtually the same thing was Charles Morgan, Jr., the director of the national office of the American Civil Liberties Union who spoke against the Wallace candidacy all the way back in 1964. A damp-behind-the-ears Birmingham attorney in September of 1963, Morgan tasted the bitter aftermath of a Wallace Sunday in Alabama. "It had been building for weeks. George Wallace put the troopers in the doorways of the schools. He made sure no students, black or white, could enter. When the federal judges ordered the schools opened, George sent the white children to private schools and paid their way with state funds. Then the judges moved the black children elsewhere. You couldn't keep a school open with twelve students in it. George was coming out with racial statements every day. Finally it climaxed in front of the Sixteenth Street Baptist Church in downtown Birmingham," Morgan said.

On that cool autumn morning, four black girls—Carole Robertson, Cynthia Wesley, Addie Mae Collins, all fourteen years old; and Denise McNair, eleven—listened to the Sunday School lesson from Matthew 5:43–44: "Ye have heard that it hath been said, Thou shalt love thy neighbor, and hate thine enemy. But I say unto you, Love your enemies, bless them that curse you, do good to them that hate you, and pray for them which despitefully use you, and persecute you."

As soon as the last word of the lesson was spoken, the girls left the classroom and went to the bathroom.

At 10:22 A.M. the bomb exploded. Later police determined between ten and fifteen sticks of dynamite had been planted under the steps of the fifty-year-old building.

More than a block away people in a restaurant, a dry-cleaning establishment, and automobiles felt the shaking of the earth.

In the church a teacher screamed, "Lie on the floor! Lie on the floor!" When another blast did not sound, the people were marched outside.

When rescue workers began clearing debris, a seven-foot pyramid of bricks was found where the girls' bathroom had been. A civil-defense captain found a child's white lace choir robe, lifted it, made a pained face, and cried, "Oh, my God! Don't look!"

The church's pastor, the Reverend John Cross, paced up and down the sidewalk. He urged a gathering crowd of disturbed black people to go home. "The Lord is our shepherd, and we shall not want," he said.

The youth in the crowd screamed back, "We gave love—and we get this!" "Love 'em? Love 'em? We hate 'em!" When the crowd did not disperse even after a warning from police, the city's six-wheeled riot tank noisily cranked its way onto the scene. Blacks pelted rocks at police, and shots were fired over the heads of the crowd.

Later in the day a group of black youths threw rocks at passing white cars. The police ordered them to stop. A sixteen-year-old boy, Johnny Robinson, ran and a policeman fired buckshot into his back. By evening the boy was dead.

On the following Monday Charles Morgan spoke out. He stood before the Young Men's Business Club and his voice boomed out. "Four little girls were killed in Birmingham Sunday. A mad, remorseful, worried community asks 'Who did it? Who threw that bomb? Was it a Negro or a white?' The answer should be 'We all did it.' Every last one of us is condemned for that crime and the bombing before it and the ones last month, last year, a decade ago. We all did it." His words ripped into the very essence of the nervous times. "Those four little Negro girls were human beings. They have lived their fourteen years in a leaderless city; a city where no one accepts responsibility; where everybody wants to blame somebody else. A city with a reward fund which grew like Topsy as a sort of sacrificial offering, a balm for the conscience of the 'good people.' The 'good people' whose ready answer is for those 'right-wing extremists' to shut up. People who absolve themselves of guilt. The liberal lawyer who told me this morning, 'Me? I'm not guilty,' then proceeded to discuss the guilt of the other lawyers, the ones who told the people that the Supreme Court did not properly interpret the law. And that's the way it is with the southern liberals. They condemn those with whom they disagree for speaking while they sigh in fearful silence." And finally he told them, "What's it like living in Birmingham? No one ever really has and no one

259

will until this city becomes part of the United States. Birmingham is not a dying city; it is dead."

Morgan went on to fight other battles, always returning to his homeland to file suits and joust with the Wallace-appointed spokesmen in the tournament of the courtroom. He believed in 1975 that the liberals had become "so pragmatic that they will never allow Wallace to take control of the Democratic party. They hold the power, and they know they have it, and they will not let go. They will hold it to the very end," he predicted.

Carl Elliott has seen no redeeming value in George Wallace since the very beginning. Elliott, who has suffered several major defeats at the hand of Wallace, has spent more than ten years paying off debts which were incurred in those defeats. An imposing figure of a man, Elliott spent thirteen years in Washington, D. C., as a congressman, and in his last five years there became a very powerful politician. He was friend and confidant to Speaker of the House Sam Rayburn and Majority Leader John McCormack. Regarded in the House as a regular Democrat, he was appointed to the House Rules Committee, through which John Kennedy's congressional program was presented. For four years, from 1961 through 1964, Elliott was the swing vote of what he remembered as "a very powerful place, and I know of no parliamentary body on earth that had the power that the House Rules Committee had then. I tried to wield that power with sense. I didn't want to make a fool out of myself or anyone else but it was a powerful position."

During Wallace's first successful gubernatorial race in 1962 Elliott said, "We had a federal judge who was raised here [Walker County] and whom I had known well and had helped to get started practicing law. We were good friends, and his name was Frank Johnson, Jr. Wallace was going around talking about all these lying judges—Frank, who was by then on the federal judiciary, in particular. Wallace was clearly talking the code talk of the Klan by then and all of the elements that went to make up the kind of opposition to the civil-rights laws. It was clear to me that all that outfit was more or less behind George."

In September of 1962, after Wallace was elected, Elliott appeared with Wallace on the platform of the Walker County Young Democrats. Following the speech Wallace showed up at Elliott's house. "He said, 'You've got to join me.' I said, 'George, I can't join you. I don't believe in the things you do. This effort of yours to tear down the judiciary and go through all this business of reinstituting a civil war, I don't go along with you. I can't join you. I *won't* join you.' He said, 'Oh, you must believe what I say.' I told him that I couldn't, and that was the end of that."

Elliott organized ten rallies in 1963 to tell the people of his congressional district that Wallace was leading them down the wrong path. "I told them it was all wrong. We were on a collision course between state and federal power which could have no beneficial results. In the first place, I said, the collision was being provoked by a man who was using it for his own ends," he said, raking his hefty fingers through salt-and-pepper longish hair.

When the state lost sufficient population in the decade between 1950 and 1960, it was determined that Alabama's number of congressmen would be dropped from nine to seven. The state legislature was given two years to redistrict. It did not, and a state-wide race was called in 1962 to lower the number from nine to eight. The candidate with the lowest number of votes would lose his seat. After his statewide campaign, Elliott was more than one hundred thousand votes ahead of the lowest man. He kept his seat.

The state legislature was given two more years by the court to redistrict and bring the number down to seven. But Wallace failed to provide the leadership and make the legislators act.

Elliott became convinced that Wallace did not move in order to ultimately defeat him. In any case Tom Bevill, also from Jasper in Walker County, ran against Elliott in the Democratic primary prior to the state-wide race. Elliott was the only incumbent in the state who had to face an opponent within his own district before moving to the state-wide contest. And his opposition had Wallace's full support.

Elliott saw Bevill's candidacy and Wallace's support of Bevill as a ploy to make him spend more money and time than any other incumbent. After he defeated Bevill, Elliott had only thirty days to cover the state. "I just couldn't swing it," he remembered. "I was trying desperately hard and my sources of money had been cut off and I had to borrow all the money that I could get my hands on to get through that campaign," he added. Shortly before the election a group called the United Conservative Coalition distributed about two hundred thousand copies of a sample ballot which announced support of every incumbent with the exception of Elliott. State troopers were enlisted to carry the ballots into every county in the state, attempting to blanket the electorate. Only three days before the election, the state's largest newspaper, the Birmingham *News*, printed the ballot on its front page with a cut line to see the story on an inside page. "It looked like the paper was saying, 'Leave ol' Carl off,'" said Elliott, who believed the publication was an unintentional mistake.

On Monday morning before the Tuesday election Elliott sucked in his pride and called Wallace. "Governor, you and I see a lot of things differently, but Alabama holds a very important place now in Congress by virtue of my seat on the Rules Committee," Elliott said. "I also told him that there was no state in the country that wouldn't give its political right arm to have the place that I have. I said these efforts that are being made to defeat me are taking that position away from

Alabama. He dismissed that. Then I said, 'Your own people are a parcel of this movement.' He said, 'Who do you accuse?' I said, 'I'm not being funny with you, Governor, and I'll tell you who they are.' I named them to him, the ones that I knew, and I told him, 'I don't know all of them now but these are the ones that I do know.' And we left it at that, he didn't do anything publicly."

When about eight hundred thousand votes were cast the following day, Elliott found himself on the bottom of the heap. He was only about five thousand votes under the second-lowest man.

Shortly after his defeat Congress named Claude Pepper of Florida, a politician who was even more liberal than Elliott, to fill the seat on the Rules Committee.

In 1966 Elliott ran for governor. One of the first to announce after young Ryan deGraffenried's death, he became immediately known as the liberal candidate to beat. His closest political ties insisted Elliott was the natural heir to the deGraffenried support. Then came the great influx of candidates. A second north Alabama moderate, Bob Gilchrist of Hartselle, who had been one of deGraffenried's closest friends and strongest supporters, threw his hat into the ring. State Attorney General Richmond Flowers, who had stuck his neck out on numerous occasions for civil rights, announced his candidacy. This was followed by a mishmash of other secondary candidates, including former governors John Patterson and Jim Folsom; a Bible-toting retired office worker named Mr. Eunice Gore; a coon hunter, lay preacher, and lawyer from Decatur, Sherman Powell, who described himself as "just an ol' country boy" and drew crowds with a go-go girl wearing miniskirt and white boots while dancing the Watusi; a strangely arrogant and proud multimillionaire from Dothan, Charles Woods, whose once-handsome face was so badly scarred in a World War II B-24 crash that plastic surgeons left him with only a dreadfully hideous mask of scar tissue; and former Agricultural Commissioner A. W. "Nub" Todd.

Challenging the field was Mrs. Lurleen Wallace, whose fighting little husband never dropped his mitts during the match. She won going away in the first primary with a clear majority.

However, Carl Elliott remembered the campaign as a nightmare from the outset. "As soon as all the candidates started entering the race I should have known what was happening," he said with a bittersweet edge to his baritone voice. "The Wallaces put up money to back Richmond Flowers to take the black vote away from me. More than two hundred thousand black votes went to him that would have gone to me. I had friends who visited him and asked him to stay out, but he said he was in too deep. The same was true with Bob Gilchrist," he added. In the end, he conceded, Mrs. Wallace did have a majority. But he pointed out that more black people might have voted if they had known one candidate had a chance.

Elliott's own campaign was riddled with what he called "syndromes of the Wallace presence." His campaign spent fifty-four thousand dollars for roadside signs advertising his candidacy, and within a few days the signs had been destroyed; some were painted over, some had the word "never" written over his face with red paint, and others had stickers pasted over his name and face. Once when his crowd left a nighttime rally in north Alabama, the cars topped a mountain to find the road covered with Cola crates which jammed under the wheels of the cars. Another Elliott worker had his new car forced off the road. The man escaped with slight injuries. His car was totally destroyed. While returning from a rally, a man and woman from a Birmingham suburb were shot at. "All those things combined made me know that the ruffian organization of the state, which I call the Ku Klux Klan, was working for the Wallaces and against me. I criticized Wallace and the Klan more than they had ever been criticized. And I'm sure that criticism brought on the trouble," he added.

His jowly face hung sadly in the shadows of the late afternoon sun in Walker County, a rough coal-mining country which he had loved dearly for more than sixty years. When he remembered the harsh defeat, which left him virtually powerless and almost a half million dollars in debt, his voice caught momentarily in his throat. But when his eyes touched the view of the younger man's vision, his spirit picked up.

This man who authored the National Defense Education Act, which has allowed millions of young people to attend school on interest-free loans, grabbed a second wind. "I don't regret ever having fought George Wallace on his own ground. If I could do it, I'd take him on again. I only wish that he had turned out to be a positive power for the state of Alabama rather than a negative power. If he had been positive I would have been for him. Since George Wallace was first elected back in 1962 we have been close to the low man on the totem pole in employment, income, and education. The U. S. Bureau of Labor Statistics has all the material on this. There's no difference now than there was then, when he was first elected. It's true that all of us have pulled ourselves up in the various categories: We have more industry, better education, and pay our teachers better. We've done all that. But in comparison with our sister states we're about the same place give or take a few points here and there. I watched a program on television the other day and it kind of struck my funnybone. The national press interviewed Wallace. They said, 'Well, Governor, how can you say how much your state has grown when your relative position hasn't improved with the passing of time?' And George said, 'We've got the best education system, we've got the best employment system, and we've got more people than ever employed in Alabama. Furthermore, the people of Alabama don't care anything about all those statistics.' "

He stood tall on the porch of his unassuming home. His great hands were sunk into the coat pockets of his slightly tattered black suit. "Sometimes when I think about the power he's got I get scared for this country," he said slowly. "It's awesome. It's really awesome," he repeated.

THE SUMMING UP

GEORGE WALLACE, who has become a legend in his own time, has continued to work so vigorously at the game of politics that if he did win the presidency it would be almost anticlimactic. As his own physician commented, he seldom stops talking on the telephone until ten-thirty or eleven at night. Often times he works until past midnight in his office in the governor's mansion. And every morning he is on the phone again in the basement exercise room in the mansion. He has not been shy about his physical problems. On the contrary, he has been fully aware of the need for news dissemination about the state of his health; if not for public information, at least for his own political well-being. "If you want to live a long and productive life, get a serious illness and take care of it," one doctor allowed. And Wallace does take care of his "illness" from daily exercising to proper dieting. "He takes much better care of himself than most men his age," said his doctor.

During the summer and fall of 1975 he practiced his speeches, getting ready for the presidential campaign. He was honing his words to that fine edge he once displayed to the delight of some and the horror of many. Using old techniques, he talked from his wheelchair toward a wall in the upstairs of the governor's mansion. He used his wife, Cornelia, as an audience of one to listen while he molded his words into shape.

267

He looked toward a future, wishing to tell the people of the country that he would be able to do what they needed done to make the United States function properly. When anyone asked him about his past, he ignored them. When anyone saw only the negative side of his candidacy, he talked about a brighter side.

He turned fifty-six years old in August of 1975, and he celebrated his birthday quietly with his family in the summer governor's mansion on the Gulf of Mexico. Wallace sat daily in the sunshine, developing an attractive tan. He did not appear to be the old man often drawn of him in the word pictures by national columnists. During his public appearances he looked stronger and stronger. He bantered with Mickey Mouse and Donald Duck at Disney World during the Southern Governors' Conference in September. He held children in his lap and smiled and talked to them. He kept up with the political goings-on throughout the country, and he showed himself adept whenever he came face to face with political enemies who wished to debate a point.

Entering the final stretch before the primaries, Wallace gained more press than any of the announced candidates. He was the most controversial and perhaps the most complex. When he became governor he inherited the state's motto, "We Dare Defend Our Rights," and since the moment he took office, he has argued, he has stood up for that motto. Others have pointed an accusing finger at him, but he has never ducked when it came to being tough. He has met his adversaries head on. More often than not he has spoken louder and longer than they. He has been thick-skinned, physically able, and always ready to rush in where more cautious men have feared to tread.

During his political life, which has encompassed at least ninety percent of his entire life, he has never been boring—except when he caught newsmen between elections and made the same tired old speeches about his growing popularity. Indeed, his popularity has grown. Too many of those who view him closely still have their minds in 1964 and 1968, while he has been moving forward, thinking about next year, the next election, and what he will do when that time draws near.

Since the very beginning he has been motivated by the future. He never made major political decisions without thinking about each and every alternative and how it would affect his future. The recurring phrase "inveterate politician" has been laid as the foundation of his personality. In his hands people, like words, have become tools of the political trade; and he has been a master at doing with them whatever he wished.

Looking back at his life, he has used the people who surrounded him to benefit himself and his career. He turned terrible political disasters into personal political assets. He worked John and Robert Kennedy like puppets in his palms during the stand in the schoolhouse door. He tried to do the same with Lyndon Johnson during the Selma-to-Montgomery-march episode, but there he ran into a person even more masterful than himself. He elected his wife governor after he had been totally defeated by the state senate. And he continues to use people in a Machiavellian sense. Although his refusal to walk out of the Democratic Convention of 1948 was obviously no expression of liberal ideology, he has attempted to prove that he was at least progressive during his youth. But even then, at twenty-nine years of age, Wallace saw the opportunity to completely control a delegation, and he grabbed it, and he made himself the spokesman for right-wing southern conservatism. Even then he was telling the Democratic party to shape up, get back into the middle of the road, and get out of the gutter on the left. His words continued to echo down through the years.

When the political scientists of the future study the microcosm of Wallace Country, they will know that when he made his decision in 1976 to run as a Democrat, or to support the Democratic ticket, or to run on a third-party ticket, he was thinking about his own future. In 1964 he was testing a virgin land, tromping with bravado over a political countryside that was new to him. But he had always enjoyed political exploring. It was second nature to him. And in 1968 it was a daring stunt to get his name on the ballot in every state; it was impossibly demanding, requiring energy and intelligence, money and fortitude. But none of these things were new to Wallace, except the money. He never thought about money; he left it to others, and ultimately that was where the problems arose within that campaign.

One might wonder what he would have done in 1972 if he had not been shot. Of course no one knows positively what he would have done. But the most educated answer would be that he would have stayed in the Democratic party if he could have mustered together enough delegates to stop McGovern's first-ballot nomination or enough to make a deal with Hubert Humphrey. If these two far-out possibilities had not worked, he might have then tried the third party. Still he would have been looking toward 1976 and what the mood of the country would be then. Nevertheless, all answers are conjecture.

What will he do in 1976? Again, he will look to his own future. He will use his own standard deductions. In attempting to prognosticate his own future, he will first determine what he might do two years hence in Alabama. His lovely wife, Cornelia, born and raised of a political dynasty [the Folsoms], could make a formidable candidate in the governor's race. He would have to determine if he could again pull off the stunt of running his wife. Most seasoned political veterans have discouraged him from such thoughts. They have pointed out that Lurleen was a mother image, while Cornelia was a vibrant young divorcée when he married her. Also, Cornelia has a strong-willed mind of her own, while Lurleen was perfectly willing to allow her husband to run the state. Wallace could also decide that it would be a good idea to run his brother Jack, who has been circuit judge in Barbour County since 1959, when George Wallace left that office. Jack, a handsome, trustworthy individual, would make an attractive candidate to carry on the Wallace name on capitol hill. With Jack in the governor's office, the older Wallace would have no trouble wheeling and dealing in political circles. In either case Wallace would have to decide shortly after the National Democratic Convention if a third-party move would be profitable on the home front. However, if he made significant changes in the Democratic platform and ticket by that time, he would decide to stay with the Democrats. If he failed to make significant changes, he could decide that the third-party route would be a more effective way to force party changes.

But these will not be the only possibilities facing Wallace's future. Also in 1978, John Sparkman will be coming up for reelection to the U. S. Senate. While many have stated in the past that Wallace was not interested in the Senate because he would be only one of one hundred voices, Wallace will need a political office from which to continue to launch his national campaigns. He could not go back to the practice of law. He was never a practicing lawyer as such. His physical handicaps will continue to make public service a necessity. He will need the office in order that his necessities will be taken care of; otherwise, he would not have the money to tend to his needs. As a student of Huey Long, Wallace has become aware of the possibilities of being a senator. With a Wallace person running the state and Wallace himself in the Senate, his political future could become even more dynamic than it has been. Also, he will not overlook the fact that Sparkman, while powerful in the upper house, will be seventy-eight years old at the time of the next election and could be vulnerable against an opponent as capable as Wallace. If he chose to run for the Senate, he would know that his best chance would be from within the Democratic party. In that case he would stay, perhaps reluctantly and perhaps silently, with the Democrats in 1976. If he bolted the party, then ran for the Senate, it would be likely that the Democratic hierarchy would put all its strength behind Sparkman.

The last and most unlikely situation to exist would be Wallace's sitting in the wings for four years waiting to have his shot at a fourth term as governor. "If he's alive, he will be running for some office," predicted an old-time Alabama politician.

By the last quarter of 1975 he had put together a magnificent mechanism in his national campaign. Out in the field he had more experts than novices working for his cause. From a youth who had worked in New Hampshire for Edmund Muskie to an MIT political economist, the organization began at last to look like a sure-enough political effort rather than a slipshod attempt at an absolutely unreal goal. Almost overnight he became the leader of the pack, and only time would tell how he would react to that precarious position.

In an exclusive interview he told a reporter with National Public Radio that 1976 would be his last hurrah. He said emphatically that he would not run again for public office. But he told confidential associates in 1968, after his wife died, that he would not seek the gubernatorial chair in 1970. When that election came around, Wallace was running.

In the meantime, Wallace packed his bags and headed for Europe, where he would meet heads of state, military leaders of the North Atlantic Treaty Organization, and the political power brokers of that continent. He had come a far distance from that impatient novice who kept bothering his friend for a foreign policy before the national television interview in 1963.

He was going to the source for his information. But while he appeared sophisticated and suave on the surface, those who knew him best believed that he would remain simply the expert on racism.

BIBLIOGRAPHY

BOOKS:

Alabama: A Documentary History. Lucille Griffith, University of Alabama Press, 1972.

Alabama Politics. Ralph Price, Vantage Press, 1973.

America Votes. Edited by Richard M. Scannon, Congressional Quarterly Press, 1970.

An American Life. Jeb Stuart Magruder, Atheneum Publishers, 1974.

An American Melodrama: The Presidential Campaign of 1968. Lewis Chester, Godfrey Hodgson, and Bruce Page, The Viking Press, 1969.

An Assassin's Diary. Arthur Herman Bremer, Harper's Magazine Press, 1973.

A Time to Speak. Charles Morgan, Jr., Harper and Row, 1966.

Atlas of Alabama. Project Director Neal G. Lineback, University of Alabama Press, 1973.

Campaign '72: The Managers Speak. Edited by Ernest R. May and Janet Fraser, Harvard University Press, 1973.

Climbing Jacob's Ladder. Pat Watters and Reese Cleghorn, Harcourt, Brace and World, 1967.

Dixiecrats and Democrats. William D. Bernard, University of Alabama Press, 1974.

Divided They Stand. David English, Prentice-Hall, 1969.

Farewell to the South. Robert Coles, Atlantic-Little, Brown, 1972.

Gothic Politics in the Deep South. Robert Sherrill, Grossman Publishers, 1968.

Bibliography

Grover C. Hall, Jr.: Profile of a Writing Editor. Judy Means Wagnon, an unpublished thesis from the University of Alabama School of Communications, 1975.

Historical Atlas of Alabama. Donald B. Dodd, University of Alabama Press, 1974.

Huey Long. T. Harry Williams, Alfred A. Knopf, 1969.

Mayor: Notes on the Sixties. Ivan Allen, Jr., with Paul Hemphill, Simon and Schuster, 1971.

My Life With Martin Luther King, Jr. Coretta Scott King, Holt, Rinehart and Winston, 1969.

Nixon Agonistes. Garry Wills, Houghton Mifflin, 1970.

Official Inaugural Program: Governor George C. Wallace. National Services, Inc., 1963.

Official Inaugural Program: Governor Lurleen Wallace. Inaugural Book Committee, 1967.

Plantation Politics: The Southern Economic Heritage. J. Earl Williams, privately published, 1972.

Portrait of a Decade. Anthony Lewis, Random House, 1964.

Racially Separate or Together? Thomas F. Pettigrew, McGraw-Hill, 1971.

Senate vs. Governor, Alabama 1971. Harold W. Stanley, University of Alabama Press, 1975.

Southern Politics. V. O. Key, Jr., Alfred A. Knopf, 1949.

The American South. Monroe Lee Billington, Charles Scribner's Sons, 1971.

The Glory and the Dream. William Manchester, Little Brown and Company, 1974.

The Deep South States of America. Neal R. Pierce, Norton, 1974.

The Intimate Story of Lurleen Wallace. Anita Smith, Communications Unlimited, Inc., 1969.

The Lost Priority. John Herbers, Funk and Wagnalls, 1970.

The Making of a President: 1968 and 1972. Theodore H. White, Atheneum Publishers.

The Mind of the South. W. J. Cash, Alfred A. Knopf, 1941.

Bibliography

The Palace Guard. Dan Rather and Gary Paul Cates, Harper and Row, 1974.

The Political South in the Twentieth Century. Monroe Lee Billington, Charles Scribner's Sons, 1975.

The Resurrection of Richard Nixon. Jules Witcover, Putnam, 1970.

The South and the Nation. Pat Watters, Pantheon Books, 1969.

The Southern Strategy. Reg Murphy and Hal Gulliver, Charles Scribner's Sons, 1971.

The Vantage Point. Lyndon Baines Johnson, Holt, Rinehart and Winston, 1971.

The Wallace Story. Bill Jones, American Southern Publishing Company, 1966.

The Wallaces of Alabama. George Wallace, Jr., as told to James Gregory, Follett Publishing Company, 1975.

Wallace. Marshall Frady, The World Publishing Company, 1968.

Y'all Come. W. Bradley Twitty, Heritage Press, 1962.

MAGAZINES:

Atlantic, Commentary, Harper's, Life, Nation, Newsweek, New Times, New York, The New Republic, The New York Times Sunday Magazine, The Saturday Evening Post, Time, and *U. S. News & World Report.*

NEWSPAPERS:

Alabama *Journal,* the Birmingham *News,* the Birmingham *Post-Herald,* the Boston *Globe,* the Charlotte *Observer,* the Montgomery *Advertiser, The New York Times,* the Philadelphia *Inquirer,* and the Washington *Post.*

TELEVISION FILM:

CBS and NBC network news.